Assessing the
Value of
E-Learning Systems

Yair Levy
Nova Southeastern University, USA

 Information Science Publishing

Hershey • London • Melbourne • Singapore

Acquisitions Editor:	Renée Davies
Development Editor:	Kristin Roth
Senior Managing Editor:	Amanda Appicello
Managing Editor:	Jennifer Neidig
Copy Editor:	Jennifer Young
Typesetter:	Amanda Kirlin
Cover Design:	Lisa Tosheff
Printed at:	Integrated Book Technology

Published in the United States of America by
    Information Science Publishing (an imprint of Idea Group Inc.)
    701 E. Chocolate Avenue, Suite 200
    Hershey PA 17033
    Tel: 717-533-8845
    Fax: 717-533-8661
    E-mail: cust@idea-group.com
    Web site: http://www.idea-group.com

and in the United Kingdom by
    Information Science Publishing (an imprint of Idea Group Inc.)
    3 Henrietta Street
    Covent Garden
    London WC2E 8LU
    Tel: 44 20 7240 0856
    Fax: 44 20 7379 3313
    Web site: http://www.eurospan.co.uk

Library of Congress Cataloging-in-Publication Data

Levy, Yair, 1970-
  Assessing the value of e-learning systems / Yair Levy.
    p. cm.
  Summary: "The book provides A guidelines approach on how to implement the proposed theory and tools in e-learning programs"--Provided by publisher.
  Includes bibliographical references and index.
  ISBN 1-59140-726-5 (hc) -- ISBN 1-59140-727-3 (sc) -- ISBN 1-59140-728-1 (ebook)
  1. Internet in education. 2. Education--Computer network resources. 3. Computer-assisted instruction. 4. Distance education.   I. Title.
  LB1044.87.L496 2006
  371.33'44678--dc22
                              2005013553

British Cataloguing in Publication Data
A Cataloguing in Publication record for this book is available from the British Library.

Dedication

To my parents, Zion & Liora
To my loving wife, Michelle
To my kids, Maya & Ethan

Assessing the Value of E-Learning Systems

Table of Contents

Preface

The target audiences of this book are researchers in the field of information systems, online learning, and distance education, as well as administrators, directors, and managers of e-learning programs. The overall objective of this book is to help administrators, directors, and managers of e-learning programs understand the potential in measuring as well as studying learners' perceived *value* of e-learning systems. Until recently most measures of systems' effectiveness done in industry looked at the "satisfaction" or users' perceived satisfaction. However, this book provides the rationale behind the limitations of measuring only learners' satisfaction in the attempt to uncover the true system effectiveness in the context of e-learning systems. Therefore, the main theory and framework behind this book talk about the limited sight most current measures in industry of system effectiveness have. Grounded in information systems' user satisfaction theory and in the context of this book, *satisfaction* is defined as *the perceived performance level users find at a post-experience point of time with e-learning systems*. The limitation surrounding the fact that learners' satisfaction is the "surrogate" measure to uncover the system effectiveness. As a result, most current measures of system effectiveness follow the notion that if two systems are compared and the users' satisfaction for one of the system is significantly higher than the other, that system is more effective for users. However, this book argues that aside from users' satisfaction there is a second dimension to system effectiveness that was largely ignored in prior literature and measures. That dimension is the users' perceived *value* of the system characteristics. Grounded in value theory and in the context of this book, *value* is defined as *an enduring core belief about the level of importance users attribute to the e-learning system*. By measuring both users' perceived *value* and users' perceived *satisfaction*, practitioners will be able to compare systems based on the multiplication of the two measures, which will provide a more accurate picture of the system effectiveness. Consequently, this book will propose a more robust measure by combining users' perceived *value* and users' perceived *satisfaction* in the context of e-learning systems in order to provide practitioners a better measure and to uncover the true effectiveness of such systems.

The framework proposed in this book is specifically in the context of e-learning systems. However, such framework is very well applicable for other types of systems. Some examples for other types of systems that may benefit from implementing the propose framework are enterprise resource planning (ERP), decision support systems (DSS), expert systems (ES), executive information systems (EIS), knowledge management systems (KMS), airline and travel reservation systems to name a few. Clearly, additional research will be needed to develop similar instruments and provide validity for such measures in the context of other systems. Additional information about this same issue will be provided in the "recommendations for future research" section of Chapter VIII, p.227.

Organization of the Book

The book is organized into eight chapters. The first chapter presents an introduction to the book by building the argument for the significance of *value* as a key construct in the assessment and measurement of e-learning effectiveness. Moreover, it provides the research questions guiding this book and rationale for studying the *value* construct.

Chapter II presents a comprehensive review of the theoretical foundation underlying the value theory used in this book. Clarifications and detail descriptions are provided on the differences between values, beliefs, attitudes and behavior. Additionally, this chapter builds the foundation behind the need for *value* assessment as a major indicator of e-learning effectiveness.

The third chapter discusses the rationale and importance for studying *value* in the context of e-learning systems. Additionally, it provides definitions of the key concepts discussed in this book, such as *value, satisfaction*, and *effectiveness*. The main streams of research in which this book is grounded, namely value theory, information satisfaction theory, and information effectiveness are also described. Supporting literature from the fields of psychology, information systems, education, marketing, and related studies are drawn upon. In particular, Rokeach Value Survey (RVS) theory, List of Values (LOV) theory, value of information systems, User Information Satisfaction (UIS) theory, End-User Computing Satisfaction (EUCS) theory, IS effectiveness theory, technology mediated learning (TML) theory, and management education literature. Review of appropriate statistical techniques is provided as the conceptual theories guiding the development and validation of the Learners' Value Index of Satisfaction (LeVIS).

Chapter IV presents the proposed overall conceptual model and strategy based upon the foundation presented in Chapters II and III. In order to develop conceptual models, extensions from the relevant literature are used along with research questions proposed in Chapter I. Additionally, the development of e-learning system's dimensions and e-learning system's characteristics are proposed based on the comprehensive literature reviewed in the previous two chapters.

Chapter V discusses the value-satisfaction grid of e-learning systems as the first tool to assess learners' perceived effectiveness of such systems. The rationale behind the value-satisfaction grid of e-learning systems as a building block in the development of the other two tools, mainly LeVIS and the effectiveness grid, is also provided.

Chapter VI discusses LeVIS as the second tool to augment the value-satisfaction grid in providing additional measures for the true assessment of e-learning systems' effectiveness. The chapter also elaborates on the use of both tools: value-satisfaction grid and LeVIS together. The chapter elaborates on the combination of the two tools to create the effectiveness grids as the ultimate measurement that provides administrators, directors, and managers, guidance on the system's dimensions and characteristics that requires additional resources or ones that are a waste and may be discarded. Chapter VI provides detail information on the development and rationale of the LeVIS tool, effectiveness curves as well as the effectiveness grids.

Chapter VII describes the case study used to validate the framework and the tools proposed in this book. The research methodology employed in this case study along with validity and reliability measures is also reviewed. In order to address the complexity of the phenomenon on hand, a three-phase research approach was taken. The first phase explores the phenomenon utilizing qualitative research methods. The data collection and data analysis procedures of phase one are discussed in this chapter. A review of survey instrument development is presented and is drawn from multiple validated instruments. The second phase covers a pilot study that used the proposed instrument. Chapter VII also includes a review of the administration and response procedures to the survey instrument, as well as the review of the quantitative data analysis procedures employed in this phase. The third phase of the case study includes the procedures of revisions and modifications needed as a result of the pilot study; followed by the administration and responses to the main study, as well as the quantitative data analysis procedures employed in the full study. Furthermore, Chapter VII includes a review of the proposed validity and reliability measures including internal validity, external validity, instrument validation, and instrument reliability. Additionally, the chapter provides the research findings along with the qualitative results gained during phase one as well as the results of the pilot and main quantitative analyses gained during phases two and three.

Chapter VIII presents the summary of results by reviewing the implications of the case study results in the context of the book and the validity it provides for the framework proposed. Additionally, it provides a "cookbook" approach for practitioners who wish to implement the framework proposed in this book in their own e-learning program. Chapter VIII concludes with the discussion of the contribution of this book, implications for research, study limitations, and recommendations for future research.

Yair Levy, PhD
Nova Southeastern University, USA

Acknowledgments

I would like to acknowledge the assistance provided by Dr. Steve H. Zanakis, Dean Joyce J. Elam, Dr. Kenneth E. Murphy, and Dr. Leonard Bliss on earlier versions of this work. I thank Professor Grigoroudis for allowing me to use the MUSA software and Dr. Michael Doumpos his time and for allowing me to use the MHDIS software. Additionally, I would like to thank Dr. Dorothy Leidner, Dr. Brian Schriner, Mr. Ed Fischer, and Dr. Christos P. Koulamas for their emotional support and advices throughout the initial stages of this journey. Moreover, I want to thank Dr. Roxanne Hiltz and Dr. Murray Turoff for their conceptual advices on the preliminary stages of this work. Additionally, I would like to thank Nili Cimand for her editorial comments on the preliminary versions of this manuscript. Finally, I would like to thank my dean, Dr. Edward Lieblein, and assistant dean, Dr. Eric S. Ackerman for their continuous support.

Yair Levy, PhD
Nova Southeastern University, USA

Chapter I

Introduction

Introduction

Many universities and private corporations are investing significant capital in e-learning systems. Full understanding of the factors contributing to learners' perceived effectiveness of e-learning systems will help institutions channel funding to effective factors and redesign or eliminate non-effective factors. However, learners' perceived effectiveness of such systems has not been fully explored in prior studies. Piccoli, Ahmad, and Ives (2001) argue that interest in e-learning environments is growing rapidly; however, "a broad framework identifying the theoretical constructs and relationships in this domain has yet to be developed" (p. 403). Alavi and Leidner (2001b) concluded that "research that helps uncover the important attributes of VLS [virtual learning systems]…will be critical to our understanding of VLS effectiveness" (p. 30). In prior study, Alavi and Leidner (2001a) also concluded that: "most of the recent attempts at studying TML [technology mediated learning] in IS [information systems] research tended to adopt an overly simplistic view of this phenomenon" (p. 9).

Consequently, the study presented in this book attempts to develop a holistic view first by querying students concerning the characteristics of e-learning systems that they value and consider important during their learning experience. Secondly, this research study attempts to understand the relationship between the value learners attribute to e-learning systems and the satisfaction learners experience with e-learning systems. It is the goal of this book to address these issues by building upon existing streams of literature to propose a framework that encompasses all dimensions (technology and support, professor, course, and learner) of e-learning systems in order to provide an assessment of learners' true effectiveness of such systems.

This book proposes measures of learners' perceived value, perceived satisfaction, for assessment of the true effectiveness of an e-learning system. *E-learning system* is defined as the entire technological, organizational, and management system that facilitates and enables students learning via the Internet (Levy & Murphy, 2002). Literature suggests that the system's effectiveness is a relative construct (Grover, Jeong, & Segars, 1996). Ultimately, it is not the number of satisfied users or the level of satisfaction that suggest the system's effectiveness. Rather, it is the extent to which users are more satisfied by the system performance with what they perceive as important. In the context of this book, e-learning systems are considered effective when learners value its characteristics as highly important and are highly satisfied by those same characteristics. Furthermore, relationships between the constructs of value, satisfaction, effectiveness, and perceived learning in the context of online learning will be explored. Following IS literature, *satisfaction* is defined as the perceived performance level users find at a post-experience point of time with e-learning systems (Doll & Torkzadeh, 1991, p. 6; Kim, 1989, p. 7), whereas following value theory, *value* is defined as an enduring core belief about the level of importance users attribute to the e-learning system (Rokeach, 1969, p. 160).

Current research in Technology Mediated Learning (TML) theory falls into two distinct streams. The first addresses the pedagogical or learning perspective, comparing the learning outcomes of online learning courses with that of on-campus courses. A number of studies have investigated the comparison of learning outcomes between online learning courses and traditional courses (e.g., Alavi, Yoo, & Vogel, 1997; Hiltz, 1993; Hiltz & Johnson, 1990; Leidner & Jarvenpaa, 1993; Piccoli, Ahmad, & Ives, 2001). These and other research studies have shown that there is no significant difference between the two modes of delivery. TML research also identifies several e-learning systems' characteristics that are essential in any assessment of such systems. E-learning systems' characteristics are defined as the attributes (or features) associated with the e-learning system. Examples of such characteristics are: quality of technical support, high network availability, ease-of-use, learners' comfort with online learning and technology, to name a few.

The second research stream addresses the system perspective, indicating learners' perceived effectiveness by comparing e-learning systems overtime, with peer systems, and with a theoretically ideal system. Very few studies address this approach in the context of distance learning (Alavi, Wheeler, &Valacich, 1995; Webster & Hackley, 1997). Webster and Hackley (1997) study learners' satisfaction of distance learning systems and suggest categorizing system characteristics into four major dimensions: technology & support, course, professor, and learner's dimension (p. 1285).

Although extensive research was done on the effect of user satisfaction on IS effectiveness for decision support systems, the relationship between *value* and *satisfaction* constructs for assessment of the true system's effectiveness is lacking. Consequently, this proposed study is unique as it will introduce the *value* construct along with the *satisfaction* construct and concentrate on the second TML theory research stream, measuring both perceived learners' value and perceived learners' satisfaction with each of the e-learning system's characteristics. Moreover, this study helps to uncover the characteristics within each e-learning system's dimension proposed by literature (technology and support, professor, course, and learners' dimension) that contribute significantly to the learners' dimension satisfaction and value measures. In addition, this study helps researchers to understand how these characteristics indicate the true effectiveness of e-learning systems.

Following Straub's (1989) recommendations for valid and sound instrument development, the case study includes three phases. The first phase includes qualitative research following Keeney's (1999) methodology in the pursuit of e-learning system's characteristics learners' value when learning online. The second phase of the research study includes an empirical assessment of such characteristics using a survey instrument on a pilot group of online learners. The survey includes satisfaction and value items for each e-learning system's characteristic: learners' dimension value and satisfaction measures with each of the e-learning system's dimension, as well as learners' overall value measure, overall satisfaction measure with e-learning system, and an overall perceived learning measure. The survey is based upon prior validated measures from education and IS literature. Following the pilot data collection, factor analysis was used to help assess and clean items that do not add to the overall validity of the instrument. The third phase of the research study includes data collection using the revised instrument on a larger group of learners using e-learning systems. Following the main data collection, a comprehensive analysis using exploratory factor analysis (utilizing principal components analysis [PCA]) was employed to construct significant factors for learners' perceived value of e-learning systems as well as to construct significant factors for learners' perceived satisfaction of e-learning systems. Following the factor analysis, learners' elicited scores were aggregated in order to develop the Value-Satisfaction grids and the Learners' Value Index of Satisfaction (LeVIS). Additional information on the development of the grids and LeVIS index is provided in Chapters IV and V. Finally, in order to provide construct validity for value and satisfaction measures, an analysis was done to look at how the overall perceived learning measure is related to the overall value, satisfaction, and perceived effectiveness of e-learning systems. Additional information is also provided in Chapters IV and V.

The remainder of this chapter is organized as follows. The next section introduces a brief review of the supporting literature for this book along with key definitions, the purpose, and importance of this book. The subsequent section addresses the research questions guiding the development of the framework proposed in this book. The expected contributions of the research study are then outlined.

Structure for the Research Study

This section will briefly discuss the significance of value and satisfaction constructs, define them and introduce the key theories and concepts to be used in this research study of learners' perceived effectiveness of e-learning systems, as well as the rationale for the research study. The subsequent two chapters will present a more complete literature review of each of the theoretical foundations for this research study. Such theoretical foundation includes the value theory, IS user satisfaction theory, IS effectiveness theory, and Technology Mediated Learning (TML) theory literature.

The concept of value refers to two distinct concepts in information systems (IS) literature. The first deals with financial value (e.g., IS value), and the second has a long history in the area of psychology, sociology, and behavioral science which deals with psychological value (e.g., value of IS). The purpose of this book is to investigate the latter in the context of e-learning systems. Rokeach (1969; 1973) in his value theory argues that "the concept of value, more than any other, is the core concept across all the social science" (1973, p. ix). He defines values as "[having] to do with modes of conduct and end-states of existence" (1969, p. 160). He also suggests that "to say that a person 'has a value' is to say that he has an enduring belief that a specific mode of conduct or end-state of existence is personally and socially preferable to alternative modes of conduct or end-states of existence" (1969, p. 160). He claims that "once a value is internalized it becomes, consciously or unconsciously, a standard or criterion for guiding action" (1969, p. 160).

Similarly, Kluckhohn (1951) defines values as "culturally weighted preferences for things, ideas, people, institutions, and behavior" (p. 388). Allport, Vernon, and Lindzey (1951) in a more specific definition suggest that "value enables one to measure the relative order of importance" (p. 6). Furthermore, Posner and Munson (1979) noted that "values describe what individuals consider to be important" (p. 10). Consistent with the literature and in the context of e-learning systems, this study defines learners' value items as measures of the importance of enduring core beliefs concerning each characteristic of e-learning systems when learning online.

Value theory (Rokeach, 1969, 1973, 1979) suggests that values are different from attitudes. Rokeach (1969) claims that values are "justifying one's own and others' actions and attitudes" (p. 160). Moreover, he elaborates, "a value, unlike an attitude, is an imperative to action, not only a belief about the preferable but also a preference for the preferable...a value, unlike attitude, is a standard or yardstick to guide actions, attitudes, comparisons, evaluations, and justifications of self and others" (1969, p. 160).

List of Values (LOV) theory (Kahle, 1983; Kahle, Beatty, & Homer, 1986) argues that Rokeach's value theory is too vague and not specific to the values of life's major roles (i.e., marriage, parenting, work, leisure, school, and daily tasks). The LOV theory, (Kahle, 1983; Kahle et al., 1986) concentrated on values consumers sought and defined consumer shopping values as "what is important to consumers." It also argues that values impact attitudes which, in turn, impact behavior (Durgee, O'Connor, & Veryzer, 1996; Kahle, 1983; Kahle et al., 1986).

User Information Satisfaction (UIS) theory (Bailey & Pearson, 1983; Ives, Olson, & Baroudi, 1983) and End-User Computing Satisfaction (EUCS) theory (Doll & Torkzadeh, 1988, 1991; Torkzadeh & Doll, 1991) suggest that user satisfaction is a "surrogate" construct for system effectiveness. However, several other IS studies define satisfaction as attitude. IS literature is not consistent regarding the differences between the construct of attitude and satisfaction. Several IS studies refers to the construct of satisfaction as synonymous to the construct of attitude (Doll & Torkzadeh, 1991, p. 6; Sethi & King, 1999, p. 93; Srinivasan, 1985, p. 244). However, other IS studies point out that the constructs of attitude and satisfaction are related, but have different meaning (Galletta & Lederer, 1989, p. 420). Allport (1935) suggests that "attitude is a state of readiness which exerts influence over one's actions." Rokeach (1969) defines attitude as "a relatively enduring organization of beliefs around an object or situation predisposing one to respond in some preferential manner" (p. 112). Conversely, Galletta and Lederer (1989) suggest that "user satisfaction is a state at a given point of time (rather than lasting trait) and ... influenced by experience" (p. 427). Srinivasan (1985) reported several studies that suggest system usage impacts user satisfaction, whereas positive or negative satisfaction impacts attitude towards the system (p. 244). Kim (1989) suggests that individual intention to use and usage of a system can be predicted by "some weighted combination of the individual's attitude toward MIS-related objects" (p. 3).

IS literature noted that a richer framework is needed based on behavioral theories, to identify and measure factors that predict attitude in order to fully understand the implications of user satisfaction on the effectiveness of information systems (Doll & Torkzadeh, 1988, 1991; Torkzadeh & Doll, 1991). As noted, Rokeach (1969, 1973) argued that the constructs of attitude and satisfaction are in a lower cognitive level than the construct of value. Value theory and User Satisfaction theory suggest that these constructs are represented in the sequence: *values* impact *attitudes* which impact *behaviors*, which in turn impact *satisfaction*. The goal of this study is not aiming at providing empirical evidence for such sequence, rather to build upon such sequence in developing a framework to indicate learners' perceived effectiveness of e-learning systems.

Although *value* is recognized by several IS researchers (Bailey & Pearson, 1983), as an important construct in the process that effects user satisfaction and user behavior, later work by Ives et al. (1983), Doll and Torkzadeh (1988, 1991), and Torkzadeh and Doll, (1991) ignored the construct of value while concentrating on the measures of satisfaction only. Earlier work in the development of UIS theory (Bailey & Pearson, 1983) proposed a model including value items evaluating the "degree of importance" as well as satisfaction items for each system characteristic. In a later work, Ives et al. (1983) suggests that "the weighted [value score] and un-weighted [satisfaction] scores are highly correlated, making the additional information provided by the importance rating unnecessary" (p. 787).

Overall, both UIS and EUCS theories argue that adding measurement of value is redundant and provide very little added information to the overall understanding of user satisfaction and users' effectiveness of IS. Several researchers criticized both UIS and EUCS theories for omitting the measurements of value (Etezadi-Amoli & Farhoomand, 1991). They claim that in some instances of information systems, measurement of value can lead to a deeper understanding especially in the event that both are uncorrelated.

Grover et al. (1996) argue that for individuals "IS effectiveness is related to the extent to which IS satisfies the requirements of organization's members" (p. 180). They also suggest three types of measurement of IS effectiveness from the individual's unit of analysis: a comparative, a normative, and an improvement measurement. The comparative measurement determines IS effectiveness by comparing the effectiveness of a particular system with "peer systems" in other organizations. The normative measurement determines IS effectiveness by comparing the effectiveness of a particular system with a "theoretically ideal system." Lastly, the improvement measurement determines IS effectiveness by comparing the effectiveness of a particular system over time.

Rokeach (1969) claims that values also refer to "an end-state of existence one can strive for … while it is often impossible to achieve giving reality" (p. 160). Thus, in the context of this study learners' overall value of e-learning system represents the theoretically ideal state of such system. Conversely, IS satisfaction is suggested as the perceived performance level of a system (Doll & Torkzadeh, 1991, p. 6; Kim, 1989, p. 7). Thus, in the context of this study learners' overall satisfaction with e-learning systems represents the perceived performance state of such a system.

Following Grover et al.'s (1996) normative approach and in the context of this study, e-learning systems are considered effective when learners value its characteristics as highly important and are highly satisfied by those same characteristics. The other two types of effectiveness measurement (comparative and improvement) proposed by Grover et al. (1996) can be derived utilizing the normative measurement, however they are not part of this study.

Galletta and Lederer (1989) suggest practitioners are interested in tools "as a mechanism to uncover user perception of strength and weaknesses [of system characteristics]" (p. 421). Valentin (2001) suggests that marketing scholars (e.g., Andrews, 1987; Ansoff, 1965; Mintzberg, Ahlstrand, & Lampel, 1998; Porter, 1991) propose using Strengths-Weaknesses-Opportunities-Threats (SWOT) grids framework to assess companies' or products' performance. Such grids provide positioning of companies or products on a 2×2 matrix to indicate success and suggest improvements, modification, fundamental changes, or elimination needed to improve such products in the marketplace. Following this approach, in the context of e-learning systems, Value-Satisfaction grids will be developed to provide actions and improvement priorities for the e-learning system characteristics and dimensions. Due to the heterogeneous nature of the e-learning system dimensions, it will be appropriate to develop a grid for each of the four dimensions proposed in literature as well as for the overall system.

The Value-Satisfaction grid proposed provides a tool to indicate action and improvement priorities for e-learning systems as well as a technique for measuring the true effectiveness of e-learning systems. In addition, an index would be useful to provide a measure of the magnitude of the implied e-learning system's effectiveness. The Learners' Value Index of Satisfaction (LeVIS) is proposed as a benchmarking tool combining the learners' perceived value and satisfaction in order to indicate the magnitude of the learners' perceived e-learning system's effectiveness. The LeVIS index combines e-learning system's *value* measures and e-learning system's *satisfaction* measures in order to provide an overall index of learners' perceived effectiveness of an e-learning system.

Summary of Research Questions

This book reports on a research study of business learners' value and satisfaction of e-learning systems as a component contributing to the learners' perceived effectiveness of e-learning systems. It asks the following research question: Is there a relationship between learners' perceived *satisfaction* and learners' perceived *value* for learners' perceived effectiveness of an e-learning system? As the main research question guiding the research study focuses on learners' perceived effectiveness of an e-learning system; finding and measuring learners' value and learners' satisfaction for each e-learning system's characteristic will be the core of this research study. It is also the goal of this study to explore the relationship between learners' overall value and overall satisfaction of each e-learning system's dimension providing indication for the assessment of learners' perceived effectiveness of the e-learning system. Therefore, seven more specific research questions are addressed:

RQ1: What characteristics of e-learning systems are important for learners?

RQ2: What are the significant factors for learners' perceived *value* of e-learning systems?

RQ3: What are the significant factors for learners' perceived *satisfaction* of e-learning systems?

RQ4: How well do the actual value measures elicited from learners fit the imputed value measures derived via data mining techniques? Which data mining technique provides the best fit and how does it compare with statistical estimation procedures?

RQ5: How is the overall perceived learning measure related to the overall value, satisfaction and perceived effectiveness of an e-learning system?

RQ6: How are aggregated learners' perceptions of the overall value and overall satisfaction of the e-learning system under this study positioned in the Value-Satisfaction grid (overall and separately for each of the four e-learning system's dimensions)?

RQ7: What is the learners' perceived effectiveness of e-learning systems (as measured by LeVIS) for each of the e-learning system's dimension (technology and support, course, professor as well as learners' dimension) and overall?

Gaining insight into the answers to these questions is challenging given the complexity of the phenomena. Nevertheless, these insights are of great value to practitioners and researchers alike. These insights are important for practitioners in order to increase student retention, reduce students' frustration with e-learning systems, extend the longevity of such programs, and provide a benchmarking tool for such systems. At the same time these insights are important for researchers in uncovering the importance of value construct in conjunction with the construct of satisfaction and their impact on the learners' perceived effectiveness of e-learning systems, while providing a general framework of the phenomenon on hand.

Contributions of the Research

The research study presented in this book provides five main contributions. IS literature include numerous studies assessing IS effectiveness by the measurement of user satisfaction mainly for decision support systems. Value theory (Rokeach, 1969, 1973, 1979) suggests *value* as a core construct across all the social science. However, *value* construct in IS effectiveness is lacking. Furthermore, Brown (1976) criticized management and organizational behavior scholars for neglecting value construct in their theories (p. 16). Therefore, the first goal of the research study is to contribute to the IS knowledge domain by identifying, defining, and articulating the relationship between *value* and *satisfaction* constructs as assessment of users' perceived IS effectiveness.

Webster and Hackley's (1997) suggest four major dimensions of distance learning systems: technology and support, course, professor, and learner's dimension. Following their approach, the second objective of the research study is to gather qualitative data from the learners' point of view on all system's characteristics and what they value or find important when learning online. Subsequently, a survey instrument was constructed to empirically assess the findings of the qualitative study and generate a list of factors that contribute to learners' overall value and learners' overall satisfaction of e-learning systems. This approach provides guidelines to other researchers on the process of gathering value and satisfaction items as well as construction of factors leading to users' perceived effectiveness of other types of systems.

Brown (1976) contends that measuring satisfaction as well as value is a major burden on the respondents and pose a burden for researchers in the data collection process (p. 20). Consequently, respondents' fatigue from long questionnaires makes it difficult for researchers to gather both learners' value and satisfaction items of e-learning systems. Currently there are statistical techniques that can impute value scores from satisfaction scores. As the proposed survey instrument includes both learners' value measures and learners' satisfaction measures on the four dimensions of e-learning systems, it provides an opportunity to assess the accuracy of such techniques in an effort to reduce respondents' time. Therefore, the third objective of the research is to provide assessment of the reliability of such statistical techniques for predicting value scores of e-learning systems from elicited learners' satisfaction scores.

IS literature provides little agreement on the methods of assessing IS effectiveness. Kim (1989) claims that "measuring MIS effectiveness is a complex task because of the difficulties of tracing and measuring the effects of MIS through a web of intermediate factors" (p. 1). Yuthas and Eining (1995) claim that "despite the importance of IS effectiveness ... research in the field has not been successful in its attempts to identify the factors that influence IS effectiveness" (p. 69). Arnold (1995) at a moment of frustration from the IS effectiveness literature said "all too often the search for an [IS] effectiveness measure has resembled [the] search for [the] Holy Grail" (p. 85). However, Grover et al.'s (1996) proposed a general approach for measurement of IS effectiveness. Therefore, following their approach the fourth objective of this research is to develop and validate the Value-Satisfaction grids as well as the Learners' Value Index of Satisfaction (LeVIS) as benchmarking tools indicating learners' perceived effectiveness of e-learning systems.

Finally as a result of the research study, a development and validation of the two benchmarking tools (Value-Satisfaction grids and LeVIS), the fifth objective of the research study provides recommendations for researchers and practitioners regarding the learners' perceived effectiveness of such systems. The LeVIS index gives researchers a system benchmarking tool without ignoring the multi-dimensionality of such systems. Therefore, the research study presented in this book helps researchers by identifying key characteristics of the four dimensions (technology and support, course, professor, and learners' dimension) that warrant attention for future studies of e-learning systems. The study also helps practitioners by providing guidelines on channeling funds to effective factors and redesigning or eliminating non-effective factors.

Chapter Summary

This chapter has introduced the motivation behind this book and the argument for the significance of *value* as a key construct in the assessment and measurement of e-learning effectiveness. Additionally, the research questions, introduction to the guiding theories, and expected contributions of the research are discussed. Finally, the five main contributions of the research study presented in this book are proposed.

Chapter II

Values, Beliefs, Attitudes, and Behavior

Introduction

In three books on issues related to the construct of *value*, Rokeach (1969, 1973, 1979) contributed significantly to the overall understanding of *value* construct as a psychological phenomenon. In his first book, titled *Beliefs, Attitudes, and Values: A Theory of Organization and Change*, Rokeach (1969) presented a philosophical argument for the importance and association of value to other psychological aspects such as beliefs and attitudes. In his second, book titled *The Nature of Human Values*, Rokeach (1973) presented his value theory and an instrument to assess value, known as Rokeach's Value Survey, or RVS, as well as the rationale and validity of his survey instrument. In a third book, titled *Understanding Human Values*, Rokeach (1979) discussed the validity of his value theory along with a review of research studies that employed his theory in different research fields. Rokeach (1969) discussed the differences between: values, beliefs, attitudes, and behaviors. He suggested that values are underlying dispositions for individual's beliefs, attitude, and behavior.

In the following section, a review of such differences is presented in the context of information systems in general and e-learning systems in particular. Although the aim of this study is not to provide empirical evidence for such a sequence (i.e. value impacts on beliefs, attitude, and behavior), the relationships presented in literature among such constructs are valuable in developing a framework to assess e-learning systems' effectiveness that is built upon value theory. Furthermore, some IS scholars include attitudes and behaviors (or system usage) as constructs contributing to IS effectiveness. However, a review of these constructs in value theory literature is essential as it suggests these are mediating constructs rather than effecting constructs such as *value* and *satisfaction*.

Values and Beliefs

Rokeach (1969) defines belief as "any simple proposition, conscious or unconscious, inferred from what a person says or does" (p. 113). He suggests that all beliefs are predisposition to action. Rokeach (1969) proposes three kinds of beliefs. The first kind is a *descriptive* or *existential* belief, which coincides with common facts. An example of such a belief is: I believe that the sun rises in the east. The second kind is called an *evaluative* belief, which coincides with an individual's evaluative judgment. An example of such a belief is: I believe this ice cream is good. The third kind of a belief is a *prescriptive* or *exhortatory* belief. Example of such a belief is: I believe it is desirable that children should obey their parents. Rokeach (1969) also proposes that individuals possess a belief system that includes the "total universe of a person's beliefs about the physical world, social world, and the self" (p. 123).

Rokeach (1969) considers a *value* to be a type of belief that is "centrally located within one's total belief system, about how one ought or ought not to behave" (p. 124). By contrast, Feather (1975), in his book titled *Values in Education and Society*, criticizes Rokeach on equating values and beliefs. He claims that beliefs are considered to be "affectively neutral"; in other words, they are not related to a particular scenario or situation. However, values are not "neutral"; they are held with a slight degree of feeling (p. 4). Feather (1975) continues to criticize Rokeach by claiming that he argues that values may be classified as prescriptive or proscriptive beliefs rather than as a descriptive or evaluative belief (p. 4). Feather (1975) acknowledges that there is no sharp distinction between evaluative and prescriptive or proscriptive beliefs. As a matter of fact, that is his core argument for criticizing Rokeach's as "one would expect a person's judgments about what is good or bad to be highly correlated with his view about what is desirable or undesirable" (p. 5). As a result, this study assumes values as core beliefs (following Rokeach, 1973), but will relate to desirables (consistent also with Feather, 1975). This issue is also mentioned later in the review of value theory in management and marketing research. Management and marketing scholars claim that Rokeach's approach is not specific enough to measure individuals' perceived values of objects, ideas, or behaviors (Kahle, Beatty, & Homer, 1986).

Values and Attitudes

England (1967) noted that "values are similar to attitudes but are more ingrained, permanent and stable in nature" (p. 54). Rokeach (1969) suggests that unlike beliefs and its similarities to values, attitudes are fundamentally different than values in the fact that values appear to be underlying cognitive reasons for attitudes. In other words, he suggests that a value is the measurable criterion, or measurable weight, by which one rates an object or situation of his or her attitude. He defines attitude as an "organization of beliefs around an object or situation predisposing one to respond in some preferential manner" (p. 112). In other words, according to Rokeach (1969), attitudes are sets of beliefs formed mainly by past experiences. Rokeach (1969) presents a previous definition by Newcomb, Turner, and Converse (1965) that "the attitude concept seems to reflect quite faithfully the primary form in which past experience is summed, stored, and organized in the individual as he approaches any new situation" (p. 116).

Rokeach (1973) criticized social psychologists for putting too much attention in the concept of *attitude* and neglecting the concept of *value* (pp. 17-23). Brown (1976) used Rokeach's Value Survey (RVS) to measure the values of managers and employees in the workplace. She concluded that when looking at factors that motivate employees, scholars should pay more attention to the construct of value as opposed to the construct of attitude. Feather (1975) suggests that one plausible explanation for such neglect is due to the variety of models and instruments proposed over the years to measure attitudes compared with the limited number of procedures and instruments available for assessing values (p. 9). He also criticizes psychologists and sociologists for confusing the two concepts, for example, value and attitude, and in some cases considers the two as synonyms (Feather 1975, p. 10). Rokeach (1973) acknowledges that the lack of clarity about the conceptual differences between values and attitudes and about their functional inter-correlation may also cause such confusion (p. 18).

Rokeach (1969) also implies that value is "seen to be a disposition of a person" and underlying person's attitude (p. 124). He later (1973) suggested that values and attitudes are different in a number of important respects (p. 18). First, values transcend specific situations whereas attitudes do not have this transcendental quality about them. Second, values serve as important criteria or standards used by persons to evaluate objects, ideas, and actions. Attitudes, on the other hand, do not have these evaluative criteria about it. Third, a person has as many values as his or her "beliefs concerning desirable modes of conduct or end-states of existence" (Rokeach, 1973, p. 18). At the same time, he believes that a person has "as many attitudes as direct or indirect modes of encounters he had with specific object or situations" (p. 18). He believes that persons have thousands of attitudes, but only a few dozen values (Rokeach, 1973, p. 18). Other scholars consider this issue to be the root of the problem with Rokeach's theory as it is not measuring specific values but only vague life existence values. This issue will be further discussed in this section.

The fourth important point Rokeach (1973) suggests about the differences between values and attitudes deals with the notion that values are centrally located in one's personality makeup and cognitive system. In contrast, attitudes do not hold such central positions in one's personality. Feather (1975) agrees with Rokeach by claiming that attitudes do not occupy the central position that values do within one's personality makeup and cognitive system. Values are the "core" and closely situated with self-conceptions whereas attitudes are less directly connected to the self (p. 10). Also, Rokeach (1973) suggests that values are determinants of attitudes, as well as behavior (p. 18). He continues to claim that "individuals derive satisfaction from expressing attitude appropriate to their personal values" (Rokeach, 1969, p. 130). Accordingly, values impact attitude and satisfaction. Rokeach (1973) acknowledges that other scholars also noted this causal relationship between value and attitude, and not as a synonym as suggested by some other scholars (Allport, 1961; Watson, 1966; Woodruff, 1942; all found in Rokeach, 1973, p. 18). Examples of other scholars include Woodruff (1942), who claimed that "attitudes are functions of values" (p. 33). Allport (1961) claimed that "attitudes themselves depend on pre-existing social values" (pp. 802-803), and Watson (1966), who claimed "attitudes express values" (p. 215).

The fifth point Rokeach (1973) suggests is that value is a more dynamic concept than attitude and has more of an immediate link to motivation. This claim is controversial and other scholars, including IS and marketing scholars, dispute it. Some suggest that *value* is an important research concept as it is believed to impact attitude, which is believed to impact behavior, which in turn impacts satisfaction (Doll & Trokzadeh, 1991, p. 6; Durgee, O'Connor, & Veryzer, 1996, p. 90). Feather (1975) disagrees with Rokeach on this issue, and claims that attitudes do impact individuals' behavior. He provides an example to support his notion: if a teenager changed his attitude towards a popular singer, most likely he or she will no longer purchase the records of that singer (p. 7). As a result, this book follows both Rokeach (1973) and Feather (1975) in assuming that values are core beliefs that are related to a mode of conduct. However, they also assume to impact attitudes, behavior, and satisfaction.

Values and Behavior

England (1967) proposed a conceptual model on the impact of value on human behavior based on data collected from nearly 1,000 American managers. He noted that "the model also indicates the two primary ways in which values can influence behavior: behavior channeling (high value on honesty and integrity) and perceptual screening (filtering and influenced interpretation)" (pp. 54-55). He concluded his study by claiming that "what is being suggested is that a manager's behavior (insofar as it is influenced by his personal values) is best explained by utilizing those things he considers important" (p. 58).

Rokeach (1973) proposes that it is essential to explore human values as it predicts human behavior. He defines behavior as "a function of the interaction between two attitudes — attitude-toward-object and attitude-toward-situation" (pp. 127-128). Knowing individuals' values will enable us to predict individuals' behavior in experimental and real-life situations (p. 122). He proposes that individual's social behavior must always be mediated by at least two types of attitudes. The first one deals with the object, whereas the second deals with the situation by which such individuals encounter the object (Rokeach, 1969, p. 126). He continues to suggest that there are two major types of behavior. The first type deals with a single act, impulse act, or what he calls "molecular act," whereas the second type of behavior deals with a whole set of acts or what he terms "molar act." An example of molar acts that go beyond a single act can include pursuing a type of occupation or majoring in a certain kind of educational degree. He suggested that values underline both molecular and molar behaviors.

"There is no reason to expect that any one value or attitude should predict behavior perfectly … behavior towards a particular object in a particular situation is a function of the cognitive interaction between the attitude activated by the object and the attitudes activated by the situation within which the object is encountered. The attitudes toward object and situation are each functionally related to a subset of values that are activated by the attitude object on the one hand and by the situation on the other" (Rokeach, 1973, p. 162).

By contrast, Williams (1979) suggested that values are an essential guidance for human behavior and also in some cases serves as a justification to explain past conduct (p. 20). He asserts that human values do influence subsequent behavior and that data from experimental studies and non-experimental studies demonstrate such consequential patterns (p. 23). He continues by pointing out that individual behavior also depends upon the individual's attitude towards the object, idea, or situation. In agreement, Connor and Becker (1979) acknowledge the relationship among value, attitude, and behavior by claiming that behavior is considered as a "manifestation of value and attitude" (p. 72).

This review of the theoretical differences between the constructs of *value*, *belief*, *attitude,* and *behavior* provides support for the significant emphasis this study puts in researching the construct of value as the underlying construct. This review also suggests that although *belief*, *attitude,* and *behavior* constructs are significant, these constructs are mediating ones rather than effecting constructs such as *value* and *satisfaction*. Definition and discussion of the construct of *satisfaction* is provided in the following chapter.

Chapter Summary

This chapter provides a brief overview on the differences between values, beliefs, attitudes, and behaviors. It has long been documented in several streams of research (i.e., information systems, marketing, education, etc.) the major confusion scholars have with some of these constructs. This chapter attempted to clarify such confusion and to provide additional clarifications on how *values* are fitting into this cognitive map in the context of information systems as well as e-learning systems.

Chapter III

Value, Satisfaction, and Effectiveness

Introduction

In this chapter, a comprehensive review of the major literature streams is presented and serves as a foundation for this book. To identify the relevant theories of *value*, this chapter starts with a discussion of the value theory from the field of behavioral research psychology and explores its implications on research in the fields of education, marketing, and information systems (IS). Rokeach's Value Survey (RVS) theory, List of Values (LOV) theory, and value of information systems are discussed as the theoretical foundation for this study of learners' perceived value of e-learning systems.

To identify the relevant theories for studying *user satisfaction* of information systems, this chapter provides a discussion of two valid theories of user satisfaction from the IS field. User Information Satisfaction (UIS) theory and End-User Computing Satisfaction (EUCS) theory are presented as the foundation for guiding the assessment measures related to learners' perceived satisfaction with e-learning systems.

In the pursuit of development of a sound instrument to assess learners' perceived e-learning systems effectiveness, this chapter continues with a discussion of IS Effectiveness theory from the field of information systems. Technology mediated learning (TML) literature from IS and education is presented (e.g., Alavi, 1994; Alavi, Wheeler, & Valacich, 1995; Hiltz & Johnson, 1990; Hiltz & Wellman, 1997; Leidner & Jarvenpaa, 1993; Marks, 2000; Piccoli, Ahmad, & Ives, 2001; Webster & Hackley, 1997).

Value

Overview and Importance of Value

The concept of value, more than any other, is the core concept across all the social science. It is the main dependent variable in the study of culture, society, and personality, and it is the main independent variable in the study of attitude or behavior. It is difficult for me to conceive of any problem social scientists might be interested in that would not deeply involve human values. (Rokeach, 1973, p. ix)

The concept of value has a long history in psychology, sociology, anthropology, political science, economics, and other fields of social research. Value theory by definition specifies what values are, what people value, and what is the ultimate function or purpose of value in human behavior. The importance of research of *value* as a cognitive construct effecting human behavior has been recognized by scholars in various fields of research (Rafaeli & Raban, 2003; Reynolds & Jolly, 1980). Many scholars, including Allport, Vernon, and Lindzey (1951); England (1967); Feather (1967, 1975); and Rokeach (1969, 1973, 1979), based their suggestions on empirical studies. Although it is important to investigate the nature of attitudes and opinions, it is more fundamental to investigate the nature of values since attitudes and opinions can often change based on experience, while values remain relatively stable over time.

Following the initial work in value theory of Rokeach (1969, 1973, 1979) and Feather (1967, 1975) during the late 1960s and 1970s, several researchers suggested that the value construct is vital for the understanding of various management and educational constructs. England (1967) claimed that value construct is a complex phenomenon. Once measured, it can be very fruitful for researchers (p. 67). Brown (1976) criticized the management and organizational behavior scholars for neglecting the *value* construct when investigating causal factors that effect employee motivation. She claims that values are basic to behavior and are communicated verbally or nonverbally both by employees and managers. Examining the fit between employees' and managers' value system can uncover the key in a successful productive workplace, whereas the lack of fit might suggest key problems leading to an unproductive workplace (p. 18). She asserts that measuring the value system of both employees and managers, and comparing the two, will provide fruitful information on how to avoid or how to resolve issues in an unproductive workplace. Kahle and Kennedy (1988) suggest that previous studies show a causal link between value, attitude, and consumer behavior (p. 50). They also claim that there is evidence in literature to suggest that "values 'cause' attitudes, which in turn 'cause' shopping behavior" (p. 54). They emphasize the significance of *value* construct by saying that "without considering the function of values in a certain context, one may be missing an important influence on behavior" (p. 55).

Information Systems (IS) literature also indicate a similar argument. Doll and Torkzadeh (1991) suggest looking at the overall domain of MIS research. They argue that the MIS research domain include two different types of investigation in the "causal chain." The first one deals with downstream, or forward, investigating the causal link starting from attitude and going downstream to the social and economical impact of IS on organizations and individuals, hence the name "downstream." The second one deals with upstream, or backwards, investigating the causal link starting from attitude and going upstream to the causal factors (see Figure 1). They suggest that most IS research studies were concentrated in the downstream type, while very little attention has been placed on the upstream of IS research. They indicate that satisfaction in the IS domain is considered synonym for attitude (p. 6). They suggest that attitude research in the MIS domain lacks clarity as it "emphasize[s] the affective rather than the cognitive (e.g., belief) dimension of attitude" (p. 5).

Durgee, O'Connor, and Veryzer (1996) suggest that "sociologists feel that values impact attitudes which, in turn, impact behavior, as follows: VALUES → ATTITUDE → BEHAVIOR" (p. 90). They also argue for the importance of value research in business disciplines as "although a person's attitude and opinions might vary and conflict from time to time and [from] situation to situation, values are felt to be relatively enduring and have stronger effects on

Figure 1. Doll and Torkzadeh's (1991) conceptual model for EUCS

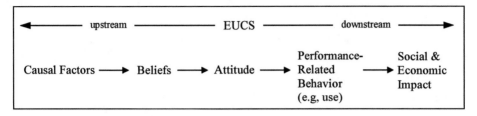

Source: Doll and Torkzadeh, 1991, Figure 1, p. 6

behavior" (Durgee et al., 1996, p. 91). The significance of value research is clearly demonstrated. However, such research is lacking in current IS literature. Consequently, this study contributes by providing the theoretical and empirical foundation for future value research in IS. The following section provides definition of value from prior literature. Subsequently, a discussion on the differences between *value* construct and other constructs such as *belief, attitude,* and *behavior* is presented. A review of instruments measuring values and studies using such instruments follows.

Definition of Value

Several definitions of the term "value" were found in literature, mainly from the field of psychology. Kluckhohn (1951) defined values as: "culturally weighted preferences for things, ideas, people, institutions, and behavior" (p. 388). England (1967) suggested that values refers to "concepts [that are] important or unimportant" (p. 57). He also noted that "personal value system makes a difference in terms of how [an individual] evaluates information … arrives at decisions — in short, how [an individual] behaves" (England, 1967, p. 53). Rokeach (1973) defined value as: "an enduring belief that a specific mode of conduct or end-state of existence is personally or socially preferable to an opposite or converse mode of conduct or end-state of existence" (p. 5). Feather (1975) criticized Rokeach's (1973) definition for using the word *belief* since beliefs are considered to be neutral, whereas one's values are neutral but are held with some degree of feeling (p. 4). He revised Rokeach's definition and suggested that values are: "beliefs about the desirables and therefore, involve some knowledge about the means or ends considered to be desirable"

(Feather, 1975, p. 5). Brown (1976) in an attempt to simplify Rokeach's definition of value suggested that value is "a belief upon which a person acts by preferences" (p. 16). Williams (1979) defined values as: "components in the guidance of anticipatory and goal-directed behavior; but they are also backward-looking in their frequent service to justify or 'explain' past conduct" (p. 20). He concluded by saying that values are "generalized criteria of desirability" (Williams, 1979, p. 28). Posner and Munson (1979) suggest that "values describe what individuals consider to be important" (p. 10). Keeney and Raiffa (1993) define values as "principles that an individual might adhere to" (p. 12). Rokeach (1969) argued that overall value, or what he called "personal value system," refers to the level of importance one places on a list of values (p.161).

Kahle and Chiagouris (1997, p. 102) suggested that a major disagreement exists among researchers in regards to the difference between the words "value" and "values." Some researchers, such as Fischhoff et al. (1980, found in Kahle & Chiagouris, 1997, p. 102), use the words "value" and "values" interchangeably, while others, such as Kahle and Chiagouris (1997), find it important to distinguish between the two. Consensus with earlier studies of value theory by other authors, such as Fischhoff et al. (1980, found in Kahle & Chiagouris, 1997, p. 102), agree that the words "value" and "values" are noticeably distinguished and refer to two different levels. Kahle and Chiagouris (1997) claim that "values" are the dimensions of "value." Similar to Rokeach's terminology, values refer to the collection of items contributing to the overall value, or what he called "personal value system."

In summary, literature suggests that values are enduring principles individuals use to evaluate the importance of objects, ideas, or behaviors. In the context of e-learning systems, this book will follow the definition of values from literature. Hence, *values of e-learning systems* are enduring principles learners use to evaluate the importance of e-learning system characteristics. Whereas e-learning system characteristics are the attributes (or features) associated with e-learning systems (e.g., quality of technical support, interaction with professor, quality of course content, learner's comfort with technology, etc.). This study also defines the term *value of e-learning systems*, similar to Rokeach's overall value, as an enduring core belief about the level of importance learners attribute to an e-learning system as a whole. In IS survey methods, *items* are defined as questions that seek to measure users' perceptions on various characteristics (e.g., those related to e-learning systems) (Bailey & Pearson, 1983; Doll & Torkzadeh, 1988, 1991; Ives, Olson, & Baroudi, 1983). Consequently, *learners' value items* are defined as measures of the importance of enduring core beliefs concerning each characteristics of an e-learning system when learning online.

Instruments to Measure Values

Rokeach (1969, 1973, 1979) developed a theoretical framework on the nature of values along with an instrument to measure them. In his second book (Rokeach, 1973), he presented an instrument to assess value (known in literature as the Rokeach Value Survey or RVS) as well as the rationale and validity of such survey instrument. The RVS was developed based on values that were gathered via interviews with groups of students. The reported values were listed alphabetically and participants were then asked to rank-order the values in terms of importance. Results provide a list of 36 values, 18 terminal and 18 instrumental values as noted in Table 1 (Rokeach, 1969, p. 169). The "terminal values," or personal and social values, and the second RVS's set of values called "instrumental values," or moral and competence values (See Table 1). The RVS is administered by asking respondents to rank order the two sets of values (terminal and instrumental separately) in their desired order of importance from 1 (most important) to 18 (least important) (Rokeach, 1973, p.27).

Table 1. Rokeach's (1973) terminal and instrumental values

Terminal Values	Instrumental Values
A comfortable life	Ambitious
An exciting life	Broadminded
A sense of accomplishment	Capable
A world at peace	Cheerful
A world of beauty	Clean
Equality	Courageous
Family security	Forgiving
Freedom	Helpful
Happiness	Honest
Inter harmony	Imaginative
Mature love	Independent
Natural security	Intellectual
Pleasure	Logical
Salvation	Loving
Self-respect	Obedient
Social recognition	Polite
True friendship	Responsible
Wisdom	Self-controlled

Rokeach (1969) suggests that *terminal values* refer to an end-state of existence one can strive for while it is often impossible to achieve giving reality (p. 160). For instance, he suggests that "a world at peace" is a terminal value (p. 175). Given reality, it is virtually impossible to achieve such an end-state of existence, or goal. However one can feel high value in such of an end-state of existence, or feel it is extremely important, and will act upon it, for example: join a world peace organization or become a diplomat helping nations achieve peace. He suggests that terminal values take the comparable form of "I believe that such-and-such and end-state of existence (i.e., salvation, a world in peace) is personally and socially worth striving for" (Rokeach, 1969, p. 160). Rokeach (1969) suggests that *instrumental values* refer to a single mode of conduct. For instance, he suggests that "helpful" is an instrumental value. One can feel high value in such single mode of conduct, or feel that it is extremely important, and act upon it. He suggests that instrumental values take the comparable form of "I believe that such-and-such a mode of conduct (i.e., honesty, courage) is personally and socially preferable in all situations with respect to all objectives" (Rokeach, 1969, p. 160).

Other philosophers suggested a more pragmatic definition of instrumental values. Johonson (1978), in his book *Modes of Value*, suggested that an instrumental value refers to an instrument when being used. He suggests, for example, that a pen has value when it is being used to write something on a stable surface; however, it does not have this status, *mode of value*, when a person tries to use it as a life-raft when he is drowning (p. 90). He also suggested that "any entity has an instrumental value when it is being used to produce a result" (p. 90). Johonson's approach is slightly different from the one taken by Rokeach; as RVS measures general values of human behavior and ignores the specific values a human might perceive in a particular object, idea, or situation. The next section will review some empirical studies using RVS.

Prior Studies Using RVS

Rokeach (1969) reported in his book some significant research findings about a study to determine values. The study included three separate parts, consisting of two test-retest time intervals. The second part of the study occurred three weeks after the first one (i.e., the first test-retest time interval of three weeks), followed by the third part of the study after three months (i.e., the second test-retest time interval of three months). Three groups of participants were used for this study. The control group A included 47 students during the first time interval (three weeks) and 32 students during the second time interval (three months). Experimental groups B and C included 135 and 178 students during the first time interval (three weeks) as well as 93 and 120 students during the second time interval (three months), respectively. A week after the first test, experimental group B listened to several lectures (as part of the class) on the significance of the two values relative to other values. Similarly, group C has also listened to several lectures (as part of the class) on the significance of two other values relative to the rest of the values. However, these two values emphasized to group C were different than the two presented to group B. By contrast, control group A did not listen to any lectures about those values. The instrument was administered to all three groups following the lecture series; once two weeks later and again three months later.

Results show that control group A had generally non-significant changes in values over the first and second test-retest. Experimental group B showed significant changes in the two values discussed in the lectures three weeks later, and a non-significant increase three months later on. Experimental group C showed significant changes in the two values discussed in that class lecture three weeks later, and non-significant increase three months later. Based on the results, Rokeach (1969) concluded that although two values out of 18 did change after three weeks, in the long run the change was non-significant. As a result, he noted that values are "enduring" over long period of time (Rokeach, 1969, p. 174). The study also shows another interesting result about the fact that values that were not discussed at all, did not change over both time intervals.

Following this discovery, in an effort to validate the reliability of individual values and the value systems (overall value) of individuals, Feather (1975) conducted a study with 77 students who enrolled in an introductory psychology course at Flinders University in South Australia. His study includes a test-retest validity check for the RVS instrument over a five-week period. The RVS instrument was administrated during the first week of the term, and again five weeks later. Results show that in general, individual values and value systems (overall value) are stable over a five-week period. Based on this, he concluded that the results are consistent with those reported by Rokeach (1969) and that the reliability test suggests that the RVS instrument is stable and reliable to measure values.

In a later study, Rokeach (1973) administered the RVS instrument to a larger group of adult Americans over 21 who registered with the National Opinion Research Center. The national sample includes respondents drawn from all levels of American society. A sample of 1,409 adult men and women was collected with about 52% women and 48% men. Results were interpreted based on several demographics indicators: gender, social class (income and education), race, age differences, religious beliefs, and political beliefs. The results showed that both terminal and instrumental values varied significantly between different levels of demographics groups (p. 93-94).

In a review of instruments to measure values, Brown (1976) suggests using RVS, but criticizes it as a major "burden on the respondents … to rank each of these [terminal and instrumental value] lists by relative importance" (p. 20). Besides posing a "burden for respondents" in the data collection process, she criticizes RVS's rank-order procedure for also limiting the data analysis techniques that can be used (p. 21). Brown (1976) concluded that when looking at factors that motivate employees, scholars should pay more attention to the construct of value and compare the "value match" between management and employees.

Three years later, Posner and Munson (1979) conducted a review of previous literature dealing with value (using RVS) and its effect on managers and employees. One study they point to shows close similarities between the values of college students and industrial engineers. In another study, they point out, a significant differences was evident between values of managers and employees. A third study in their review shows a significant difference between values measured with RVS instrument of ministers, purchasing executives, and scientists.

Several years later, Thompson, Levitov, and Miederhoff (1982) conducted a study to assess the construct validity of the RVS instrument. They suggest that "values play an important role in education and psychology because values are central to personhood" (p. 899). They claim that previous studies have been less extensive in their quest to assess such construct validity. In their study, 174 adult education students enrolled in a university in the Southeastern US were administered the RVS instrument in a rating scale. Principal components analysis (PCA) was conducted with a Varimax rotation following the same steps Rokeach (1973) included in his study of 1409 respondents. Thompson et al. (1982) suggest that their results contradict Rokeach's (1973) results that the 36 values are independent of each other. They claim that results of their study show that values do overlap and therefore ranking such values may limit substantially the results (p. 902-903). They point out that the RVS instrument is by nature a ranking instrument, and as such it has two major limitations.

The first one deals with the fact that once a respondent ranked an item as the most important (or ranked it as number 1) by default, all other items are ranked lower. They assert that persons find many values as "almost equally desirable" but cannot rate them as equally important due to the nature of the instrument (p. 903). The second limitation Thompson et al. (1982) suggest of RVS deals with the fact that ranked data should not have been analyzed in factor analysis as factor analysis is not suitable for such data. They concluded that the ranking of values "'dishonors' the psychological reality of value perception" and that the rating of values seems more appropriate when measuring value perceptions (Thompson et al., 1982, p. 903). After a comprehensive review of value literature, Ng (1982) suggests that rating procedure of values is more suitable over the original RVS ranking procedure, especially for cross-cultural studies of values. He also sided with Thompson et al. (1982) regarding the two major limitations of the original ranking RVS instrument discussed. Furthermore, an additional obvious disadvantage of ranking measures over rating measures is that the distance between any two consecutive ranks is exactly one, whereas the differences of their rating measure can vary widely.

Chapman, Blackburn, and Austin (1983) conducted a study to investigate the validity of converting the rank order RVS data to a rate order. They claim that the rank order data provides a major challenge for researchers in terms of analyzing the data and that "rank ordered data cannot easily be entered into regression or other multivariate analysis" (p. 419). They also claim that due to that limitation, the "relationships between people's value structure and other attitudes or behaviors have often been unexplored" (p. 419). Their sample included 63 faculty members in the area of science, social science, and humanities at the University of Michigan. Each respondent was asked to rank order RVS value items and also rate each value item on a 1-8 scale, from least important (1) to most important (8). In analyzing the data, the rank order were also converted to a normal distribution (i.e., rated data) trough a transformation into Z scores corresponding to the division into 17 equal areas (18 boundary points) under the normal curve (p. 420). Their aim was to test the converted rank data (or "hypothetical rating") with the actual rating data. Results show that both the converted rank data (or "hypothetical rating") and the actual rating data were highly correlated. They concluded by claiming that their findings support the validity that the procedure of rating values is at least as applicable and suitable as ranking values (Chapman et al., 1983, p. 421).

Prescott and Hopkins (1984) conducted a study to investigate the relationships between value, attitude, and behavior of educators. Their sample size included 103 special educators who were enrolled in the department of education at a university in the Chicago metropolitan area. The Minnesota Attitude Inventory (MTAI) instrument was used to assess attitude, while RVS was used to assess value. Their results show that there is significant evidence linking teachers' values and attitudes. They claimed that some teachers' values may provide significant support for (or mediators of) attitudes about classroom behavior (Prescott & Hopkins, 1984, p. 58).

In an effort to predict college academic achievement, Coyne (1988) conducted a study using RVS instrument on college students. The sample size included 518 students enrolled in introductory psychology classes at Washington State University. Respondents also allow researchers to access their high school GPA and college aptitude test scores. The results show that RVS shades little as a predictor of academic success, whereas high school data is a more promising predictor. Coyne (1988) attributes his results on the rank-order nature of RVS and concluded that such a measure brings major difficulty to researchers. As a result researches should opt to transform the rank scale into an interval rating scale (p. 171).

Payne (1988) also criticizes RVS for its ranking order procedure and suggests that rating procedure of values is more appropriate when a research investigates the nature of value perceptions. He suggests that "knowledge of the characteristics and limitations of value ... measures allow business educators to make better selection of possible supplements to traditional instructional methods" (p. 273). He also criticizes RVS for being too vague, especially in the case of research in academic fields and points out several limitations of RVS instrument. First, respondents are constrained to a standard set of values that may not effectively describe values that they recognize and view as important. Second, values are being suggested to respondents which may not actually be part of their cognitive worlds. Third, there can be issues involving respondent agreement concerning definition, connotations, or meanings of terms used in the RVS items. Payne (1988) claims that some scholars found the application of a Likert-type scaling procedure that they have used with the RVS, to be as reliable as the ranking procedure developed by Rokeach. This application, he suggested can "bring with it great information about intensity of values, quicker administration, and availability of parametric statistical analysis" (p. 275). Consequently, a rating measure of values will be proposed in this study in the development of the value instrument. Doing so will allow respondents to answer the survey much quicker and enable better statistical analysis of the data. Table 2 presents a summary of literature related to Rokeach's Value Survey (RVS) that was reviewed and its major findings or contributions.

Table 2. Summary of literature related to RVS

Study	Methodology	Sample	Instrument/ Constructs	Main findings or contribution
Rokeach, 1969	Theoretical, Case study, & Survey	360 college students in three groups (one control & two experimental)	RVS	Some minor changes were observed after three weeks and non-significant changes after five months. Thus, values are enduring!
Feather, 1967	Theoretical & Survey	77 students (introductory psychology)	RVS	Individual values and value system (overall value) are stable over five-week period. Reliability test suggests that the RVS instrument is stable and reliable.
Rokeach, 1973	Theoretical & Survey	1409 adult American men & women	RVS	Both terminal and instrumental values vary significantly between different levels of demographics groups.
Brown, 1976	Theoretical	Commentary	RVS	**RVS ranking is "a burden for respondents" and data analysis.** Scholars should pay more attention to the construct of *value* and compare the "value match" between management and employees.
Posner & Munson, 1979	Theoretical	Commentary	RVS	Value and value system do significantly from managers and employees.
Thompson, Levitov, & Miederhoff, 1982	Theoretical & Survey	174 adult education students enrolled in a university in the Southeastern US	RVS in a rating scale (not ranking as the original RVS items are)	Results of the Factor Analysis don't match Rokeach's (1973) results. **They argue that rating is more appropriate than ranking.**
Ng, 1982	Theoretical	Commentary		**Rating is more appropriate than ranking.**
Chapman et al., 1983	Theoretical & Survey	63 faculty members	RVS in both ranking & rating	**Rating values is at least as applicable and suitable as ranking values.**
Prescott & Hopkins, 1984	Theoretical & Survey	103 special educators	MTAI instrument used to assess attitude, RVS was used to assess value	Some teachers' values may be important support for or mediators of attitudes about classroom behavior. **Values → Attitude → Behavior**
Coyne, 1988	Theoretical & Survey	518 students at Washington State University	RVS	RVS add little as a predictor of academic success. **Researchers should opt to transform the rank scale into an interval rating scale.**
Payne, 1988	Theoretical	Commentary	RVS	**Argued that Likert-type value scaling was found to be as reliable as the ranking procedure.**

List of Values (LOV)

The work done by Rokeach laid the foundation for other theories of value and the empirical work on the impact of value on other cognitive constructs such as attitude, behavior, and satisfaction. Several researchers have used and validated the RVS in several fields of study (Chapman et al., 1983; Coyne, 1988; Payne, 1988; Posner & Munson, 1979; Thompson et al., 1982). Nevertheless, some criticize RVS for its rank-order nature as well as for not being specific enough for many other fields of study (Beatty, Kahle, Homer, & Misra, 1985; Kahle, Beatty, & Homer, 1986). As a result, some scholars sought to develop alternative approaches and measurement instruments. One such instrument is the List of Values (LOV) developed by Kahle et al. (1983, 1986) for assessment of values in advertising and market research purposes. LOV is grounded in the theoretical foundation of Rokeach's (1969, 1973, 1979) and Feathers' (1975) work on values. They suggest that RVS is not specific enough for the values of life's major roles (i.e., marriage, parenting, work, leisure, school, and daily tasks). Initially, Kahle (1983) approach was to modify RVS's terminal values into a smaller subset of values that were both generalized across important situations and that were easier to administer. A study with 2,264 Americans respondents was conducted by the Survey Research Center in the Institute of Social Research at the University of Michigan. Respondents were asked to rank what they considered as the first and second most important value from a list of values. A list of nine values was generated to form the LOV instrument. In this instrument, respondents asked to rank order the list of nine items. They concluded that the LOV instrument is comparable to RVS due to its raking assessment method of individual's values (see the list in Figure 2).

Beatty et al. (1985) conducted a study to validate the initial LOV instrument in comparison to the RVS instrument. They developed a questionnaire made out of three parts. The first part included the two subsections: (1) RVS questions and (2) LOV questions both in ranking formats. The second part of their instrument included a variety of consumption questions such as the frequency of consuming different things (cold breakfast, hot breakfast, coffee, sweets, etc.), frequency of engagement in different activities (watching TV, golfing, fishing, attending movies, attending the opera, visiting art galleries, etc.). Finally, the third part of their instrument included questions associated with gift-giving attitudes and behaviors on Likert-type items. The entire questionnaire took approximately 30 minutes to complete. The questionnaire was administered to 356 freshman and MBA-level students. Their results show that

"'LOV' items appear to have construct validity when contrasted with the widely used RVS items" (Beatty et al., 1985, p. 189). Such results indicate that indeed more specific value instruments are appropriate, especially for other fields of study than psychology. They also suggest that their findings support empirically the validity of LOV and the impact of values on attitude and behavior for consumers (p. 192). They concluded that since LOV is an easier instrument to administer than RVS and it appears to be equally valid to RVS, then it is a more appropriate measurement of values of consumers.

Kahle et al. (1986) conducted another study to validate the LOV instrument. A sample of 112 students enrolled at the University of Oregon, including international students from 25 countries was used. In their study, they normalized the LOV ranking results in order to convert it to rating format. Doing so is consistent with previous literature as ranking format is difficult to analyze in statistical methods. The results suggest that this method might have decreased the power of the LOV items found in their results, however, it was needed to better analyze the data (p. 408). They indicated that a rating LOV instrument will help other researchers investigating this phenomenon.

In order to develop a rating rather than ranking LOV instrument, Kahle and Kennedy (1988) conducted a study introducing a rating LOV instrument. The rating LOV instrument included the same nine-item values as the original LOV instrument. The only difference was that in this instrument respondent were asked to rate the value items, rather then rank it. They propose asking respondents to rate each item on a Likert-type scale from 1 (Very Unimportant) to 9 (Very Important) (see Figure 2). Converting the LOV instrument to a rating format, they claim, will not only help to administer the Instrument, but also enable an effective analysis of the data.

Durgee et al. (1996) conducted a study to seek new values from consumers. Theoretically grounded in RVS and LOV, their methodology included qualitative assessment of values. A group of 55 mothers, aged 30 to 50, were interviewed for approximately 25 minutes. The results suggest five highest ranked values: good health, family security, happiness, freedom, and moral goodness. They concluded that it is essential for scholars to identify and track key values, and understand their impact on attitude and behavior (Durgee et al., 1996, p. 99).

In summary, it is suggested that RVS is more vague and broad, and not focused enough for specific fields of study. It is also evident that the ranking of value items provide a major challenge for respondents and researchers alike. Therefore, this study proposes a survey instrument to measure values in the

Figure 2. Kahle and Kennedy's (1988) instrument of rating LOV

The following is a list of things that some people look for or want out of life. Please study the list carefully and then rate each thing on how important it is in your daily life, where 1 = not at all important, and 9 = extremely important.

		Very Unimportant		Very Important
1.	Sense of Belonging		1—2—3—4—5—6—7—8—9	
2.	Excitement		1—2—3—4—5—6—7—8—9	
3.	Warm Relationships with Others		1—2—3—4—5—6—7—8—9	
4.	Self-Fulfillment		1—2—3—4—5—6—7—8—9	
5.	Being Well Respected		1—2—3—4—5—6—7—8—9	
6.	Fun and Enjoyment of Life		1—2—3—4—5—6—7—8—9	
7.	Security		1—2—3—4—5—6—7—8—9	
8.	Self-Respect		1—2—3—4—5—6—7—8—9	
9.	A Sense of Accomplishment		1—2—3—4—5—6—7—8—9	

Source: Kahle and Kennedy, 1988, Table 2, p. 52

Table 3. Summary of literature related to LOV

Study	Methodology	Sample	Instrument/ Constructs	Main findings or contribution
Kahle, 1983	Theoretical, Case study, & Survey	2,264 Americans conducted by the University of Michigan	Based on RVS's instrumental values	LOV instrument nine values: 1. Self-Respect 2. Sense of Accomplishment 3. Being Well Respected 4. Security 5. Warm Relationships with Others 6. Sense of Belonging 7. Fun and Enjoyment in Life 8. Self-Fulfillment 9. Excitement
Beatty, Kahle, Homer, & Misra, 1985	Theoretical & Survey	356 freshman and MBA level students	LOV, RVS, attitude & behavior measures	LOV is an easier instrument to administer than RVS, it appears to be equally valid to RVS, and it is more appropriate for measurement of values of consumers. **Values → Attitude → Behavior**
Kahle, Beatty, & Homer, 1986	Theoretical & Survey	112 students from University of Oregon	LOV	Normalized the LOV ranking results in order to convert it to rating format. Doing so is consistent with previous literature as ranking format is difficult to analyze in statistical methods.
Kahle, & Kennedy, 1988	Theoretical	Commentary	LOV with 1-9 Likert-type scale (rating)	**Values → Attitude → Behavior**
Durgee, O'Connor, & Veryzer, 1996	Theoretical & Survey	55 mothers, aged 30 to 50	Combination of values from the RVS and LOV instruments	**Values → Attitude → Behavior** (p. 90) The 5 highest ranked values are: 1. Good Health 2. Family Security 3. Happiness 4. Freedom 5. Moral Goodness

context of e-learning systems using rating scale. Additional information on the development of the survey instrument is provided in Chapter VI. Table 3 presents a summary of literature related to LOV that was reviewed in this section and its major findings or contributions.

Review of Value-Related Studies from the Fields of OR, IS, and Education

Another significant stream of research in the area of value theory is the value of information systems in the field of operations research (OR) and information systems (IS). This include: the value of information systems (King & Epstein, 1983) and the theory of consumer value (Keeney, 1994; 1999) based on theoretical foundation of Keeney and Raiffa (1993).

King and Epstein (1983) conducted a study to develop a linear model assessing the value of information systems as a function of IS characteristics. Their empirical work includes a study of "managers in two firms and their assessment of the importance of IS characteristics, the level of satisfaction produced by various levels of each IS characteristic, and the overall value of the total systems" (p. 34). Based on previous literature, they claimed that the value of information system is conceptually based on multi-characteristic approach (King & Epstein, 1983, p. 34).

The main purpose of King and Epstein's (1983) study was to explore whether it is practical to apply multi-characteristic linear value models in assessing the value of IS. The primary focus of their study was on the "evaluative judgment" of managers who use IS in their decision-making process. Furthermore, they wanted to determine consistency between the overall evaluations of "total systems" of managers and a derived overall value from a linear model that incorporates managers' evaluation of the IS characteristics. A second main focus of their study was to compare the validity of a rank-order procedure and the interval-scale rating of each item and determine whether ranking is superior to rating. If it is not superior, they claim, then the simpler ordinal rating can greatly facilitate the implementation of the multi-characteristic approach (p. 35). For this purpose, they proposed the following linear model for the assessment of the overall value of IS:

$$W = V_1 S(a_1) + V_2 S(a_2) + ... + V_{10} S(a_{10}) \qquad (1)$$

Where the V_i are the value measures, or relative importance weights, attached to the IS characteristic a_i and the $S(a_i)$, are the satisfaction valuation of each characteristic a_i. W in Equation 1 represents the overall system value, which they assume as a linear combination of the value measure and the valuation of the satisfaction of all 10 characteristics (King & Epstein, 1983, p. 35). This study proposes a model constructed in a similar way in the context of e-learning systems. However, note a major distinction in the fact that the multiplication of value and satisfaction yields the overall perceived effectiveness, rather than just the overall value. Moreover, the proposed model in this study adds to the body of literature by examining also a non-linear approach, utilizing logistics regression analysis. Additional information is provided in Chapter VII as part of the data analysis of the case study.

King and Epstein (1983) noted that in a previous experimental field study with 60 managers in a manufacturing firm, the values (or importance) associated with IS characteristics were collected and analyzed. The results yielded 10 characteristics associated with the overall value of IS. These include: reporting cycle, information sufficiency, information understandability, freedom of bias, reporting delay (timeliness), system reliability, decision relevance, cost efficiency, comparability (format, consistency), and quantitativeness (quantifiability). Data from this study was analyzed along with new data from a second firm (Firm B, service).

In both firms, middle managers were asked to evaluate each of the systems they utilize for the 10 characteristics using the same instrument for each characteristic. The title of the instrument (see "<Reporting Cycle>" in Figure 3) labeled the name of a given characteristic measured. For each characteristic, respondents were given a typical decision-making context from their area of expertise. Respondents were asked individually to assess the satisfaction that they would derive from each characteristic on a five-point Likert-type scale and at the same time select a point on the satisfaction scale on a continuous scale between "Greatest Satisfaction Possible" and "Lowest Satisfaction Possible." The satisfaction scores for each of the 10 characteristics are the $S(a_i)$ noted in Equation 1. Respondents were also asked to mark a point on the scale to the right from 0 to 100 to describe their perceptions of the relative 'importance' of each characteristic (King & Epstein, 1983, p. 37).

Following the previous procedure, respondents were given another instrument and were also asked to make an overall evaluation of the total system. They were asked about the overall level of satisfaction and the overall level of importance, the weight or value similarly to the one obtained via Figure 3.

Figure 3. King and Epstein's (1983) instrument to measure IS characteristics

<Reporting Cycle*>

Please indicate the relative satisfaction you would receive in the case of each type of *reporting cycle* described below.

The *reporting cycle* relates to the frequency with which formal measurement of observations of events are made. Such informational inputs for the decision process you will perform will be generated

	SUBJECTIVE SATISFACTION SCALE		
	GREATEST		
Extremely frequent, such as whenever a specified event	SATISFACTION	--------	100
occurs.	POSSIBLE	--	90
		--	80
Very frequently.		--	70
		--	60
Moderately frequently		--	50
		--	40
Fairly infrequently.		--	30
		--	20
Very infrequently.	LOWEST	--	10
	SATISFACTION	--------	0
	POSSIBLE		

King and Epstein's (1983) instrument was a combination of 10 sections, one for each of the system's characteristics. Each section includes the structured measure noted in this figure, while the title of the section noting the name of each characteristic and the explanations associated with each characteristic were different.

Finally, respondents were asked to rank order all the characteristics related to each of the IS in order to generate the ranking scale.

Data from both firms totaled 236 system evaluations. Out of that, 180 evaluations were completed by 60 middle managers from Firm A (the manufacturing company) over three different systems and 56 evaluations were completed by eight managers from Firm B (the service company) over seven different systems. Their results show that the analysis of the data provides a high correlation (0.992 for Firm A and 0.969 for Firm B) between the results drawn from the ranking items and the rating items. Based on that, the implication of their results demonstrate that there is little added by using "cumbersome procedure's such as the ranking procedure in the measurement of values" (pp. 41-42). This is further evidence to support the approach that this study takes by using rating value items. King and Epstein (1983) also noted that although their model is based on linearity assumption, it "suggest[s] that the 'mental models' of the respondents may, in fact, be nonlinear" (King & Epstine, 1983, p. 40). Consequently, this study explores both linear and non-linear models.

Keeney and Raiffa (1993) proposed a multiple-objectives preferences and value tradeoff theory. Keeney (1994) describes in detail the foundation of their value theory and the rationale for defining, outlining, and measuring values. Keeney and Raiffa (1993) suggested that a value model refers to an objective or utility function when uncertainties are involved in any chosen alternative. Accordingly, there are two major types of value functions. The first type of value function is called an *ordinal value function*, representing the case where one is interested only in ranking alternatives. The second type of value function is called a *measurable value function*, representing the case where one is interested in the strength of preference for some alternative over another. RVS is an example of ordinal value function, as the instrument is measuring the relative ranking of all; consequently, values and tradeoffs between values are not needed.

Keeney and Raiffa (1993) suggest that value models include values with quantitative relationships. They claim that the key for building a value model is the set of characteristics appropriate for the phenomena at hand (Keeney, 1994, p. 795). They also propose a process of refining the model. The first phase of the process comes from a combination of literature review and interviews of individuals associated with the phenomena. The second phase quantifies the model and assesses "its reasonableness by examining how it performs in situation well understood" (p. 796). A third phase that assesses the validity and performs modification of the model until the model adequately reflects the appropriate phenomena. This study follows these steps. Additional information is provided in Chapter VII.

Keeney and Raiffa (1993) suggest that in the field of decision science, a decision usually includes many objectives or goals that "maximize some function of the effectiveness of the decision relative to the objectives and the relative importance of the objectives" (p. 796). They suggest that in order to find the optimum solution, one must maximize this "weighted effectiveness," where the weighting factors are the values of each objective or goal. Appropriately, they define four important independence concepts: additive independence, preferential independence, utility independence, and weak-difference independence.

Additive independence refers to the event where attributes' preferences for the consequences (the values) depend solely on the individual levels of the separate attributes rather than on the manner in which the levels of the different attributes are combined.

Preferential independence refers to the event where a pair of attributes is independent of other attributes if preferences for levels of these two attributes do not depend on levels of any of the other attributes.

Utility independence refers to the event where an attribute's preferences for risky situations (i.e., lotteries) involving probabilities of different levels of that attribute do not depend on a fix level of any of the other attributes.

Weak-difference independence refers to the event where an attribute's preference differences between pairs of levels of that attribute does not depend on a fixed level of any of the other attributes.

Based on the four independence concepts, Keeney and Raiffa (1993) suggest two major structures for the development of the overall value function. The first one is an additive value model, which deals with the event where all combinations of attributes are additive independent. In that case, the overall value faction must have the additive form, similar to Equation 1 (shown earlier) suggested by King and Epstein (1983). The second structure is a multiplicative value model, which deals with the event where each pair of attributes is preferentially independent of the others and one attribute is utility independent of the others. In that case, the overall value function must have the multiplicative form (Keeney, 1994, p. 796-797; Keeney & Raiffa, 1993). For example, suppose a given system has four characteristics. If the decision-maker (or user) did not care how the value level of *each* characteristic combined with the value level of all other characteristics, this implies that overall value is determined by simply adding up the value levels for all four characteristics. Hence, the overall value is an additive value model. However, suppose for the same system, the decision-maker (or user) did not care how the value levels of *each pair* of characteristics are combined and did care how a combination of the value level of *each* characteristics is effected by the value level of other characteristics. In this case the overall value is determined by multiplicity of the value levels for all four characteristics. Hence, the overall value is a multiplicative value model (Keeney, 1994, pp. 796-797).

Keeney (1999) conducted a study to develop a value model specifically for consumers' value of Internet commerce. The theory of consumer value provides indication for attributes or objectives involved with a person's reasons for conducting transactions via the Internet (Keeney, 1999). His methodology includes three steps. The first step includes the development of a list of customer values. He conducted interviews with "over 100 individuals about their values with regards to purchasing goods and services over the Internet versus the alternatives" (p. 536). The sample included diverse group of people with over 20 nationalities, of ages 18 to 65 with approximately 75% under the age of 35, some of which had experienced Internet purchasing and others had no experience. After completing all of the interviews, a list of values was generated. Duplicate values were eliminated and similar values were combined. This resulted in a comprehensive list of more than 100 values. The first phase of this study closely followed such methodology in order to collect a list of values of e-learning systems.

The second step in Keeney's (1999) study included the development of a quantification process to express each value in a common form. He categorized the values of this step into two major categories: means values and fundamental or ends values. In the third step, he organized the values by their relationships. In this step, Keeney (1999) suggested evaluating the relationships between the means and ends values. In constructing such a network, he asserts, one can see how the means values are indicating several tradeoffs (see Figure 4). As the overall goal is to maximize customer satisfaction, by maximizing the sum of the fundamental values will enable achieving such a goal. Also, he suggests that the list of the fundamental values form the "complete value proposition of an Internet purchase to a prospective customer" (Keeney, 1999, p. 536). This methodology was taken in a study conducted by Keeney and McDaniels (1999) on a gas company in British Colombia to help identify and structure values for integrated resource planning project in the firm.

Keeney (1999) proclaims that the means-ends values network (Figure 4) is a good starting point for companies who wish to investigate the overall value of their Internet products or services. At this step, he claims that each company can alter the values based on their specific products or services. Some fundamental values such as cost, privacy, and purchase time would be generic to all Internet products or services, while other fundamental values may vary, depending on the nature of the product or service at hand (p. 538).

Keeney (1999) concluded that in order to apply the results of the model proposed, it is necessary to convert the meaning of each of the objectives seen

Figure 4. Keeney's (1999) means-ends values for Internet commerce

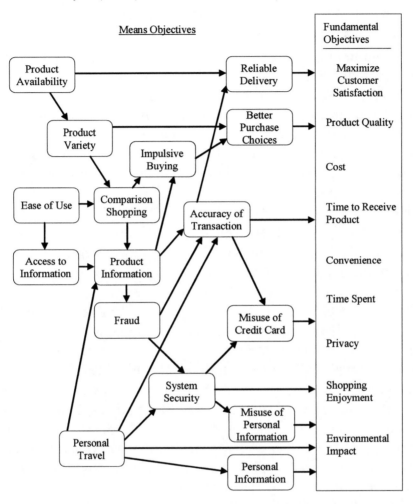

in Figure 4 to a more specific term dealing with the product or service under investigation. He suggests that doing so, can provide companies insightful information on their overall value of Internet shopping to the consumer (p. 541). Keeney's work is significant as one of the goals of this study is to gather a list of values specifically for e-learning systems. Furthermore, his three key steps provide general framework for development of a reliable instrument to measure values. Consequently, this study followed the first step proposed by Keeney (1999) to qualitatively generate an initial list of values as the preliminary step for the development of instruments to measure values. Additionally, this study uses several characteristics/values in similar form (i.e., security, cost, product quality, ease-of-use, access to information, product availability, product information, etc.). Additional information is provided in Chapter IV.

A significant stream of research in the area of value theory from the field of education based on Feather's work (1967, 1975) was covered in the *Rokeach's Value Survey (RVS)* section. However, another study from the field of education conducted by Marks (2000) is relevant to this section due to its approach of developing a model to predict overall value. Marks (2000) attempted to explore factors that predict the overall value of on-campus courses. In his work, he claims that the overall course value is indistinguishable from the overall course effectiveness (p. 109). Marks' (2000) work is fruitful especially in the context of this study.

Marks' (2000) study included two phases. The first one was a development of a preliminary survey instrument with items from various factors identified in previous studies of teaching effectiveness (e.g., perceived learning, perceived value, enthusiasm, course organization, group interaction, individual rapport, breadth of coverage, exams/grades, assignments, workload/difficulty, and clarity) (p. 113). The preliminary instrument was administered to 700 students enrolled in business courses at a regional Midwestern university. The results were analyzed with exploratory factor analysis which identified 13 items that loaded significantly (larger than 0.5 on the main factor and not larger than 0.3 on any other factor) were selected for further analysis. Five factors were identified based on the thirteen items that influence students' perceived overall course value. These include course organization, workload and difficulty, expected fairness of grading, liking and concern of instructor, and perceived learning (see Figure 5). Student attitudes towards course organization, course difficulty, workload, and attitude towards the course content as well as attitude of the instructor were found to influence overall course value.

The second phase of his study includes administering the 13-item instrument plus one overall course value item to 2,200 students enrolled in business courses at a regional Midwestern university. Marks (2000) proposed measuring the fit between the five-factor model resulted from the exploratory analysis (first phase) and the five-factor model resulted from the confirmatory analysis (results of the second phase). Marks (2000) suggests that his results show a good fit with valid Cronbach's α (Marks, 2000, p. 110). The results of Marks (2000) are significant for this study as such factors are being used in similar form in the development of the survey instrument to assess learners' perceived value and satisfaction with e-learning systems. Moreover, several key course char-

Figure 5. Marks' (2000) structural model for overall course value

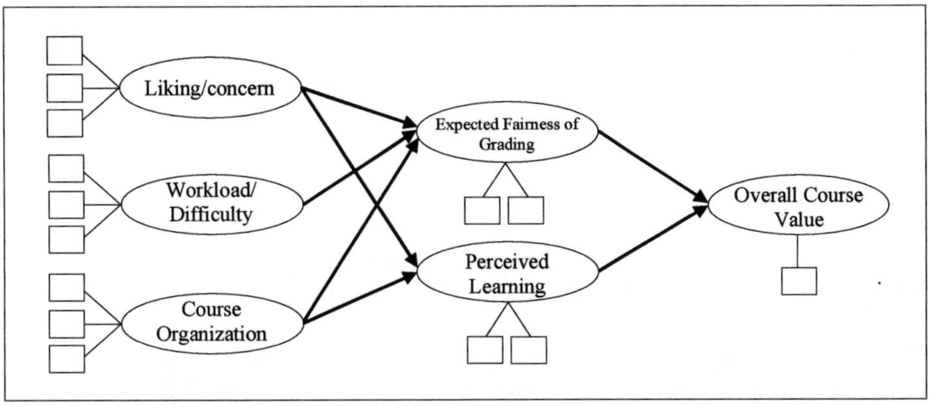

Source: Marks, 2000, Figure 3, p. 113

Table 4. Summary of literature related to value in OR, IS, and education

Study	Methodology	Sample	Instrument/Constructs	Main findings or contribution
King & Epstein, 1983	Theoretical, Case study, & Survey	236 systems evaluation of 68 managers in two firms	10 IS characteristics: reporting cycle, information sufficiency, information understandability, freedom of bias, reporting delay (timeliness), system reliability, decision relevance, cost efficiency, comparability (format, consistency), quantitativeness (quantifiability)	**Development of linear model to measure overall value of IS based on 10 characteristics. Rating and ranking values results provide highly correlated overall value of IS Hence, rating of values is appropriate. No need to use difficult procedures such as the ranking procedure. Nonlinear models of overall value may be more appropriate.**
Keeney & Raiffa, 1976; 1993	Theoretical	Commentary	Additive value model Multiplicative value model	**Provide roadmap for the development of overall value models**
Keeney, 1999	Theoretical & Case study	Over 100 individuals	Development of a means-ends value network to assess overall value of Internet shopping to the consumer	The process to gather values from respondents The process of combining a list of values The process of quantifying values in non-linear models
Marks, 2000	Theoretical, Case study, & Survey	700 students in phase 1 2200 students in phase 2	Development of 13-item survey instrument of factors effecting **overall course value**	Five main factors effecting **overall course value:** 1. Course organization 2. Workload and difficulty 3. Expected fairness of grading 4. Liking and concern of instructor 5. Perceived learning

acteristics that were proposed by Marks (2000) are included in similar form in this study. Such characteristics include: Liking/concerns, workload/difficulty, course organization, perceived learning, and overall course value. Table 4 presents a summary of literature related to OR, IS, and education that was reviewed in this section and its major findings or contributions.

User Satisfaction

In the effort to improve the success of information systems (IS), several scholars suggested that IS effectiveness is one of the most important concepts in the IS research field (Ives et al., 1983; Kim, 1989; Srinivasan, 1985). Furthermore, many scholars acknowledge that measuring IS effectiveness is an extremely difficult task (Bailey & Pearson, 1983; Baroudi & Orlikowski, 1988; Doll & Torkzadeh, 1988; Ives et al., 1983; Seddon & Yip, 1992; Srinivasan, 1985). Ives et al. (1983) noted that measuring IS effectiveness is "generally not feasible" (p. 785). Consequently, one should measure user satisfaction with IS as a "surrogate" for measurement of IS effectiveness. Measurement of user satisfaction is more feasible as well as generally more accepted (Ives et al., 1983). As a result, during the 1980s and early 1990s there was a major effort to establish an IS user satisfaction measure. Bailey and Pearson (1983) introduced a tool to develop and analyze computer user satisfaction. Their study sparked two major streams of user satisfaction measures. The first one, named user information satisfaction (UIS), was introduced by Ives et al. (1983), and the second one, named end-user computing satisfaction (EUCS), was introduced by Doll and Torkzadeh (1988) shortly after. The next two sections will provide a thorough review of these two streams of research along with criticism and limitations of such satisfaction measures. Such review is essential as the instrument proposed in this study, also seeks to assess learners' satisfaction with e-learning systems and will be grounded on such studies.

User Information Satisfaction (UIS)

The user information satisfaction (UIS) is grounded in research performed by Bailey and Pearson (1983). It introduced a list of 39 characteristics affecting computer-user satisfaction. In an effort to develop a computer user satisfaction measurement tool, they suggested looking at the research progress that psychologists have made in the area of employee satisfaction. They suggest that satisfaction in a given situation and is the sum of one's feelings or attitudes toward a variety of characteristics effecting that situation (p. 531). Furthermore, they define satisfaction as the sum of the user's weighted reactions to a set of characteristics" (Bailey & Pearson, 1983, p. 531).

An initial list of 36 characteristics attributing to individuals' satisfaction with IS was recognized by Bailey and Pearson (1983) from previous computer and user interface literature. Once the list was completed, tests for completeness and accuracy were run. Three groups of data processing professionals reviewed the list and recommended adding two more characteristics. The extended list then was compared with interview results of 32 managers in several organizations. Finally, they concluded that the expanded list is complete for the measurement of computer user satisfaction. Their conclusion was based on the fact that results from their interviews with managers suggested the same set of characteristics as the extended list found in literature and the list suggested by three professional groups.

At the same study, once the interviews were completed, respondents were shown the list of the IS characteristics they proposed and were asked to rank order the characteristics by the importance relative to their own satisfaction (Bailey & Pearson, 1983, p. 532). Based on the results, they concluded that individuals' ranking "strongly suggest that individuals differ in the characteristics that affect their perception of satisfaction" (p. 532). Also, each respondent was asked to provide their overall satisfaction with the overall system on a 7-interval Likert-type scale from "extremely satisfied" to "extremely unsatisfied." Based on the interviews outcome, they concluded that another characteristic should be added, from a final total of 39 items.

In order to measure empirically their proposed list, Bailey and Pearson (1983) selected to use a semantic differential technique. This technique uses differential between the pairs of adjectives and is believed to measure individuals' perceptions on a seven-interval scale ranging from a positive to a negative adjective. For example, when looking at measurement of sufficiency of information provided from IS, they proposed to measure a pair scale of *sufficient* and *insufficient* allowing the user to place their selection on the seven intervals between the two indicated ends. For each characteristic, they also proposed adding another semantic differential pair, important-unimportant, to measure "the weight given to the characteristics" (p. 534). Figure 6 provides a sample of the semantic differential pair scale for one of the

Figure 6. Bailey and Pearson's (1983) semantic differential questionnaire items

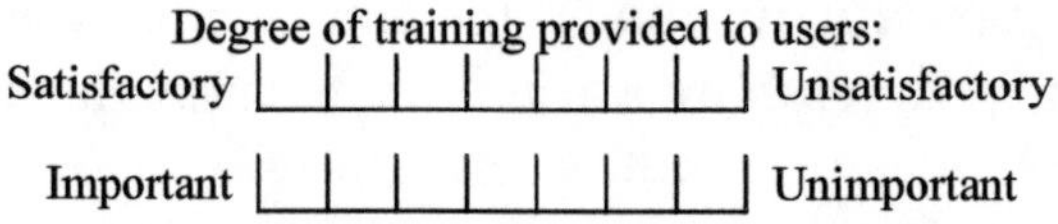

Degree of training provided to users:

Satisfactory | | | | | | | | | Unsatisfactory

Important | | | | | | | | | Unimportant

characteristics proposed by Bailey and Pearson (1983). This resulted in two items for each of the IS characteristic, one measuring the satisfaction level and the other measuring the value (or level of importance). This study follows such guidelines in the development of the instrument. Additional information is provided in Chapter VII.

In follow-up research, Ives et al. (1983) attempted to improve internal consistency and reliability by creating an abbreviated survey instrument and eliminating characteristics with the lower correlations to the overall measure and the measurement of the importance level of the characteristics to the user. They imply that a system usage or user behavior with the system, either mandatory or voluntary, can also serve as an indicator for system success in certain cases.

In looking at previous measures of IS satisfaction, Ives et al. (1983) acknowledge that several scholars examined a single item measuring IS satisfaction. Such measurement, as they criticize, is very limited and provides very little directions for practitioners and researchers on venues of improving such systems (p. 786). They recommend looking at two major types of factors: the IS product and the IS support. They suggest, among other things, measuring factors related to the quality of information and system content.

In the process of simplifying the measurement of user satisfaction, Ives et al. (1983) omitted the key measure component, the measurement of the level of importance in their development of the user information satisfaction (UIS) instrument. They claim that they omitted these measures because "the weighted [values] and un-weighted [satisfaction] scores are highly correlated [n=280], making the additional information provided by the importance rating unnecessary" (p. 787). This resulted in an instrument that can be administered faster but is limited in its ability to measure the effectiveness of IS. Ives et al. (1983) stated that the "degree of importance" or value, is redundant and provides very little added information to the overall understanding of user satisfaction. They also criticize Bailey and Pearson's (1983) instrument for developing the instrument on a small sample size of 29 managers and the fact that the same 29 managers were previously involved with the development of the list of factors the instrument was to measure (Ives et al., 1983, p. 787).

Several researchers criticized Ives et al. (1983) for omitting the key measure component the degree of importance of the measured characteristics in their UIS instrument. Etezadi-Amoli and Farhoomand (1991) claim that in some instances of information systems, measurement of the degree of importance can lead to a deeper understanding, especially in the event that both the satisfaction and the degree of importance, or value, are uncorrelated. This study, among other things, addresses this major issue by developing, testing reliability, and proposing a model that assumes that the two constructs (value and satisfaction) are uncorrelated. It also shows that measuring the degree of importance, or value, alongside the measurement of satisfaction is a crucial piece in our overall understanding of the users' perceived effectiveness of any IS, let alone e-learning systems. Moreover, since there has been such a great concern in the literature that the two constructs (satisfaction and value) may come highly correlated, this study proposes to measure both the linear correlation, using Pearson correlation, as well as non-linear correlation, using η correlation. Additionally, this study proposes a method to impute the overall system satisfaction and overall system value, and proposes models that will enable future prediction of *overall value* and *overall satisfaction* for systems under study. Additional elaboration on the techniques is provided in Chapter VII.

Ives et al. (1983) took Bailey and Pearson's (1983) instrument along with a revised short form instrument and administered it to 800 production managers in several US manufacturing companies. A total of 280 managers completed the UIS measure and 200 (25%) completed both UIS instrument and the UIS short-form instruments. After proposing a methodology to eliminate items, a two-fold validation was used to measure the validity and reliability of the new 13 item short-form UIS instrument. They found that the Pearson correlation of two instruments was only 0.54 (n = 200). However, they state that "these correlations provide substantial evidence that the short-form questionnaire is a sound general measure of Bailey and Pearson's original UIS" (Ives et al., 1993, p. 791). They concluded that there has been a long and apparent lack in the IS research field in providing an adequate mechanisms to evaluate IS effectiveness. As the major role of IS research field is to aid IS practitioners, it is essential to continue seeking ways of measuring IS effectiveness. Ives et al. (1983) stated that measuring IS satisfaction provides an indication for IS effectiveness. Therefore, they claimed that the proposed short-form UIS is a good step towards that direction, while future studies on the validity, reliability and reduction of items are needed.

Baroudi and Orlikowski (1988) attempted to reaffirm the reliability and validity of the short-form UIS instrument proposed by Ives et al. (1983). They employ the short-form UIS measure in an attempt to indicate the effectiveness of IS by evaluating the IS user satisfaction in a study conducted with 358 employees from 26 companies in the New York City area. About half of these organizations are financial institutions while the rest include companies in various fields such as accounting, advertising, education, government, media, retail, and such. It is important to note that Baroudi and Orlikowski (1988) supported Ives et al.'s (1983) omission of the items that measure the importance (or value items) that Bailey and Pearson (1983) used in their original instrument, by claiming that "they [the value items] provide no additional information" (Baroudi & Orlikowski, 1988, p. 47). As discussed earlier, this issue was strongly criticized by other scholars. This study also takes the position that this key omission caused the IS scholars to miss in the attempt to get the true grasp of measuring IS effectiveness. Moreover, it is one of the central arguments of the value theory (Kahle et al., 1983, 1986; Rokeach, 1969, 1973) that by neglecting the value construct in the assessment of any social science, researchers and practitioners alike can totally "miss the boat," which in the IS literature resulted in high quality instruments that measure only half of the key phenomenon. Additional information and clarifications of this central claim is provided in Chapter IV.

In the process of reducing respondents' time when answering the UIS instrument, Baroudi and Orlikowski (1988) believed it is best to provide respondents with questions that are "minimal verbal," while making a reference for the measured characteristic instead of asking a full question. This helps minimize confusion and uncertainty about the true meaning of the question (p. 55). Rather than asking confusing or unclear long text questions, the survey instrument that was developed in this study followed such guidelines by providing the name of the e-learning systems characteristics.

In an effort to explore the validity of Ives et al.'s (1983) UIS instrument, Galletta and Lederer (1989) conducted a study with 92 executive MBA students, who were senior managers with at least 10 years of managerial experience and users of information systems in their firms. They suggested that other scholars have long established an empirical support to demonstrate that feelings and beliefs lead to behavioral intention, which in turn lead to actions (usage). At the same time, they claimed that scholars also conducted studies to empirically support the notion that voluntary usage of information systems increases when user satisfaction increases (p. 421).

Galletta and Lederer (1989) criticize Ives et al.'s (1983) for the changes made to Bailey and Pearson's (1983) UIS instrument and claimed that "some potentially important items from the 39-item instrument [Bailey and Pearson's (1983) UIS instrument] were dropped" (p. 422). They present their concerns with the revisions made by Ives et al. (1983) to the original UIS instrument over several issues. One such concern has to do with "item heterogeneity." As the nature of the UIS instrument to measure heterogeneous items from several different dimensions of IS, they argued that summing up all the items poses limitation of the revised scale. They also suggested that conducting a Cronbach's α reliability test for such heterogeneous instrument has no meaning. Another suggestion was that the "alpha ... should be used only for the homogeneous tests" and that "if the test measures a variety of traits, spatial, and quantitative skills are actually quite heterogeneous" (Galletta & Lederer, 1989, p. 423). They claimed that Ives et al.'s (1983) 13-item UIS instrument appears to include several heterogeneous factors, therefore their meaning of the overall alpha score is not valid as "only alpha scores for individual factors are meaningful" (p. 423).

Galletta and Lederer's (1989) study include three groups: a control group (n = 27), a "failure" group (n = 38), and a "success" group (n = 27). They added two more overall satisfaction questions to the original Ives et al.'s (1983) 13-item UIS instrument. The questions asked respondents to answer their overall satisfaction level with each of the three main factors (IS product, IS support, and user involvement). A fourth question provides an overall measure (global question) of satisfaction with the entire IS environment. The instrument was administered to all three groups; once at the beginning of the class session and again at the end of the class (two and a half hours later). They suggest that "because user satisfaction is a state at a given point of time (rather than lasting trait) and more easily influenced by experience, a shorter [time] interval was required" (Galletta & Lederer, 1989, p. 427). During that time interval, the control group had a lecture of finance with no IS related content. The "failure" group was presented with lecture and class discussions about failures of information systems. At the same time, the "success" group was presented with lecture and class discussions about the success of information systems.

Galletta and Lederer (1989) results showed that the Cronbach's α scores for the main factors of the six administration groups (test/retest for each group over three groups) were comparable with previous studies (p. 430). They claimed that "this study provides evidence that an instrument [Ives et al.'s (1983) UIS] previously accepted as reliable is, in fact, unreliable" (p.433). They also suggested that future instruments should seek a deeper understanding of the constructs impacting IS satisfaction and that "evaluation might be more reliably conducted through more behaviorally-based measures" (p. 434). Accordingly, this study addresses this core issue by measuring both value and satisfaction in attempt to propose a reliable measure of IS effectiveness.

In another effort to propose a valid and reliable measure of IS user satisfaction from accounting information system, Seddon and Yip (1992) compared three types of IS user satisfaction instruments: UIS, end-user computer satisfaction (EUCS, which is addressed in the next section), and a new instrument that they developed. They acknowledged that some researchers had serious concerns about the reliability of the UIS instrument (Galletta & Lederer, 1989). At the same time they criticized EUCS for omitting several important aspects of IS such as satisfaction from technical support. Their proposed instrument of IS user satisfaction from accounting information systems was based on all 13 measures of Ives et al.'s (1983) short-form UIS instrument along with 10 measures of Doll and Torkzadeh's (1988) EUCS. The instrument was pre-tested in three face-to-face interviews with 100 responds from a random sample of 200 Australian firms with over 200 employees. They used multiple linear regression models including all measured satisfaction items in order to predict the overall user satisfaction. Their results indicate that Doll and Torkzadeh's (1988) EUCS provide the best outcome (with $R^2 = 0.72$, n = 100), while their proposed instrument provides intermediate results (with $R^2 = 0.46$, n = 100). Whereas Ives et al.'s (1983) sort-form UIS instrument demonstrated the lowest accuracy in predicting the overall satisfaction using multiple linear regression model ($R^2 = 0.33$, n = 100) (Seddon & Yip, 1992, p. 90). Although their results are based on linear models, they concluded that Doll and Torkzadeh's (1988) EUCS appears to be the most adequate measure of overall user satisfaction with this type of system. Additional information about EUCS is provided in the subsequent section in this chapter. It is important to note that most of the models developed in prior IS literature on satisfaction measures are based on linearity assumption. This study seeks to take this notion further and seek to develop both linear models using multiple linear regression techniques and non-linear models using logistics regression techniques. Additional information about this issue is provided in Chapter VII.

Kettinger and Lee (1994) criticize Ives et al.'s (1983) UIS instrument for omitting the measurements of IT service. Similarly to other scholars (Baroudi & Orlikowski, 1988), they acknowledge that Ives et al.'s (1983) UIS instrument has a limitation due to the fact that it mainly focuses on large centralized transaction systems that were available during the late 1970s and early 1980s. Consequently, the UIS instrument has less validity and reliability in "today's personal computing and network-based service environment" (Kettinger & Lee, 1994, p. 738). Thus, they proposed a new instrument named user satisfaction with the information services function (USISF) that combines Ives et al.'s (1983) short-form UIS instrument and the consumer service quality instrument (known as "SERVQUAL") from the marketing research field. Kettinger and Lee (1994) proposed adding five more constructs from SERVQUAL (tangibles, reliability, responsiveness, assurance, and empathy) to the short-form UIS instrument. Their results indicated that only two dimensions of service quality (reliability and empathy of IS service) out of the five are valid for IS settings. They suggest that IS scholars should consider including the two (reliability and empathy of IS service), which are not measured in Ives et al.'s (1983) UIS instrument, to any new measure of user satisfaction with information systems. They provide clarification of the two dimensions of service quality (reliability and empathy of IS service) in the IS context. Accordingly, they state that *IS service reliability* deals with the hours of operations the service is provided, the quality of the system in use, and the overall availability of the system to end users. Additionally, *IS service empathy* deals with the service level provided to end users and the adequate care by the service staff. In this study, both key factors of IS service quality (IS service reliability and IS service empathy) will be addressed in the context of e-learning systems. Service reliability will include items addressing the adequacy of the hours of operations of technical support provided to learners. Additionally, service reliability will include items addressing the reliability of the e-learning systems, the network to access the system, along with the availability of the system for learners. Moreover, service empathy in the context of this study includes items that address the service level provided to learners from both the technical support and pedagogical aspect (by the professor) along with the quality of such service. Table 5 presents a summary of literature related to user information satisfaction (UIS) that was reviewed in this section and its major findings or contributions.

Table 5. Summary of literature related to UIS

Study	Methodology	Sample	Instrument/Constructs	Main findings or contribution
Bailey & Pearson, 1983	Theoretical, Case study, & Survey	32 (Interviews) & 29 (questionnaires) from managers in several organizations	39 items (seven-point semantic differential) Measuring satisfaction level + **the weight given to the item**	The initial work of measurement of IS user satisfaction.
Ives, Olson, & Baroudi, 1983	Theoretical, Case study, & Survey	280 managers in production US manufacturing companies	UIS Long-form (39-items) & Short-form (13-item) seven-point semantic differential scale	UIS 13-item instrument. **Didn't measure "level of importance" or weights, claimed highly correlated to satisfaction items.**
Baroudi & Orlikowski, 1988	Theoretical & Survey	358 employees in 26 companies in the New York area	Revised UIS 13-item, seven-point semantic differential scale with items presented as "**minimal verbal**" **expression**	Reliability test of 13-item UIS. **Concluded that the 12-item UIS is a reliable measure of user information satisfaction.**
Galletta & Lederer, 1989	Theoretical & Survey	92 Executive MBA students	UIS 13-item instrument + overall questions for each of the three factors	**UIS 13-item instrument is unreliable!** Feeling & beliefs → behavior & usage and also: behavior → satisfaction
Seddon & Yip, 1992	Theoretical & Survey	100 responds from a random sample of 200 Australian firms with over 200 employees	Compared three types of IS user satisfaction instruments: UIS, EUCS, and their own	Concluded that Doll & Torkzadeh's EUCS appears to be the most adequate as a measure of overall user satisfaction with general ledger accounting systems.
Kettinger & Lee, 1994	Theoretical & Survey	342 students (Grad & UG)	UIS + IS Service Quality (measured by SERVQUAL instrument)	Adding IS **Service Quality** to UIS model Service related measures are essential. **Two key measures (sig): - Service reliability - Service empathy**

End-User Computer Satisfaction (EUCS)

A second stream of research resulted from Bailey and Pearson's (1983) study and initiated with the study conducted by Doll and Torkzadeh (1988). They introduced a new measure of user satisfaction, called the end-user computing satisfaction (EUCS), to measure IS satisfaction. Doll and Torkzadeh (1988) claimed that most of the existing UIS instruments are geared towards the evaluation of a specific application, rather than end-computing in general. Their aim was to develop a measurement to assess the satisfaction of end users with

IS in general, rather than IS professionals, who deal with data processing systems or a specific application. They propose six goals for the development of EUCS instrument. These goals include: focus on satisfaction with the information product provided by a specific application; include items to evaluate the ease of use of a specific application; provide Likert-type survey items as an alternative to semantic differential scaling; short instrument that is easy to administer and appropriate for both academic research and practice; ensure confidence across a variety of applications (i.e., adequate reliability and validity). Finally, the last goal of their development of EUCS was to enable researchers to explore the relationships between end-user computing satisfaction and plausible independent variables. Such plausible independent variables may include user computing skills, user involvement, end-user data processing (EDP) support policies and priorities, to name a few (Doll & Torkzadeh, 1988, p. 260).

Doll and Torkzadeh (1988) indicate that other scholars describe the changing role of computing users by distinguishing between two types of user roles: *primary role* and *secondary role* (Davis & Olson, 1985). The *primary role* user uses the system output, the reports, in the decision process. The *secondary role* user is responsible to enter the data and to generate reports, without using such reports for their jobs. Doll and Torkzadeh (1988) claim that computer users have changed their role in the past two decades, consequently, they defined "end-user computing" as the person who combines the two roles of developing the reports as well as utilizing the system output (the reports) to aid in the decision-making process. Consequently, they defined "end-user computing satisfaction" (EUCS) as "the affective attitude towards a specific computer application by someone who interacts with the application directly. EUCS can be evaluated in terms of both primary and secondary user roles" (Doll & Torkzadeh, 1988, p. 261).

Doll and Torkzadeh (1988) also indicate that user information satisfaction focuses on the primary user role, whereas the secondary user satisfaction varies by application. It is the primary role, that most IS studies of user satisfaction, including UIS, were focused on while very little attention and research was done in the area of the secondary user satisfaction. They criticize both Bailey and Pearson (1983) and Ives et al. (1983) for measuring the primary user role, as their sample size included only middle managers and production managers who mainly use the system output (the reports) in aiding their decision-making process and were not involved in the process of developing such reports from the systems. As the role of users change towards end-user role, in particularly the role of managers, there is a growing need to measure the satisfaction of both primary and secondary roles, which Doll and Torkzadeh (1988) claim their EUCS instrument was designed to measure.

After a comprehensive review of previous literature of user satisfaction, Doll and Torkzadeh (1988) collected 31 items to measure end-user perception of IS satisfaction. They added seven more items to measure ease-of-use of the application along with two overall measures to assess overall satisfaction and overall success. Thus, they created a 40-item instrument using a 5-point Likert-type scale. A structured interview questionnaire was also developed to measure qualitative data on users' perceived satisfaction from the IS studied. Doll and Torkzadeh's (1988) sample size included 96 users (no responds rate reported) from five different firms: a manufacturing firm, two hospitals, a city government, and a university. After analyzing the pilot study results and in an attempt to help eliminate unreliable survey items, they developed another scale from the two overall satisfaction and overall success items. The sum of these two overall items was then used as a "criterion scale" (p. 264). Using this "criterion scale." Doll and Torkzadeh's (1988) claim, will enable elimination of unreliable survey items by removing survey items that its correlation with the new calculated "criterion scale" was below 0.4. A sample size of 618 responses from IS end users was obtained, with an "average of 2.5 responds per application" or in other words, a 40% response rate. Using their proposed "criterion scale," they eliminated fifteen items from the original proposed instrument and ended up with the an instrument that contains 23 survey items. Five additional survey items were also eliminated as "they represented the same aspects with only slightly different wording" (Doll & Torkzadeh, 1988, p. 264). The remaining 18 survey items demonstrated high reliability (with Cronbach's $\alpha = 0.94$) and a correlation of 0.81, $n = 618$, with the new "criterion scale" they developed.

Doll and Torkzadeh (1988) performed exploratory factor analysis to identify the factors or components associated with IS end-user satisfaction. They attempted to label the resulting factors in a precise and non-ambiguous way. Although three strong factors resulted from the analysis, they felt that five factors were more interpretable for IS end-user satisfaction. These five factors were named: content, accuracy, format, ease-of-use, and timeliness. The exploratory factor analysis suggests that these five factors explained 78% of the total variance in the collected data. A number of survey items had factor loading above 0.3 or 0.4 on several factors, which can be an indicator for survey items that may be ambiguous, unclear, or not reliable and reduce the overall clarity between the factors proposed. Doll and Torkzadeh (1988) suggested that although these items are potentially excellent measures of the overall end-user satisfaction, including these items in the survey instrument will "blur the distinction between factors" (p. 266). Consequently, five other survey items were eliminated from the analysis resulting in a 12-item scale survey instrument to measure EUCS with a reliability of overall Cronbach's $\alpha = 0.92$. They concluded with a review of the implication of the 12-item survey instrument for practitioners along with recommendation for interpretation of the results. Again as noted before, the overall reliability measure may not be the accurate reliability measure for heterogeneous items as in the EUCS (Galletta & Lederer, 1989, p. 423). A more accurate measure would have been to conduct a Cronbach's α reliability test for all survey items in each of the factors. Thus resulting in an accurate and valid reliability measure as the survey items within each factor are, by the nature of the results of factor analysis, are homogeneous. Consequently, this study performs an individual Cronbach's α reliability test for all survey items in each of the resulted factors in order to provide an accurate and valid reliability of survey instrument proposed. Additional information about the development of the survey instrument, the validity and reliability is provided in Chapter VII.

In an attempt to further validate the reliability of the EUCS instrument, Torkzadeh and Doll (1991) conducted a test-retest study with 41 respondents. Respondents were asked to answer the 12-items EUCS instrument across three different points in time, applied in two time intervals: namely, short-range interval (two and a half hours) and long-range interval (two weeks). By doing so, they suggested, the short-range respondents may subconsciously remember and instantly mark scores similarly to their answers in the first time they responded to the EUCS instrument. While in the long range, they claimed, it is less likely that respondents will remember their previous scores for a particular question, thus, provide a more accurate result. They continue to suggest that "any discrepancy in scores during this longer period could more closely be associated with the instrument's lack of stability" (Torkzadeh & Doll, 1991, p. 29). The sample includes the same group of 41 MBA students with "considerable work experience." The instrument was administered over two test-retest periods with three points in time. Respondents were asked to evaluate the decision support system used in class and provide other demographics information along with the 12-item EUCS instrument. Based on the results of this study, Torkzadeh and Doll (1991) conclude that the 12-item EUCS instrument is "internally consistent and stable" and that it does not "elicit a substantial reactivity effect [Inflation or deflation of results by respondents]" (p.36). They criticize Ives et al.'s (1983) UIS instrument for measuring general satisfaction rather than measuring satisfaction from a specific application, as they claim their EUCS does. According to Torkzadeh and Doll (1991), the unique research design with the incorporation of the short-range and long-range time intervals provide further evidence for the stability and reliability of the EUCS instrument (pp. 36-37).

Etezadi-Amoli and Farhoomand (1991) in their commentary piece criticize Doll and Torkzadeh's EUCS for having "several problems in the area of measurement" (p. 1). Etezadi-Amoli and Farhoomand (1991) based their main argument on two major flaws. The first major flaw of EUCS instrument deals with the measuring scale. They suggested that the EUCS instrument is measuring "frequency" of satisfaction rather that "extent of satisfaction" in IS applications (Etezadi-Amoli & Farhoomand, 1991, p.1). The second major flaw of the EUCS instrument, as they pointed out, is the elimination of the "scale evaluating the degree of importance of each item to the respondent" similarly to the one included in the original Bailey and Pearson's (1983) instrument. The lack of inclusion of such scale prevents Doll and Torkzadeh's (1988) EUCS instrument from measuring the "silent beliefs" of respondents' satisfaction with the application (p. 1). The two main flaws proposed by Etezadi-Amoli and Farhoomand (1991) are indeed valid and will be the central aim of this study. This study goes to the heart of these two issues and proposes assessment tools that does not have these two flaws by measuring the extent of satisfaction from e-learning systems as well as by measuring the value (or level of importance) learners attribute for each of the e-learning systems characteristics.

In their study, Etezadi-Amoli and Farhoomand (1991) used Doll and Torkzadeh (1988) data and conducted confirmatory factor analysis to validate the results. They reported that "the fit was found to be inadequate" (p. 3). They concluded that Doll and Torkzadeh's (1988) EUCS instrument "cannot be used unequivo-cally because of the above methodological and conceptual problems" (p. 4). Other scholars also criticized EUCS instrument for omitting measurement of important satisfaction aspects of IS. Additionally, Seddon and Yip (1992) criticize Doll and Torkzadeh's EUCS for lacking the measurement of the technical support as well as users' knowledge and involvement with the IS (p. 78). They criticize both UIS and EUCS for claiming to measure the general users' satisfaction, where in fact there is very little agreement in the variables each instrument (UIS and EUCS) measure.

Figure 7. Four EUCS models proposed by Doll et al. (1994)

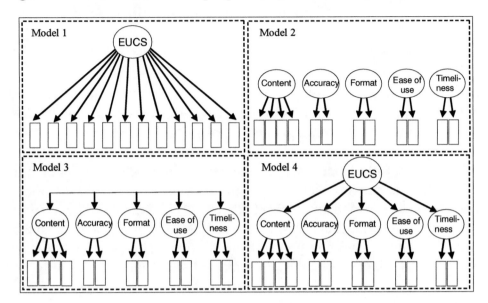

In a later article responding to Etezadi-Amoli and Farhoomand's (1991) criticism, Doll, Xia, and Torkzadeh (1994) conducted a confirmatory factor analysis to further indicate the reliability of their EUCS instrument. They suggest exploring four different models of EUCS based on the overall EUCS index and the five factors found in their previous work: content, accuracy, format, ease-of-use, timeliness. The goal of their study was to evaluate which model would produce the best fit and the most reliable results.

The first model suggests one first-order factor, namely overall EUCS index. The second model suggests five first-order factors (the five factors) uncorrelated, without the overall EUCS index. The third model suggests five first-order factors (the five factors) correlated, without the overall EUCS index. The fourth model that was proposed by Doll and Torkzadeh (1988; 1991), include five first-order factors (the five factors), and one second-order factor, the overall EUCS index. Figure 7 illustrates the four models proposed by Doll et al. (1994). They propose comparing the four models using goodness-of-fit measures.

Following the same data collection methodology as Doll and Torkzadeh's (1988), Doll et al. (1994) collected data from 409 computer end users (responds rate not reported) from 18 organizations and 139 different computer applications. As one of the initial goals of EUCS was to measure the general end-user computer satisfaction, rather than a specific type of computer application, they claim that "the large number of organizations and the variety of applications support the generalizability of the findings" (Doll et al., 1994, p. 456).

Based on their results, Doll et al. (1994) suggested that model three (five first-order factors correlated without EUCS) provide the best fit, although model four [five low-order factors and one higher-order (EUCS) index as a global factor, (their original model)] provides slightly lower results than model three, it is more applicable. In fact, model three resulted in an extremely better result than models one and two. Since model three provides better results than model four, Doll et al. (1994) claimed that IS theory suggests another overall users satisfaction construct, hence "model 4 is of greater theoretical interest than model 3" (p. 457). They also point out that the overall user satisfaction (their proposed EUCS index) of model four explained 74% of the variation in the first five-order factors in model three. Therefore, they concluded that the validity and reliability of the 12-item EUCS survey instrument is the same regardless of the model selected (Doll et al., 1994, p. 457). Similarly, this study constructs the Learner's Value Index of Satisfaction (LeVIS) index using one high-order factor and four lower-order dimensions that was validated by this study.

Hendrickson, Glorfeld, and Cronan (1994) conducted a study to further validate the test-retest findings of Doll and Torkzadeh (1991) results. Whereas the Doll and Torkzadeh (1991) test-retest study was done over two time intervals, short-range (after two hours) and long-range (after two weeks), Hendrickson et al. (1994) believe that the long-range time interval is insufficient to measure the stability of the instrument. Therefore, their study included measurement of the stability of the 12-item EUCS instrument over a two-year time frame. The first data collection conducted in 1990 included respondents from 32 mainframe end users and 35 PC end users. The second data collection conducted in 1992, included respondents from 22 mainframe end users and 22 personal computer (PC) end users.

The results of the Hendrickson et al. (1994) study show that "reliability over two years indicate that the EUCS instrument is stable and reliable" (p. 659). They also point out that their results are comparable to those reported by the test-retest reliability study of Doll and Torkzadeh (1991). Hendrickson et al. (1994) do, however, acknowledge that the results for PC end users provide lower than expected Pearson's correlation between the test and retest scores (0.63, n = 22), whereas results for mainframe end users provide Pearson's correlation (0.74, n = 22), which is slightly better. Hendrickson et al. (1994) suggest that the lower than expected results for PC end users might have resulted due to the application at hand and due to the lower number of hours users reported using the applications; whereas mainframe end users reported higher number of hours using the applications. Thus, they assert that "users' perceptions might tend to be more stable when evaluating systems with which they are more familiar and possess a better understanding" (Hendrickson et al., 1994, p. 663). Hendrickson et al. (1994) concluded by agreeing with previous literature that "In general, the results of the current study's reliability assessment over two years indicate that the EUCS instrument is stable and reliable" (p. 659).

Lee, Kim, and Lee (1995) conducted a study to empirically test the relationship between end-user ability, EUCS, end-user IS acceptance, system utilization, and job satisfaction. They used EUCS instrument to assess end-user satisfaction with IS. Data collection includes a sample size of 236 end users, or a 37% response rate, from 11 large companies (300 employees or more) in the state of Nebraska. Their results show a significant impact of system utilization on IS satisfaction and end-user ability on both system utilization and IS acceptance. In addition, a very strong impact IS acceptance was demonstrated on system utilization and IS satisfaction. They concluded that a causal link can be established between system utilization (usage), IS satisfaction and job satisfaction.

Palvia (1996) points out that both UIS and EUCS were developed for large organization, whereas small-businesses computing satisfaction (not end-user) varies from these main theories. In his study, he reviewed UIS and claimed it to be inappropriate for small business. However, he suggested that EUCS is a better starting point in the development of IS satisfaction instrument for small businesses. He suggests adding several constructs to Doll and Torkzadeh's (1991) 12-item EUCS instrument to make it more appropriate in measurement of small businesses computing satisfaction. The additional constructs include measures of: productivity, hardware adequacy, software adequacy, system security and integrity, documentation, vendor support, and training and education. Palvia's (1996) preliminary instrument based Doll and Torkzadeh's (1991) 12-item EUCS instrument included 48-items, which grouped in 13 factors. A sample size of 108 companies responded, out of 1353 or an 8% response rate. Eight companies were not considered small and were dropped from the study, resulting in an even 100 respondents. After exploratory factor analysis and item correlation Palvia (1996) eliminated several questions and derived the final instrument. Thus, Palvia (1996) proposed a survey instrument containing 23 items and three overall questions. He concluded that small businesses have significantly different factors associated with IS satisfaction than end users in large businesses (Palvia, 1996, p.156).

McHanry and Cronan (1998) conducted a study to validate EUCS instrument for simulation systems and decision support systems (DSS). Data was collected from a sample size of 411 developers and end users of computer simulation applications. Respondents had over six years of simulation experience and a relatively high level of usage of such applications. McHanry and Cronan (1998) results are comparable with the results reported by Doll and Torkzadeh (1988). They concluded by claiming that their data indicates that the EUCS instrument is valid and reliable also in measuring simulation systems and DSS (McHanry & Cronan, 1998).

The extensive review (mentioned earlier) of instruments of IS satisfaction is crucial as it provides a solid foundation for the survey instrument that this study proposes. The survey developed in this study is based on the structure and development of both the EIU and EUCS satisfaction measure. It is using the existing knowledge from the previously-mentioned literature to ensure the development of a sound and valid e-learning systems satisfaction instrument. Furthermore, the survey instrument proposed in this study also includes measures of value by providing robust theoretical rationale along side the measures of e-learning systems satisfaction. Additional information on the development of the instrument is provided in Chapter VII. Table 6 presents a summary of literature related to EUCS that was reviewed in this section and its major findings or contributions.

IS Effectiveness

A conceptual model of IS effectiveness has long been an important goal of the IS research community. Review of literature in the area of IS effectiveness and IS success yield that there is little agreement in literature on the definition of IS effectiveness, let alone how to measure it (Arnold, 1995; Grover, Jeong, & Segars, 1996; Kim, 1989; Seddon & Yip, 1992; Sethi, Hwang, & Pegles, 1993; Srinivasan, 1985; Yuthas & Eining, 1995). Kim (1989) claimed that "measuring MIS effectiveness is a complex task because of the difficulties of tracing and measuring the effects of MIS through a web of intermediate factors"

Table 6. Summary of literature related to EUCS

Study	Methodology	Sample	Instrument/Constructs	Main findings or contribution
Bailey & Pearson, 1983	Theoretical, Case study, & Survey	32 (Interviews) & 29 (questionnaires) from managers in several organizations	39 items (seven-point semantic differential scale). Measuring satisfaction level + **the weight given to the item**	The initial work of measurement of IS user satisfaction.
Doll & Torkzadeh, 1988	Theoretical, Case study, & Survey	618 end users from five different firms: a manufacturing firm, two hospitals, a city government, and a university	12-item (five-point Liket-type scale) **five factors (78% of variance): content, accuracy, format, ease-of-use, and timeliness.**	12-item EUCS instrument. **Didn't measure "level of importance" or weights, claimed highly correlated to satisfaction items.**
Etezadi-Amoli & Farhoomand, 1991	Theoretical	Commentary	EUCS	Criticize EUCS for: 1. Measuring "frequency" of satisfaction rather that "extent of satisfaction" from the application. 2. Not considering the attitude-behavior chain.
Torkzadeh & Doll, 1991	Theoretical	Commentary	EUCS	Causal factors→beliefs→attitude (satisfaction)→behavior (usage)→social and economic impact
Doll, Xia, & Torkzadeh, 1994	Theoretical & Survey	409 computer end users from 18 organizations & 139 different computer applications	Test-retest of EUCS w/Confirmatory Factor Analysis on EUCS, proposed four models: 1. One first-order factor, (overall EUCS). 2. Five first-order factors *uncorrelated*, without the overall EUCS. 3. Five first-order factors *correlated*, without the overall EUCS index. 4. Five first-order factors and one second-order factor, the overall EUCS	Model three provide better results than model four, but claimed that model four is of greater theoretical interest than model three. **Concluded that the validity and reliability of the 12-item EUCS measure is the same regardless of the model selected.**
Hendrickson, Glorfeld, & Cronan, 1994	Theoretical & Survey	57 (32 mainframe & 35 PC end users) in 1990 44 (22 mainframe & 22 PC end users) in 1992	Test-retest of EUCS over two-year period	Reliability assessment over two years indicate that the EUCS instrument is stable and reliable
Lee, Kim, & Lee, 1995	Theoretical, Case study, & Survey	236 end users from 11 large companies in the state of Nebraska	EUCS, plus: End user ability, System utilization (or usage), IS Acceptance, Job satisfaction	System utilization (or usage)→ IS satisfaction → Job satisfaction
Palvia, 1996	Theoretical & Survey	100 small businesses	23-item + three overall items based on EUCS for small businesses. Factors including: Software adequacy, Software maintenance, Information content, Information accuracy, Information format, Ease-of-use, Timeliness, Security & Integrity, Productivity, Documentation, Vendor support, Training & education	Small businesses have significant different factors associated with their IS satisfactions than end users in large businesses.
McHanry & Cronan, 1998	Theoretical & Survey	411 developers and end users of computer simulation applications	EUCS	EUCS instrument is valid and reliable also in measuring simulation systems and DSS.

(p. 1). Seddon and Yip (1992) acknowledged that "the measurement of IS effectiveness has proven very difficult" (p. 75). Yuthas and Eining (1995) claimed that "despite the importance of IS effectiveness ... research in the field has not been successful in its attempts to identify the factors that influence IS effectiveness" (p. 69). Arnold (1995), at a moment of frustration from the IS effectiveness literature, said "all too often the search for an effectiveness measure has resembled search for Holy Grail" (p. 85). Many other scholars claimed that IS effectiveness is extremely difficult to measure and researchers should be better off measuring various constructs that serve as "surrogates" for IS effectiveness such as satisfaction, attitude, usage, and behavior (Bailey & Pearson, 1983; Baroudi & Orlikowski, 1988; Doll & Torkzadeh, 1988; Ives et al., 1983). However, Seddon and Yip (1992) criticize both UIS and EUCS on the notion that both are suggested as "surrogate" measures of IS effectiveness, whereas none of them actually provide evidence to suggest such linkage. Furthermore, other scholars suggest that there is major confusion among IS scholars on the constructs related to IS effectiveness and their relationships. Additionally, they advocate for the development of reliable approaches and instruments to measure IS effectiveness (Kim, 1989; McHanry, Hightower, & Pearson, 2002; Seddon & Yip, 1992; Srinivasan, 1985; Yuthan & Eining, 1995). Nonetheless, Seddon and Yip (1992) propose that "different measures of effectiveness are needed for different systems" (p. 78). Consequently, this study suggests that a complete measurement of IS effectiveness must include measures of the "causal factors," the values (see Figure 1 for Doll and Torkzadeh's [1991] conceptual model for EUCS), and end result construct, the user satisfaction. Further discussion is provided in Chapter IV. Subsequently, a review of the various definitions of IS effectiveness is presented, followed by a review of relevant literature of e-learning systems effectiveness.

Doll and Torkzadeh's (1988) suggestion that, ideally, the effectiveness of an IS should be determined by its effect on the organization's competitive advantage and/or the productivity of decision-makers. Kim (1989) defines IS effectiveness, based on previous literature, as "the extent to which the MIS contributes to accomplishment of organizational objectives" (p. 7). As the main application of IS systems in the early- to mid-1980s concentrate around decision-making, Kim (1989) suggested that "MIS effectiveness can be assessed by the contribution of MIS to accomplishment of decision-making effectiveness, productivity, interpersonal relations, job satisfaction, etc." (p. 7). Stone (1990) defines IS effectiveness (he termed it "evaluation of IS") as "the process of determining if, how, and why an IS contributes to organizational productivity"

(p. 2). He suggested that, by definition, this is a post-implementation evaluation and that productivity is only one of the reasons for evaluation. Grover et al. (1996) suggested three different definitions of IS effectiveness based on previous literature and the unit of analysis. The first one is based on the "goal-centered" approach, which defines IS effectiveness "as the degree to which the objectives of systems, or the organizational unit utilizing the systems, are achieved" (p. 180). The second definition is based on the "system-recourse" approach and defines that "IS effectiveness is determined by the attainment of a normative state [ideal case] rather than the achievement if specific task objectives" (p. 180). The third definition of IS effectiveness Grover et al. (1996) proposed, is based on Ives et al. (1983) approach and "imply that IS effectiveness is the extent to which IS results in changes in organizational effectiveness" (Grover et al., 1996, p. 180). As the use of IS change from decision-making support to communication and eventually to learning environment, so does the definition of IS effectiveness. In the context of this study, an e-learning system is considered effective when learners perceive its character-istics as highly important and are highly satisfied by those same characteristics. More specifically, IS effectiveness of e-learning systems can be assessed by the comparison between the "causal factors," the values, and learners' satisfaction of such systems. Additional information about this definition and the theoretical rationale is presented in Chapter IV.

Srinivasan (1985) suggested an instrument to measure user perceived effec-tiveness of large corporate planning systems, based on assessment of user satisfaction. He reported that previous work suggests that there is a positive association between system use and some measures of user satisfaction (p. 244). He also suggested that attitude is considered as an important component of user satisfaction with IS. Based on unpublished work of his colleagues (Jenkins & Ricketts, found in Srinivasan, 1985, p. 245), Srinivasan (1985) postulated five key dimensions that impact overall IS effectiveness: report content, report format, problem solving, problem solving, input procedure, and system stability (see Figure 8). His study includes a pilot phase with both interviews and empirical assessment of the five key dimensions proposed in two large organizations. The intent of the study was to investigate how IS usage affects these five dimensions. It is important to note that the type of IS examined in this study was a typical system that was in place during the 1980s. Additionally, it is also important to note that in these types of systems the end user rarely interacted with the system. Instead, a technical group performed all of the analyses and generated the reports from the system based on predefined

Figure 8. Srinivasan's (1985) five key dimensions of IS effectiveness

Report Content	Problem Solving
- Accuracy of report contents	- Usefulness for identifying problems
- Relevancy of report contents	- Usefulness for selecting alternatives
- Adequacy report contents	- Power of modeling
- Understandability report contents	- Flexibility of modeling
Report Format	**Input Procedure**
- Quality of format	- Ease-of_use
- Timeliness of report	- Documentation
- Mode of presentation	- Interface
- Sequencing of information	- Editor characteristics
System Stability	
- Response time	
- Error proneness	
- Reliability of the system	
- Accessibility/availability of the system	

requirements that the end user, typically the decision-maker or manager, provided a head of time (p. 246). The main phase of their study included a sample of 29 individuals from 29 different companies in various MIS and non MIS management positions. Contradicting to previous literature, his results show that frequency of system usage is not significantly correlated with any of the five key dimensions of the perceived effectiveness (p. 247). He concluded that IS usage is not always positively associated with IS effectiveness, as previous research implies (p. 252). Clearly the results of this study should be taken in the context of the users of that time (i.e. during the 1980s, as noted earlier) as most of these respondents did not interact with the system regularly which most likely affected the results of this study.

In an attempt to clarify the confusion regarding IS effectiveness, Kim (1989) suggested that most previous literature that claimed to provide measures of IS effectiveness, based it only on IS user satisfaction. After reviewing previous literature in the area of user satisfaction of IS, attitude towards IS, and IS usage, he claimed that literature implied that individual's beliefs about MIS related objects determine the individual's attitude toward the system. Furthermore, the "weighted combination of the individual's attitude toward MIS-related objects" along with the individual's intention of user the system, is a predictor of IS usage (p. 3) (see Figure 9).

DeLone and McLean (1992) reviewed merely 180 empirical studies from IS literature and organized these diverse research efforts by developing a taxonomy to categorize such efforts. They identified six categories of IS

Figure 9. Kim's (1989) user attitude as a determinant of MIS usage

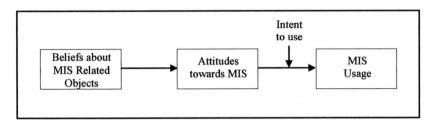

Source: Kim, 1989, Figure 2, p. 4

effectiveness (they called it "IS success") including system quality, information quality, system usage, system satisfaction, individual impact, and organizational impact (see Figure 10). They noted five major conclusions resulting from their study. First, IS effectiveness is a multidimensional and interdependent phenomenon. As a result, DeLone and McLean (1992) claim that careful attention should be placed in defining and measuring of each aspect of IS effectiveness. Second, dimensions of IS effectiveness should be based on empirical studies and, where possible, grounded and based on previous validated measures. Third, despite the numerous attempts to measure IS effectiveness directly or indirectly; scholars should attempt to reduce these measures and come up with validated comparable measures. Fourth, measures of individual and organizational impact should be a part of the overall IS effectiveness measure. Lastly, "this success [IS effectiveness] model clearly needs further development and validation before it could serve as a basis for the selection of appropriate IS measures" (DeLone & McLearn, 1992, p. 88).

Pitt, Watson, and Kavan (1995) attempted to answer the fifth aspect DeLone and McLean (1992) suggested. They claimed that the model proposed by DeLone and McLean (1992) lacks the service quality of IS. Pitt et al. (1995) argued that due to the changing role of MIS department from a product development to a service provider, service quality should also be added to the model of IS effectiveness. They proposed using SERVQUAL, "an extensive applied marketing instrument for measuring service quality" (p. 183). Their study includes a sample of 685 managers from three different companies: African financial institution, British accounting firm, and US IS service company. Pitt et al. (1995) concluded that as the nature of MIS departments is

Figure 10. DeLone and McLean's (1992) IS success model

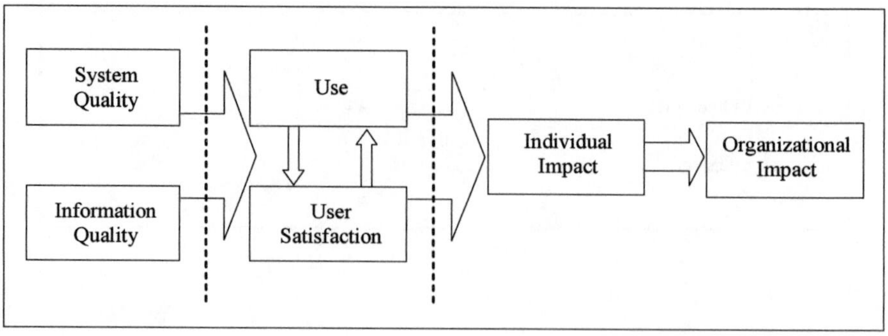

Source: Delone and McLean, 1992, Figure 1, p. 87

changing and the increase use of personal computers, IS departments are becoming more service oriented. As a result, an assessment of the service component of IS is essential for overall measurement of IS success or effectiveness (Pitt et al., 1995, p. 183).

In an effort to investigate the adequacy of various surrogate measures of IS effectiveness, Yuthas and Eining (1995) conducted an empirical study of user satisfaction and system usage on 59 undergraduate MIS students. They argued that decision performance is the "most direct and relevant measure of IS effectiveness" (p. 70). Furthermore, they claimed that their results "provide empirical support for the argument that user satisfaction and system usage cannot be used as substitutes for decision performance," or as they suggested, cannot provide adequate measures by itself for IS effectiveness (Yuthas & Eining, 1995, p. 70). Consequently, they proposed using measures of decision-making performance as indicator for IS effectiveness and compare it to perceived IS satisfaction, and system usage. Yuthas and Eining (1995) conducted a laboratory experiment where participants performed an inventory task with the support of a computerized accounting information system. They concluded that their results indicate that user satisfaction and system usage are not appropriate constructs for decision performance in the measurement of IS effectiveness (Yuthas & Eining, 1995, p. 81). Yuthas and Eining (1995) also suggest that until basic definition of IS effectiveness has been accepted, conclusions drawn from this or other research studies "should be carefully stated to focus on the outcome actually measured rather than on IS effectiveness or success" (p. 82).

Arnold (1995) conducted a study to validate Yuthas and Eining's (1995) approach on a group of students completing an inventory control task (sample size not reported). He noted that based on previous literature, a more appropriate research approach in measuring IS effectiveness should investigate it as a multidimensional construct with usage, satisfaction, and decision-making sub-constructs (p. 86). Arnold (1995) uses Yuthas and Eining's (1995) two measures (IS satisfaction, system usage) to predict a decision-making performance. According to this approach (Yuthas & Eining, 1995), a decision-making performance is assumed as the single predictor of IS effectiveness or success. Results of Arnold's (1995) study also show similar mixed results and inability to demonstrate the link between IS satisfaction, system usage, and decision-making performances. He concluded that "disappointment in part from the study's failure to integrate recent models of IS success" (Arnold, 1995, p. 90).

Grover et al. (1996) criticize scholars for emphasizing the organizational perspective only of IS effectiveness and neglecting the measurement of IS effectiveness of individual user. They praise DeLone and McLean for their model that encompasses user satisfaction and usage, but claim that their model provides limited approach to investigating the general phenomenon of IS effectiveness. They claim that "each criterion and associated approach [in previous literature] measures only portion of the total construct space of IS effectiveness" (Grover et al., 1996). They suggest that beyond the two major units of analysis (individual vs. organizational) due to the nature of information systems, there are three main evaluative judgments one can classify IS effectiveness under. The first perspective is *comparative judgment* that attempts to compare the effectiveness of a particular system with other "similar systems." The second perspective is *normative judgment* that attempts to compare the effectiveness of a particular system with "standards of best practice" or an ideal system. The third perspective is *improvement judgment* that attempts to compare the improved effectiveness of a particular system over time (see Figure 11). Grover et al. (1996) conducted a comprehensive review of over 100 articles from eight publications between 1980 and 1994 and categorized each over the six classes based on their conceptual rubric. They concluded the review by stating that the IS effectiveness research stream has several fragmented research efforts and their general frameworks encompass all possible IS effectiveness perspectives (Grover et al., 1996, p. 187).

This study follows the definition proposed by Grover et al. (1996) and concentrate only on the individual unit of analysis by measuring the normative

Figure 11. Grover et al. (1996): The construct space for IS effectiveness

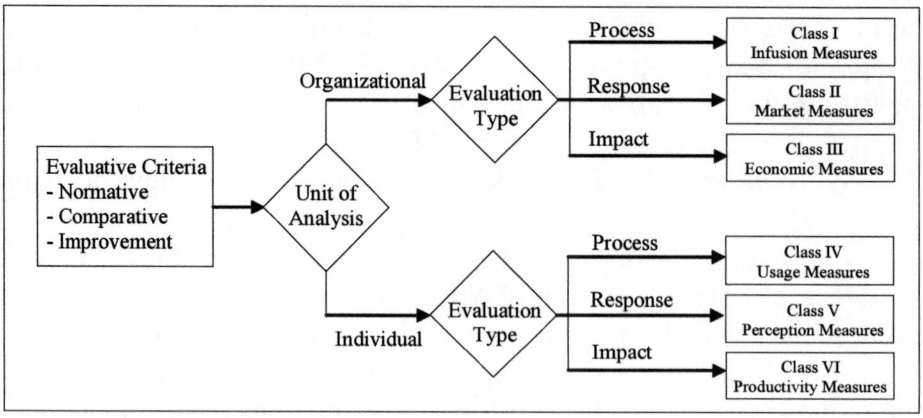

Source: Grover et al., 1996, Figure 1, p. 182

approach of IS effectiveness in the context of e-learning systems. It is not the intent of this study to explore the organizational unit of analysis at all, as the proposed model is an exploration of the learners' perceived effectiveness, rather than organizational effectiveness. Additionally, this study proposes the use of both learners' perceived satisfaction with e-learning systems and learners' perceived value of e-learning systems as a theoretical base for the measurement of such an individual unit of analysis. Moreover, the other two measures of effectiveness proposed by Grover et al. (1996) can be derived from the normative approach. Additional information is also provided in Chapter IV.

In a commentary article, DeLone and McLean (2002) summarized the progress in the area of IS success since their 1992 study. They acknowledged that the role of IS has changed over the last decade and progress towards measurement of IS effectiveness was made (p. 1). They claimed that "the measurement of information systems success or effectiveness is critical to our understanding of the value and efficacy of IS management actions and IS investment" (DeLone & McLean, 2002, p. 1). After a comprehensive review of previous studies utilizing or criticizing their 1992 model, they proposed a new revised model, similar to the one suggested by Pitt et al. (1995) with one minor change: collapsing the "organizational impact" and the "individual impact" constructs to "net benefits" construct (see Figure 12).

Figure 12. DeLone and McLean's (2002) reformulated IS success model

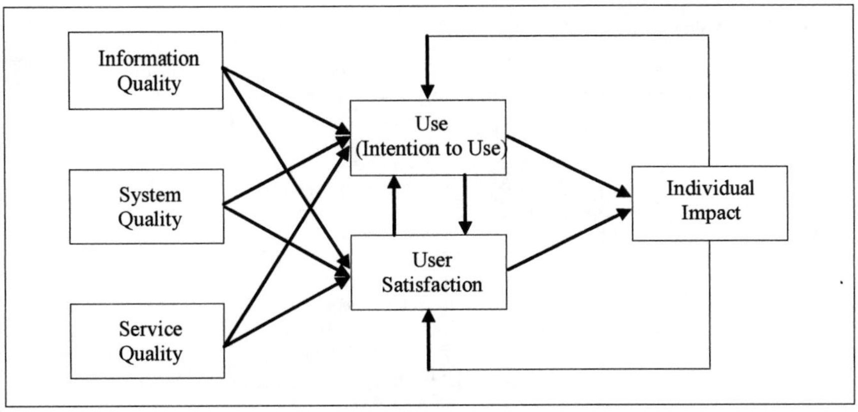

Source: Delone and McLean, 2002, Figure 3, p. 9

McHanry, Hightower, and Pearson (2002) express that IS effectiveness is not a binary mode where it can only be characterized as a "yes" or "no" proposition. They suggest that a particular system may be viewed as effective by some stakeholders and as non-effective by others. Because most systems include a variety of characteristics and may serve a range of needs, it is impossible to classify a system in a binomial fashion. Thus, they suggest, "it becomes necessary to classify it [IS effectiveness] on continuum of values ranging from failure to success" (McHanry et al., 2002, p. 504). Thus, this study attempts to develop a framework to evaluate IS effectiveness specifically in the area of e-learning based on multidimensional aspects of such systems. The proposed framework provides a measurement tool based on the various dimensions and variety of characteristics of e-learning systems grounded in the reviewed literature that is presented in this section. In order to make the assessment tool more specific for e-learning systems, the following section provides a review of the Technology Mediated Learning (TML) theory and literature that deals with e-learning systems. Table 7 presents the major findings and contributions found in the literature studies reviewed in this section, which are related to IS effectiveness.

Table 7. Summary of literature related to IS effectiveness

Study	Methodology	Sample	Instrument/Constructs	Main findings or contribution
Srinivasan, 1985	Theoretical, Case study, & Survey	Pilot study of two companies (sample not reported) Main study: 29 IS & non IS managers	- Report Content (accuracy, relevancy, adequacy, understandability) - Report Format (quality, timeliness, presentation, sequencing of info.) - Problem solving (usefulness to identify problems, usefulness to selecting alternatives, power of modeling, flexibility of modeling) - Input Procedure (ease of use, documentation, interface, editor) - System Stability (response time, error proneness, reliability, accessibility/availability)	System use → user satisfaction Not always, for old DSS where users rarely interact with the system!
DeLone & McLean, 1992	Theoretical	Commentary (180 articles from IS field)	Develop a taxonomy to categorize all IS efforts and how they impact IS effectiveness (or success)	Six main categories: - System quality - Information quality - System usage - System satisfaction - Individual impact - Organizational impact
Pitt, Watson, & Kavan, 1995	Theoretical & Survey	685 managers	D&M (1992) IS Success model + IS Service Quality (measured by SERVQUAL instrument)	Adding IS **Service Quality** to D&M's model Service related measures are essential for IS success or effectiveness.
Yuthas & Eining, 1995	Theoretical, Case study, & Survey	59 undergraduate MIS students	- Decision making (accuracy) & Performance (speed) - Satisfaction (perception) - System usage (nature & extent)	User satisfaction and system usage are **not** appropriate surrogates for decision performance in the measurement of IS effectiveness.
Arnold, 1995	Theoretical & Survey	Students completing an inventory control task (sample size not reported)	Yuthas & Eining 1995	Same results as Yuthas & Eining 1995. User satisfaction and system usage are **not** appropriate surrogates for decision performance in the measurement of IS effectiveness.
Grover, Jeong, & Segars, 1996	Theoretical	Commentary (over 100 articles from IS field)	Built on D&M (1992) IS Success model	Two units of analysis for IS effectiveness: Organizational effectiveness & Individual effectiveness
DeLone & McLean, 2002	Theoretical	Commentary	D&M (1992) IS Success model + IS Service Quality	Reformulate the original D&M (1992) IS Success model. Combine individual & org. impact into "net benefits" and add IS service quality construct.

E-Learning Effectiveness

The growing interest in e-learning for academia and corporations resulted in a rich stream of research in e-learning systems (Salmon, 2000). There have been numerous research studies that look at comparing learning outcomes between on-campus courses, vs. online learning courses, videoconferencing, satellite broadcasting, or other forms of distance courses (e.g., Alavi, Wheeler, & Valacich, 1995; Leidner & Jarvenpaa, 1993, 1995). There also has been a significant number of research studies comparing learners' perceived satisfaction of online learning with that of on-campus learning (e.g., Piccoli, Ahmad, & Ives, 2001; Webster & Hackley, 1997). In the context of this research study, a closer look will be given later to the literature stream from the IS discipline as well as the distance learning literature from education. A review of such literature will provide the foundation for this study in the collection and assessment of the characteristics and dimensions of e-learning systems as suggested to be crucial in the assessment of IS effectiveness by McHanry et al. (2002).

Hiltz and Johnson (1990) conducted a study aimed at understanding learners' satisfaction from various systems and characteristics of distance learning. They claimed that "the theoretical goal is to demonstrate the utility of systems ... in explaining variance in satisfaction" (Hiltz & Johnson, 1990, p. 741). Moreover, they suggested that measurement of e-learning system satisfaction is needed to indicate IS effectiveness. However, they criticize Bailey and Pearson (1983) as well as Ives et al. (1983) for developing measures of IS satisfaction that are not applicable for e-learning systems. They suggest that the UIS and EUCS instruments measure dimensions that "makes no sense" when applied to communication tools such as e-mail, videoconferencing, or e-learning systems (p. 740). Therefore, Hiltz and Johnson (1990) claimed that in order to develop a valid instrument to measure satisfaction with e-learning systems characteristics, certain features should be included such as: access problems to the system, experiences of the user, and the cost of using the system (p. 741).

After a review of 12 prior studies, Hiltz and Johnson (1990) constructed a pilot survey that included a list of 54 survey items: 23 semantic differential items measuring learners' satisfaction, 14 Likert-type survey items measuring group satisfaction, and 17 Likert-type survey items measuring satisfaction with the e-learning systems. The sample of the pilot survey included a nice group of 359 learners using four different e-learning systems. Their results are summarized in Table 8. It shows that individual characteristics and system differences (espe-

Table 8. Hiltz and Johnson's (1990) characteristics and features of e-learning systems

User Characteristics Variable	Group & Task Variables	Online Experience Variables
Attitude towards computers:	Group variables:	Technology barrier:
- Dull (vs. stimulating)	- Group member*	- Terminal access*
- Unreliable (vs. reliable)**	- Size of group	- Documentation (quality of
- Difficult (vs. easy)**	- # of people known in the	information)
- Media satisfaction (frustration	group	- Cost to reach the system
with the system)**	- # of friends in the group*	- Cost to use the system*
Expectations from the system:	- Communication frequency**	- Complicated**
- Expected time (sys usage)*	- Like the group (attitude	- Poor design**
- Motivation to use	towards the group)**	
- Ease-of-use**	- Group competition	Socio-emotional limits:
- Friendly	- How satisfied with	- Phone problems
- Frustration**	communication**	- Not like (to use the system)**
- Expected time saving**	- How important to	- No one (with whom one wishes
- Expected productive**	communicate**	to communicate)
- Expected efficiency**		- No interest (in subject)
- Expected quality**	Leadership variables:	- Other activities
- Expected useful	- Leadership skills	- Not worth**
- How enter (data input	- Leadership hinder use	- Just trying
yourself or by someone else)	- Task characteristics	
- Incentive	- Task importance**	Use & social ties:
Individual skills &	- Enjoy task**	- Time (use of system)*
demographics:		- No. of others (interaction with)
- Computer experience**		- Friends (communicate with)**
- Sex**		- Get know on the system*
- Age**		
- Education**		
- Position		
- Typing skills		
- Hours work**		

Significant at p < 0.05
**Significant at p < 0.01*

cially quality of information from the system) are the strongest predictors of satisfaction with e-learning systems (Hiltz & Johnson, 1990, p. 760). Their results also show that attitudes towards the group and frequent communications with the group are the strongest predictors of satisfaction with e-learning systems. They also suggest that "cost of online time…interfere with the ability of the user to feel comfortable" (p. 760). Furthermore, group mates' attitudes play a significant role in the overall feeling of satisfaction from the system. Hiltz and Johnson (1990) concluded that "characteristics of the learners and the social context of the application (cultural, group task characteristics) will strongly influence its acceptance and use" (p. 760). The current study will utilize Hiltz and Johnson's (1990) interesting results in the development of the characteristics and factors, however, in the context of newer type of e-learning systems.

In the research stream of technology mediated classrooms, Leidner and Jarvenpaa (1993) investigated the enhancement of learning as a result of computer use in university classrooms. Although their study targeted only the use of information systems in the classroom, some of the key results are relevant for this study of e-learning systems. They claimed that prior literature presented evidence that computer-assisted instruction (CAI) leads to more efficient learning and generally improves the attitude of students. Furthermore, they claim that CAI has shown to increase students' perceived learning and more active engagement in learning (Leidner & Jarvenpaa, 1993, p. 25). They also suggest that CAI provides students many learning tools such as drill and practice, test taking, simulations, course content, facilitate feedback, as well as pace and sequence control of students. They suggest that prior literature indicates that instructor's attitude, the cognitive preference of the user, and the capabilities of the system has shown to be a significant factors in the overall students' perceived learning (p. 26). Their study was aimed at providing insight into how computer-based technology is implemented in university classrooms and how computer-based teaching methods may effect classroom interactions.

In order to gain knowledge about such study goals, Leidner and Jarvenpaa (1993) conducted case studies over 15-week periods of three courses that were meeting in classrooms equipped with individual computers for each student, as well as a computer and projector for the instructor. The three courses were part of an MBA program, where all three courses contained three exclusive groups of students. Two of the three sections in their study were the same course taught by a team-pair instructors ($n_1 = 23$; $n_2 = 17$). The third section was taught by a third instructor ($n_3 = 20$). Leidner and Jarvenpaa (1993) propose looking at four dimensions: students, instructors, electronic classrooms, and the course itself.

Following both qualitative and quantitative data analyses, Leidner and Jarvenpaa (1993) concluded that their results are in accordance with prior research and suggested that students are motivated to learn more when they are given more control over their learning pace and material (p. 46). They also suggested that their results are concurrent with prior research where instructor attitude is a key factor influencing perceived learning (p. 49). Leidner and Jarvenpaa (1993) concluded by suggesting a theoretical model for future research of such phenomenon by incorporating four major dimensions: course content, technology, instructor factors, and student factors. They also proposed that future research needs to determine the important characteristics that make computer mediated learning more effective than traditional learning (p. 49). This study follows such proposed dimensions in the development of the instrument to assess the value and satisfaction of e-learning systems in order to provide the effectiveness of such systems. Additional information on the development of the e-learning systems dimensions is provided in Chapter IV.

Alavi (1994) conducted a study to investigate whether the use of group decision support systems (GDSS) in a collaborative learning process enhances student learning and evaluation of classroom experience. She claimed that prior literature in the area of collaborative learning suggest that *learning effectiveness* is measured in terms of students' perceptions of their learning and their evaluation of their classroom experience. In her study of 127 MBA students, Alavi (1994) compared three groups of MBA students attending the same course (Introduction to MIS) and taught by the same instructor. All three groups used the same course syllabus, same textbook, and the same assignments. Two groups attended a classroom equipped with GDSS ($n_1 = 77$), while the third group attended a regular classroom with no technology capabilities in it ($n_2 = 48$). Results indicated that there was no significant difference in the demographics characteristics of the students between the two groups (students attending the course with the GDSS and the students attending the course without the GDSS). A survey instrument was developed based on Hiltz's preliminary work to include measures of learning items as well as course evaluation items. After conducting a principal components analysis (PCA), Alavi (1994) proposed that the measure of perceived learning should include items based on three aspects: the perceived skill development, perceived learning, and students' interest in subject matter. The measure of the perceived course evaluation included survey items on class evaluation and student interactions. She concluded that students who used GDSS in support of their group learning activities demonstrated a higher perceived learning and interest in learning than students who did not use GDSS. Her results are consistent with prior literature in the field of collaborative learning, suggesting that e-learning systems can enhance students' perceived learning. Consequently, such course evaluation measures will also be included in the development of the instrument proposed by this study.

Leidner and Jarvenpaa (1995) suggested that researchers interested in e-learning systems should draw upon well-established variables from psychology and education research rather than creating new variables (p. 280). They also suggested some future research challenges in the e-learning systems area. One major challenge that this domain is still facing, deals with the need to look at the e-learning systems as a medium that facilitate learning in various learning models rather than comparing one model of learning without technology to the same model with technology (p. 286). Another major challenge Leidner and Jarvenpaa (1995) suggest, deals with the need to look at issues beyond the instructor and technology and include also aspects of the course content and students' characteristics. They claim that there is little research that elaborates on all such factors related to instructor, technology, course content and students' characteristics that might effect the success of such systems. Furthermore, Leidner and Jarvenpaa (1995) argue that "little is known about the prerequisites of effective application … in [online] learning environments" (p. 286). Consequently, it is the aim of this study to address these challenges by developing a framework to encompass all four dimensions (technology & support, course, instructor, and learner) in order to indicate learners' perceived effectiveness of e-learning systems.

Alavi et al. (1995) conducted an exploratory study of collaborative learning via desktop videoconferencing. Their study was based on two theoretical foundations: the Media Richness theory and TIP (Time, Interactions, and Practice) theory. In the context of their study, the Media Richness theory suggests that the richer the delivery medium is, the higher the students' perceptions of learning, skills enhancement, and satisfaction will be. Similarly, TIP theory suggests that the longer the interactions and practices are provided to groups of students to perform a task, the higher students' perceptions of learning, skills enhancement, and satisfaction will result (Alavi et al., 1995, p. 297). Alavi et al. (1995) suggested that *collaborative learning effectiveness* is the dependent variable measured in terms of students' learning achievements, satisfaction with the learning process and outcomes, and the emotional climate of the learning environment (defined in terms of student-to-student interactions and feeling towards the group or class) (p. 301). They also proposed that collaborative learning effectiveness is higher for face-to-face students in comparison with students who collaborated via desktop videoconferencing. Furthermore, they propose that collaborative learning effectiveness is higher for students who collaborated locally via desktop videoconference in comparison with students who collaborated via distance desktop videoconferencing.

In their field experiment, Alavi et al. (1995) included 120 MBA students from two universities. Students were attending the same course with the same professor and comprised of the same case studies in order to control the internal validity. Students were assigned into groups of four and each group was assigned to one of the three types of collaborative learning environments: one face-to-face and two types of distance learning systems. One distance learning system included several teams of students on the same campus using desktop videoconferencing from one room to another on the same campus. The other distance learning system included several teams of students using a collaborative learning environment over a distance (600 miles) in two separate universities. Their results indicate that the three environments had no significant difference in terms of the perceived learning. However, their results indicate that respondents who participated in the distance desktop videoconferencing environment demonstrated the highest level of critical thinking achievement.

In a commentary paper, Ives and Jarvenpaa (1996) suggested some scenarios for the future of business education and research as a result of the growing popularity of the Internet. They claimed that future students attending business degrees via online systems will greatly benefit from advantages such as "lower cost (for travel and classrooms), greater convenience, security, flexibility, and the ability to ignore time differences and geographic distances" (Ives & Jarvenpaa, 1996, p. 35). They also claimed that online students in the future will take more control over their learning pace. E-learning systems will enable business schools to shift from "just-in-case" education whereby students are provided in advance with education that they might need in the future, to "just-in-time" education. Whereby, students are provided with the skills they currently need and apply it immediately to the tasks at hand in their workplace. They predicted that this will change the way students study from learning by memorization to learning by doing (Ives & Jarvenpaa, 1996, p. 35).

Ives and Jarvenpaa's (1996) study provides several key aspects and characteristics associated with e-learning systems such as the cost of taking the courses, the ability to travel and work while attending courses, security, flexibility, and the ability to ignore time differences and geographic distances. Consequently, all such e-learning system characteristics were incorporated into the current study and empirically tested by measuring students' perceived satisfaction and value of such characteristics. Additional information is provided in the following chapter.

In another case study of a synchronized videoconference course between two universities, Alavi, Yoo, and Vogel (1997) conducted a study exploring the effect of partnership between two instructors from two universities using the same technology. The technology included videoconferencing for in-class learning and Internet-based tools (Lotus Notes) for out-of-class learning. In their study, Alavi et al. (1997) looked at the impact of the use of technology on student achievement, learning, and satisfaction for in-class and out-of-class learning. Perceived learning was measured by a revised 23-item survey based on the instrument proposed by Hiltz and Johnson (1990). Students' assessment of the learning experience was based on their evaluation of student-to-student and instructor-to-student interactions. The study included 25 MBA students in one university and 21 MBA students in the other university. The two instructors interacted and developed an overlapping course where one professor delivered the first half of the course and the other professor delivered the second half of the course. As a result each group of students' experienced half of the course when the professor's lecture was done via synchronized videoconference, and the other half of the course, the professor was locally present. To augment the in-class learning, a Lotus Notes server was provided to enable asynchronous student-to-student and instructor-to-student interaction.

Alavi et al. (1997) identify two main stakeholders, namely the student and the instructor, along with non-human factors such as course content and interactions. Their results show that "overall the students gave their learning in the networked classrooms relatively high ratings (a grand mean score of 4.41 out of a maximum of 5)" (Alavi et al., 1997, p. 1322). Furthermore, in regards to in-class learning, Alavi et al.'s (1997) results suggest that students viewed their learning via the distance networked classrooms as appropriate as via local learning. In regards to out-of-class learning, their results suggest that "students perceived outcomes of electronic learning and traditional face-to-face collaborative learning did not differ" (Alavi et al. 1997, p. 1323). Additionally, Alavi et al. (1997) suggested that content quality, instructor-to-student, and student-to-student interactions enhanced student's learning experiences (p. 1323). Their observation is consistent with prior literature in suggesting that perceived learning via distance networked classrooms is at least as appropriate as traditional face-to-face learning.

Webster and Hackley (1997) studied teaching effectiveness in a videoconference-oriented distance learning settings. They surveyed students attending 29 technology mediated distance learning courses over two semesters by instructors at six North American universities. The courses were in a variety of subjects including accounting, chemistry, computer science, engineering, mathematics, physics, political science, and sociology. The courses had an average of 16 students per course. In this highly cited study of the assessment of distance education from the students' perspective, Webster and Hackley (1997) proposed looking at four dimensions similar to the ones proposed by Leidner and Jarvenpaa's (1993) that includes: technology, instructor, course, and student. The first dimension relates to *technology* and includes characteristics such as: the reliability of the technology, the quality of the technology, perceived media richness, and location. The second dimension refers to characteristics related to the *instructor* and includes characteristics such as: instructor's attitude, teaching style, and the instructor's control over the technology and the students. The third dimension referred to *course* and includes characteristics such as: quality of course content and availability of course content. As the nature of the study was videoconference, the number of student locations was also measured as a course characteristic; however, it is not applicable in the study of e-learning systems. The last dimension of Webster and Hackley's (1997) study referred to *student* and includes characteristics such as: students' comfort with the technology and the attitude of their classmates. This study follows Webster and Hackley's (1997) conceptual model in looking at the four dimensions of e-learning systems and augments it by building a framework that combines both the measure of learners' perceived satisfaction and value of e-learning systems.

Webster and Hackley's (1997) study included both qualitative and quantitative data collection. The qualitative information included observations of class meetings both in local areas (same location as the instructor) and remote regions. It recorded the video quality, teaching style, and students' behavior (such as reading a newspaper or taking notes during class time). Additionally, informal interviews were conducted with students and instructors before and after class sessions, as well as via e-mail. Following the interviews, a survey instrument was developed based on the qualitative information to collect the quantitative data. The survey included 104 items with a seven-point Likert-type scale ranging from 1 (strongly disagree) to 7 (strongly agree). Webster and Hackley (1997) included multiple dependent variables (measures were based on several items in the survey) including: involvement and participation, cognitive engagement, technology self-efficacy, attitude toward the technology, usefulness of the technology, attitude towards distance learning, and relative advantage of distance learning. The independent variables included reliability of the technology, quality of the technology, perceived medium richness, instructor's attitudes, teaching style, control over technology, number of student-locations, comfort with image, and classmates' attitude.

This study also assesses the independent variables measured by Webster and Hackley (1997) such as stability of the technology, quality of the technology and the course, instructor's attitude, and so on. However, this study uses some of the dependent variables proposed by Webster and Hackley (1997) as independent variables in assessing learners' perceived satisfaction and value of

Table 9. Webster and Hackley's (1997) results of linear regression analysis

Independent Variables	Dependent Variables						
	Involvement & Participation	Cognitive Engagement	Technology Self-Efficacy	Attitude Toward the Technology	Usefulness of the Technology	Attitude Towards Distance Learning	Relative Advantage of Distance Learning
Reliability of the Technology	-0.01	0.01	0.02	0.21***	0.12	0.11*	0.05
Quality of the Technology	0.00	-0.05	0.11	0.12*	0.09	0.14**	0.13*
Perceived Medium Richness	0.25***	0.28***	0.29***	0.29***	0.33***	0.23***	0.26***
Instructor's Attitudes	0.06	0.06	0.17*	0.12*	0.09	0.11*	0.14*
Teaching Style	0.32***	0.22**	0.06	0.12*	0.01	0.19***	0.04
Control Over Technology	0.04	0.16*	0.00	0.16*	0.22***	0.10	0.14*
Number of Student-Locations	-0.15**	-0.01	-0.15**	-0.07	-0.01	-0.05	-0.16**
Comfort with Image	0.21***	0.10	0.15**	0.05	0.15**	0.10*	0.20***
Classmates' Attitude	0.16*	0.19**	0.09	0.10	0.07	0.24***	0.08
F	26.54	18.65	15.14	37.76	25.07	40.22	23.01
Adjusted R^2	0.50	0.41	0.36	0.59	0.48	0.60	0.46

Numbers in the table are standardized regression coefficients, t values of independent regression slopes.

*p < 0.05

**p < 0.01

***p < 0.001

Source: Webster and Hackley, 1997, Table 2, p. 1296

e-learning systems. The rationale for such a proposal is based on the value theory and IS Satisfaction theory literature reviewed earlier suggesting that such variables are needed in the assessment of system effectiveness. Among such independent variables included in this study are: student involvement and participation (student-to-student interaction), attitude toward the technology, attitude towards online learning, and relative advantage of online learning.

Webster and Hackley's (1997) quantitative data included respondents from 247 students representing 69% of all students attending the 29 technology mediated distance learning courses. They analyzed the quantitative data with canonical correlation incorporating all dependent and independent variables. As the results were significant, Webster and Hackley (1997) suggested conducting an individual multiple linear regression analysis for each dependent variable (see Table 9).

Webster and Hackley (1997) claimed that their results indicated that the main influences on the students' outcome were students' comfort with the technology, instructor control, quality of the technology, instructors' attitude, and teaching style. In their study, teaching style included items such as "the instructor encouraged questions from students," "the instructor encouraged student interactions," and so on. In this study, such survey items will refer to the instructor's characteristics. However, two other items used in their measurement of teaching style included statements such as: "there was a good balance between formal presentation and interaction" and "the instructor allowed adequate time for students to respond." These statements are not appropriate in the study of e-learning systems. Such items are not appropriate as the nature of most current e-learning systems is mainly asynchronous, unlike some of the studies reviewed earlier (Alavi et al., 1995; Alavi et al., 1997; Webster & Hackley, 1997), that are mainly videoconferencing and synchronous in nature. As a result, the construct teaching style was not termed specifically as part of this study; however, the appropriate items will be part of the characteristics in the instructor's dimension. Webster and Hackley's (1997) results also supported the notion that the reliability of the technology is positively related to the learning outcomes. Furthermore, the quality of the technology was shown to be positively related to the learning outcomes. Both reliability of the technology and quality of the technology will be incorporated as part of this study as it is highly applicable for the study of e-learning systems.

Carswell, Thomas, Petre, Price, and Richards (1999) had a case study in which they investigated students' opinions on Internet technologies that transformed the distance learning experience. From the students' perspective, their study looked at the shift from pre-Internet correspondence distance learning to an Internet-based distance learning or e-learning. Their case study reviews the process that was involved in understanding the requirements of distance learning students and how such students can be supported when transitioning from the pre-Internet correspondence learning to Internet based e-learning. Several factors that forced institutions to move from the pre-Internet correspondence learning towards e-learning were proposed by students. These factors included: the need for faster and more flexible access to course information, ability to submit assignments from anywhere, increased interactions with the instructor and other students, and reduced feelings of isolation. Carswell et al.'s (1999) study included 300 students in two groups taking the same computing course at the Open University in the UK. One group included students taking the course via correspondence learning, mainly using paper based assignments, regular mail, and phone communications. The second group included students taking the same course via e-learning system using electronic file exchange, e-mail, discussion forms, and chat capabilities. A survey instrument was sent to the students attending the correspondence course via regular mail and to the e-learning students via e-mail. The survey instrument included assessment of: students' Internet and computer skills, students' comfort with online learning and technology, students' difficulty with subject matter, students' attitude towards technology and learning, and other general demographics information.

Results from Carswell et al.'s (1999) case study suggested that students attending the e-learning course reported a higher number of student-to-student and instructor-to-student interactions than those who attended the correspondence course. Students' Internet and computer skills were not reported as a barrier for learning in the e-learning group. However, quick and high quality technical support was suggested as a key system characteristic in increasing the students' positive experience for the ones attending the e-learning course. As a result, student-to-student interactions, instructor-to-student interactions, as well as quick and high quality technical support will be included as e-learning system characteristics in this study.

Bures, Abrami, and Amundsen (2000) conducted a study in assessing students' motivation to learn online. They suggested assessing the students' acceptance of learning online by measuring the use and frequency of interactions. A survey instrument including 13 items was adapted from prior literature to measure student motivation and satisfaction with e-learning systems (see Table 10). The post-course instrument included a 5-point Likert-type scale ranging from 1 (strongly disagree) to 5 (strongly agree). The measure of online course use was based on the frequency of messages posted to the system by the students. Furthermore, the frequency of students' messages that were required and students were graded on was analyzed separately than students' messages that were posted voluntary and were not counted towards their final grade.

Respondents to the survey included 79 graduate-level students from four on-campus courses utilizing e-learning systems and one fully online course. Aside from standard Pearson correlation measures, no statistical analyses were conducted. Bures et al. (2000) claimed that "we did not collect a sample size large enough to permit the constructions of meaningful regression models" and that they "feel it is not called for [statistical analysis] as this study aims to describe rather than conclude" (p. 610). However, they suggested that motivated students are more likely to be active in the online course. Additionally, students who felt more knowledgeable with technology felt more

Table 10. Bures et al.'s (2000) items to measure student satisfaction with e-learning systems

1.	Learning to use CMC[*] was easy[±]
2.	Using CMC was frustrating
3.	CMC was an effective way to learn the course content[±]
4.	Online messages written by instructors and TAs helped me learn the course content[±]
5.	Using CMC provided me with useful peer support[±]
6.	Small-group online activities did not improve the quality of my education
7.	I learned a great deal more in this course because of CMC learning activities[±]
8.	Using CMC facilitated my work with other students in the course
9.	I learned a great deal more because of the use of CMC
10.	Adequate instructions was provided in the external access of CMC[±]
11.	Inadequate instruction was provided in the use of CMC
12.	The use of CMC in the course motivated me to learn the course material[±]
13.	I would not voluntarily take another course utilizing CMC

Source: Bures et al., 2000, Table 3, p. 608

[±]*Such characteristics were used in a similar form in this study.*

[*]*Computer-mediated communication (CMC) refers to e-learning system termed in this study.*

satisfied with learning online and the e-learning system. Furthermore, students who felt more knowledgeable with technology were more likely to be active in the course especially for non-graded messages (Bures et al., 2000, p. 614).

Bures et al. (2000) also commented in their study limitation that their study lacks investigation of student values (p. 616). They commented that when considering a measurement of outcome expectations, it is important to know what students value. Although not included in their study, they suggested, that "even if students believe that using [e-learning systems] will help them learn the course content (high outcome expectation), they may not value learning the course content (low value of outcome), and thus may not be motivated to use it" (p. 616). Clearly this study is aimed at addressing this exact issue by assessing both the value as well as the satisfaction of learners in e-learning systems in order to indicate the learners' perceived effectiveness of such systems.

Piccoli, Ahmad, and Ives (2001) conducted a study to develop a framework of e-learning systems effectiveness in the context of basic information technology skills training. They define e-learning systems as "computer-based environments that are relatively open systems, allowing interactions

Figure 13. Piccoli et al.'s (2001) dimensions and antecedents of e-learning system effectiveness

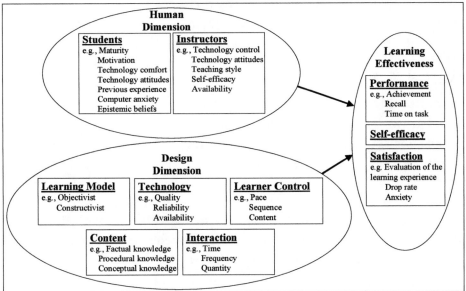

Source: Piccoli et al., 2001, Figure 1, p. 406

and encounters with other participants, and providing access to a wide range of resources" (Piccoli et al., 2001, p. 402-403). They claimed that the domain of e-learning systems propose a major challenge for researchers as there is a large number of constructs and the relationships of such constructs are complex (p. 409). Therefore, for simplicity of their study, Piccoli et al.'s (2001) approach is to investigate the *learning effectiveness* between an on-campus and online course where participants are assigned randomly to each course, rather than self selective as in most cases reported in prior literature. They proposed two main dimensions of e-learning systems: human dimension and design dimension.

The human dimension includes variables such as student characteristics and instructor characteristics; while the design dimension includes five variables: learning model, technology, learner control, content, and interaction. Piccoli et al. (2001) also proposed an overall framework where the human and design dimensions impacted the learning effectiveness. They proposed measuring *learning effectiveness* based on three constructs: students' performance (grade, recall, and time on-task), self-efficacy, and learner satisfaction (see Figure 13). Students' grades on midterms and final exams provided a measure of achievement. They suggested that historically, in the field of education, learning effectiveness has been measured in terms of students' achievement and satisfaction. Self-efficacy was added as a learning effectiveness variable due to the context of their study and "due to the relevance to IT skills development" (Piccoli et al., 2001, p. 410).

One noticeable limitation of Piccoli et al.'s (2001) model is the lack of characteristics that deals with technology support. The quality, availability, and responsiveness of technical support was proposed by other researchers as one of the key constructs in any assessment of IS (Baroudi & Orlikowski, 1988; Ives et al., 1983; Pitt et al., 1995). Furthermore, in their discussion of the students' characteristics, they claimed sources for lack of motivation for students are "work or family constrainers" (Piccoli et al., 2001, p. 405). However, in their general framework or instrument, no measurement associated with work or family support is observed.

Piccoli et al.'s (2001) study included four sections of the same course, introduction to IS, taught by two instructors, where each taught one section online and one section on-campus. Students were not able to decide if they wish to participate in the on-campus or online section, they were assigned by the instructor of the course. Initially, 192 participants were assigned to the four sections of the course; due to dropouts, 146 undergraduate students took part in their study. The assessment included a preliminary survey at the beginning of the course to measure demographics, attitude towards computer use, previous experience with computers, expectation for the course, and self-reported knowledge of course material. Piccoli et al.'s (2001) preliminary results suggest that no significant difference between the treatment and control group were evident in the preliminary survey.

A second survey instrument to assess self-efficacy and satisfaction was measured at the end of the course. The satisfaction instrument is a revised version of Green and Taber's (1980, found in Piccoli et al., 2001) instrument that was originally developed to measure individuals' satisfaction with GDSS and was revised for their study. One immediate limitation of using such instruments is the appropriateness of the instrument in the context of e-learning systems and its content validity. It is the core of this study to draw upon previous literature in order to develop an appropriate and justified instrument to assess learners' satisfaction with e-learning systems as well as perceived learners' value of e-learning systems with high construct validity.

As part of the analysis of their results, Piccoli et al. (2001) suggests using two control variables: gender and instructor. They claim that prior research suggests that perception of technology usefulness and ease of use differs between genders, hence controlling for the gender differences may be beneficial in the exploratory process of the study. Their results suggest that although online students consistently outperformed their counterparts in the on-campus courses, the score differential was not statistically significant. Online students reported slightly higher self-efficacy than students in the on-campus course. Furthermore, their study results show that students attending the two online courses were significantly less satisfied with their learning experience than students attending the two on-campus courses (Piccoli et al., 2001, p. 416). They suggest that the fact that students in the online courses were slightly dissatisfied was due to the fact that they were assigned to an online course rather than self-selecting their attendance in this type of a course. They acknowledge that a prior pilot study they conducted included 20 students interested in taking a course via an e-learning system, and their satisfaction measures showed different results. "These self-selected students responded enthusiastically to the [e-learning systems] and reported very high level of satisfaction with the learning process" (Piccoli et al., 2001, p. 420).

Alavi and Leidner (2001a) in their research commentary article in *Information Systems Research (ISR)* provided a general call for the IS community to invest in research related to e-learning systems as "the need for research in this area [e-learning systems] lags well behind the flux of activity in practice" (p. 2). They suggest that an e-learning system "is defined as an environment in which the learner's interactions with learning material (reading, assignments, exercises, etc.), peers, and/or instructors are mediated through advanced information technologies" (Alavi & Leidner, 2001a, p. 2). They criticize the IS community for lacking a "theoretically grounded and rigorous research to guide the development of these [e-learning] environments" (p. 2).

In a review of the state of e-learning systems' research, Alavi and Leidner (2001a) suggest that most studies show a non-significant difference when comparing online courses with on-campus courses. They also suggest that consistent with research in on-campus settings, research in online settings has shown that student characteristics have an important influence on the learning experiences and outcomes. Furthermore, they claim that cognitive and psychological constructs have been shown to positively correlate with learning outcomes. Moreover, student's comfort with technology observed as a factor in their behavior in videoconferencing systems (Alavi & Leidner, 2001a, p. 4).

It is the main thesis behind this book to address such issues, including a development of a theoretically grounded and rigorous research based on psychological constructs such as *value* and *satisfaction* to provide a general framework in e-learning systems or more specifically in e-learning systems research.

Alavi and Leidner (2001a) suggest that while great progress has been made in the research of e-learning systems, they believe that further research is needed to expand our knowledge in the field. They claim that "most of the recent attempts at studying e-learning systems in IS research tend to adopt an overly simplistic view of this phenomenon" (p. 9). Furthermore, they criticize that the IS research community put too much emphasis on the comparison of groups of learners attending courses via e-learning systems and traditional on-campus courses. Moreover, they criticize that "program and university levels of analysis have been largely ignored" (Alavi & Leidner, 2001a, p. 9). One example for that, they point out, is the evaluation of specific courses rather than an evaluation of a whole program. They suggest that studying a whole program as a unit of analysis rather than a course will "deepen our understanding of the technology mediated learning (TML) phenomenon, inform the design and effective TML environments and expand the breadth of potential research" (Alavi & Leidner, 2001a, p. 9).

This research study addresses the major issues proposed by Alavi and Leidner (2001a). The proposed study builds on previous literature in e-learning systems by looking at the program level to provide an assessment of the satisfaction and value of e-learning systems from the learners' point of view across several courses. Such comparison has never been previously done in the research of e-learning systems. Table 11 presents a summary of literature related to e-learning effectiveness that was reviewed in this section and its major findings or contributions.

Chapter Summary

This chapter provided an extensive review of studies serving as the theoretical foundations upon which this study is based. This study proposes measures of learners' perceived value, perceived satisfaction, and perceived effectiveness of e-learning systems. Grounded in literature from Technology Mediated Learning (TML) theory, an *e-learning system* is defined as the entire techno-

Table 11. Summary of literature related to e-learning effectiveness

Study	Methodology	Sample	Instrument/Constructs	Main findings or contribution
Hiltz & Johnson, 1990	Theoretical, Case study, & Survey	359 users of four different CMCS systems	Multi-dimensional instrument over three major areas: - User Characteristics (Attitude towards computers, Expectations from the system, Individual skills, & demographics) - Group & Task (Group variables, Leadership variables) - Online Experience (Technology barrier, Socio-emotional limits, Use & social ties)	Characteristics of the users and the social context of the application (cultural, group task characteristics) will strongly influence its acceptance and use.
Leidner & Jarvenpaa, 1993	Theoretical & Case study	Three courses, 60 MBA students	Case study 450 five-minute intervals coded for: 1. The material being discussed 2. The teaching method used 3. The interaction in the class	Students are motivated and learn more when they are given **more control** over their learning pace and material **Instructor attitude** is a key factor influencing perceived learning (p. 49). Suggested future research to use four major dimensions: - Course content - Technology - Instructor factors - Student factors
Alavi, 1994	Theoretical & Survey	127 MBA students	A survey instrument to measure: Perceived learning - The perceived skill development - Perceived learning - Students' interest in subject matter Perceived course evaluation - Class evaluation - Student interactions	Students who used GDSS in support of their group learning activities demonstrated a **higher** perceived learning and interest in learning than students who did not use GDSS.
Leidner & Jarvenpaa, 1995	Theoretical	Commentary	Five types of learning models: - The objectivist - The constructivist - The cooperative - The cognitive information processing - The socioculturism	Proposed taxonomy of IS tools that address the five learning models.
Alavi, Wheeler, & Valacich, 1995	Theoretical & Survey	120 MBA students Used three environments: 1. Face-to-face 2. Local desktop videoconferencing 3. Distance desktop videoconferencing	Collaborative learning effectiveness measured in terms of: 1. Students' learning achievements 2. Satisfaction with the learning process and outcomes 3. The emotional climate of the learning environment - Students-to-student interactions - Feeling towards the group/class	Three environments had **no significant difference** in terms of the learning achievements. Participants in the distance desktop videoconferencing environment demonstrated **the highest level of critical thinking** achievement.
Ives & Jarvenpaa, 1996	Theoretical	Commentary	- Lower cost (for travel and classrooms) - Greater convenience - Security - Flexibility - The ability to ignore time differences and geographic distances	E-learning systems will help business schools to shift from "just-in-case" education to "just-in-time" education. Online students in the future will take more control over the learning pace.

Table 11. Summary of literature related to e-learning effectiveness (cont.)

Study	Methodology	Sample	Instrument/Constructs	Main findings or contribution
Alavi, Yoo, & Vogel, 1997	Theoretical, Case study, & Survey	46 MBA students	Perceived learning was measured by a revised 23-item questionnaire based on Hiltz's (1988) instrument. Students' assessment of learning experience was based on their evaluation of **student-to-student** and **instructor-to-student** interactions.	Identified two stakeholders: - Student - Instructor Identify two major factors: - Course content - Interactions Students gave their learning in the networked classrooms **relatively high ratings (4.41 out of 5).** Students perceived outcomes of electronic learning and traditional face-to-face collaborative learning did not differ.
Webster & Hackley, 1997	Theoretical, Case study, & Survey	29 technology-mediated distance learning courses 247 students (69%)	Multi-dimensional instrument with 104 items over four dimensions: - Technology - Instructor - Course - Student (Linear Regression Analysis)	**Reliability of the technology** is positively related to the learning outcomes. The **quality of the technology** is positively related to the learning outcomes.
Carswell, Thomas, Petre, Price, & Richards, 1999	Theoretical, Case study, & Survey	300 students Two groups: 1. Corresponding Learning 2. Online Learning	Case study - Students' Internet and computer skills - Students' comfort with online learning and technology - Students' difficulty with subject matter - Students' attitude towards technology and learning - Interactions - Other demographics	- Faster and more flexible access to information - Ability to submit assignments from anywhere - Increased interactions - Reduced feeling of isolation Online learning students reported higher number of **student-to-student** and **instructor-to-student** interactions.
Bures, Abrami, & Amundsen, 2000	Theoretical & Survey	79 graduate-level students from four on-campus courses and one online course	- Survey instrument includes 13-items - Frequency of graded messages - Frequency of voluntary messages	Motivated students are more likely to be active in the online course. Students who felt more knowledgeable with technology felt more satisfied with learning online **"it is important to know what student value."**
Piccoli, Ahmad, & Ives, 2001	Theoretical & Survey	146 undergraduate students Two online courses Two on-campus courses	**Human dimension** - Student characteristics - Instructor characteristics **Design dimension** - Learning model - Technology - Learner control - Content - Interaction **Learning effectiveness** - Students' achievement - Students' satisfaction - Self-efficacy	Controlling for the **gender** differences may be beneficial in the exploratory process of the study. **No statistical significant** difference in scores between online & on-campus students. Self-selected students responded enthusiastically to e-learning systems and reported **very high level of satisfaction** with the learning process.
Alavi & Leidner, 2001a	Theoretical	Commentary	- **Student characteristics** have an important influence on the learning experience and outcomes - Cognitive and psychological characteristics are positively correlate with learning outcomes. - Student's comfort with technology impact behavior in videoconferencing systems	IS community for lacking a **"theoretically grounded and rigorous research** to guide the development of these [e-learning systems] environments." "Most of the recent attempts at studying TML in IS research tend to adopt an overly simplistic view of this phenomenon." **"Program and university levels of analysis have been largely ignored."**

logical, organizational and management system that facilitates and enables students learning via the Internet. Technology Mediated Learning theory suggests various e-learning systems characteristics as part of any assessment of such systems. E-learning systems *characteristics* are defined as the attributes (or features) associated with e-learning systems. Examples of such e-learning system characteristics include quality of technical support, high network availability, ease-of-use, users' comfort with online learning and technology, and so on. Given the nature of the phenomenon on hand it is appropriate to draw upon the four major streams of literature including: value, user satisfaction, IS effectiveness, and e-learning systems. These research streams are extracted from heterogeneous literature including psychology, marketing, operations research, information systems, general education, management education, and distance education and they have all been reviewed in this chapter.

Value theory provides the psychological foundation including definition, rationale, and significance of value construct for this study. Review of definitions of value from psychology, marketing, and IS suggests several synonyms for users' value. Such synonyms include importance, preference, weights, and desirability. Based on review of such definitions and in the context of e-learning systems, this study defines *value* as an enduring core belief about the level of importance users attribute to e-learning systems. Consequently, *learners' value items* (survey items) are defined as the measures of the importance of enduring core beliefs concerning each characteristic of e-learning systems when learning online.

Early studies in value theory suggested that ranking is the only appropriate method of assessing users' value items (Feather, 1967, 1975; Rokeach, 1969, 1973). Some scholars suggested that the use of ranking impose burden for respondents during data collection and even more burdens on scholars in the data analysis process (Brown, 1976; Coyne, 1988; King & Epstein, 1983; Ng, 1982; Thompson et al., 1982). Following studies incorporated such suggestions and looked at the comparison between rating and ranking. Results from such studies suggest that the Likert-type rating value scaling was found to be as reliable as the ranking scale, while providing quicker administration and better data analysis capabilities (Chapman et al., 1983; King & Epstein, 1983; Payne, 1988; Thompson et al., 1982). Thus, this study uses a Likert-type rating scale for the assessment of value items.

IS Satisfaction theories (UIS theory and EUCS theory) provide the foundation including definition, rationale, and significance of satisfaction construct for this study. Based on the extensive review of numerous studies from IS and in the context of e-learning systems, this study defines *satisfaction* as the perceived performance level users find at a post-experience point of time with e-learning systems. Consequently, *learners' satisfaction items* are defined as the measures of perceived performance levels learners find at a post-experience point of time with each of the e-learning systems characteristics. The extensive work done during the 1980s and early 1990s on IS user satisfaction was reviewed in this chapter, and provided several instruments in the assessment of user satisfaction. However, some scholars suggest that IS research has omitted the measurements of the degree of importance (or value), forgoing the opportunity for a deeper understanding of IS phenomenon (Etezadi-Amoli & Farhoomand, 1991, p. 1). Consequently, this study is grounded upon such IS instruments by augmenting it with appropriate measures of characteristics of e-learning systems, along with employing an appropriate measure of the level of importance (value) to each item.

IS Effectiveness theory provides the foundation, rationale, and significance of the effectiveness construct in this study. Extensive review of literature in the area of IS effectiveness suggests that there is little agreement in the literature on the definition of IS effectiveness, let alone how to measure it (Arnold, 1995; Grover et al., 1996; Kim, 1989; Seddon & Yip, 1992; Srinivasan, 1985; Yuthas & Eining, 1995). However, some scholars suggest that user satisfaction and system usage are not enough in the assessment of IS effectiveness (Arnold, 1995; Yuthas & Eining, 1995). Grover et al. (1996) suggest a promising framework to assess IS effectiveness that is based on three types of measurements of IS effectiveness from the individual's unit of analysis: a comparative, a normative, and an improvement measurement. Based on Grover et al.'s (1996) general framework, this study defines *comparative system effectiveness* as a comparison of an e-learning system with a peer e-learning system, *improvement system effectiveness* as a comparison of an e-learning system over time, and *normative system effectiveness* as a comparison of an e-learning system with a theoretically ideal e-learning system. Grounded on value theory, IS Satisfaction theory and IS Effectiveness theory are reviewed in this chapter, this study considers *e-learning system* as *effective* when learners value its characteristics as highly important and are highly satisfied by those same characteristics.

TML theory provides the general foundation and e-learning systems characteristics for this study of assessing value of e-learning systems. The instrument proposed in this study is mainly developed based on previous studies of TML

(Alavi, 1994; Alavi et al., 1995; Alavi et al., 1997; Alavi & Leidner, 2001a; Bures et al., 2000; Carswell, et. al., 1999; Hiltz & Johnson, 1990; Ives & Jarvenpaa, 1996; Leidner & Jarvenpaa, 1993, 1995; Piccoli, Ahmad, & Ives, 2001; Webster & Hackley, 1997).

TML theory suggests four extended dimensions categorizing e-learning system characteristics into heterogeneous measures of: technology and support, course, professor, and learner dimension (Webster & Hackley, 1997). Based on such an approach, this study utilizes such four dimensions by assessing learners' dimension measures (satisfaction and value) in the development of models to appropriately predict learners' overall measures (satisfaction and value). *Learners' dimension satisfaction measure* is defined as the aggregation of all perceived learners' satisfaction items with each dimension. Similarly *learners' dimension value measure* is defined as the aggregation of all perceived learners' value items with each dimension. Moreover, *learners' overall satisfaction* (overall satisfaction) is defined as the aggregation of all four learners' dimension satisfaction measures. Similarly *learners' overall value* (overall value) is defined as the aggregation of all four learners' dimension value measures.

The theories and models reviewed in this chapter provide an extensive theoretical foundation necessary to develop the proposed framework and address the research questions posed in Chapter I. Chapters IV, V, and VI build upon the theories and models reviewed in this chapter to develop a conceptual research model and a set of tools to assess the learners' perceived value and satisfaction of e-learning systems in order to provide a measure of perceived effectiveness of such systems. Chapter VII details the research methodology and case study that implements the research model. Chapter VIII ends this book by providing a discussion and conclusions of the whole study.

Chapter IV

The General
Conceptual Model

Introduction

In this chapter, a general theoretical model is proposed that links learners'
satisfaction and learners' value of e-learning systems in order to assess
learners' perceived effectiveness of such systems. The central research question in this study is: Is there a relationship between learners' perceived
satisfaction with e-learning systems and learners' perceived *value* for learners' perceived effectiveness of e-learning systems?

The significance of the *value* construct in the context of e-learning systems has
never been evaluated. How the *value* of e-learning systems relates to other
constructs, such as *satisfaction* with e-learning systems and ultimately whether
the value of e-learning systems can be used to indicate learners' perceived IS
effectiveness remains open. In this chapter, a general conceptual model or
framework is proposed to address this phenomenon in the context of e-learning
systems. The proposed model or framework will provide procedures to

identify and measure the key constructs (satisfaction with e-learning systems, value of e-learning systems, and effectiveness of e-learning systems). This chapter also defines precisely the individual characteristics and four major dimensions (categories) for evaluating value of e-learning systems and satisfaction with e-learning systems based on comprehensive literature reviewed in Chapters II and III. Additionally, this chapter proposes five specific research questions that are addressed in Chapter VII. Two additional specific research questions are proposed in Chapters V and VI.

Overview of the Proposed
General Conceptual Model

The review of value theory presented in Chapter II highlights the relationships between major conceptual constructs associated with the *value* construct. Research from the fields of psychology and marketing suggest that *value*, *attitude*, *behavior*, and *satisfaction* constructs are closely related. Many studies in both psychology and marketing as well as in the field of information systems have explored the relationships between these constructs. Results of such research suggest that these constructs are related in the sequence: *value* impacts *attitude* that impacts *behavior*, which in turn impacts *satisfaction* (Beatty, Kahle, Homer, & Misra, 1985; Durgee, O'Connor, & Veryzer, 1996; Feather, 1967, 1975; Kahle & Kennedy, 1988; Prescott & Hopkins, 1984; Rokeach, 1969, 1973). The goal of this study is not to provide empirical evidence for such a sequence, rather it is to use this sequence to develop a framework that predicts learners' perceived effectiveness of e-learning systems based on the learners' perceived value and satisfaction associated with such systems. Furthermore, although this book will use only two of the constructs in this sequence (*value* and *satisfaction*), the significance of *attitude* and *behavior* should not be underestimated. Information systems researchers investigated the sequence of *attitude*, *behavior*, and *satisfaction*; however the *value* construct was largely ignored due to its complexity (Etezadi-Amoli & Farhoomand, 1991, p. 1).

Grover, Jeong, and Segars (1996) suggested that over the years, the information systems research efforts have developed "robust (reliable and valid) instruments that can be used to measure … beliefs, attitudes, and perceptions associated with IS characteristics" (p. 179). Noticeably missing in their review and categorization of over 100 articles from the information systems field, in particular with user perceptions on systems, are studies that deal with the *value* construct. There are several studies proposing measurements as an instrument to assess the financial value of information systems (Ahituv, 1980). However, none actually explore the psychological construct of *value* even though many scholars outside the field of information systems suggest the significance of *value* as a causal factor to *attitude*, *behavior* (usage), and *satisfaction* constructs (Allport, Vernon, & Lindzey, 1951; Brown, 1976; Feather, 1967, 1975; Kahle & Chiagouris, 1997; Kahle & Kennedy, 1988; Rokeach, 1969, 1973). The model proposed here will include *value* as a central construct as well as *satisfaction* to indicate how these constructs can be used for learners' perceived effectiveness of e-learning systems.

Grover et al. (1996) state nicely that for an individual unit of analysis, "IS effectiveness is related to the extent to which IS satisfies the requirements of organization's members" (p. 180). They also suggest three types of measurements of IS effectiveness from the individual perspective: a comparative, a normative, and an improvement measurement. In the context of this study, the *comparative measurement* determines the e-learning systems effectiveness by comparing an e-learning system with peer e-learning systems. The *improvement measurement* determines information systems effectiveness by evaluating an e-learning system over time. Lastly, the *normative measurement* determines e-learning systems effectiveness by comparing the existing state of an e-learning system with a theoretically ideal e-learning system or the desirable state of the e-learning system.

The theoretical framework proposed here takes the *normative* view of information systems' effectiveness in the context of e-learning system by developing measures of individual users' perceptions of the current state of an e-learning system and measures of users' perceptions of the desired state of an e-learning system. An assessment of the users' perceived current and desired measures will enable an analysis of the magnitude of e-learning system effectiveness. A comparison of e-learning systems can be derived by using the *normative measurement* over peer e-learning systems. Additionally, an assessment of the *improvement* in e-learning systems effectiveness can be derived from the assessment of the *normative measurement* for a given e-learning system over time. Consequently, the model proposed in this study concentrates on the *normative* view solely. Following Grover et al.'s (1996) approach (see Figure 11 in Chapter III), the unit of analysis of this study focuses on the learner or individual perspective in the context of e-learning systems.

Research in the field of information systems, specifically in the area of information systems satisfaction, suggests that user's information systems satisfaction instruments provide measures of the users' perceived *performance* level of a system (Doll & Torkzadeh, 1991, p. 6; Kim, 1989, p. 7). Bailey and Pearson (1983) suggested that measuring respondents' overall satisfaction provides an indication of the performance level of a system after their experience with the system (p. 532). Therefore, in the context of this study, *satisfaction* is defined as perceived performance level that users find at a post-experience point of time with an e-learning system. Accordingly, *learners' overall satisfaction* with e-learning systems represents the learners' overall perceived performance state of such systems.

Research in the field of value theory suggests that value instruments provide measures of the users' perceived desired state of ideas or things (Rokeach, 1969, p. 160). Therefore, in the context of this study, *value* is defined as "an enduring core belief about the level of importance users attribute to e-learning systems." Accordingly, *learners' overall value* of e-learning systems represent the learners' perceptions of the desirable state of such systems.

To measure the *normative* system effectiveness, an analysis of the *learners' perceived satisfaction* with e-learning systems and *learners' perceived value* of e-learning systems is needed in order to indicate the level of effectiveness of such a system. Such normative assessment can be done at the various levels associated with the system (including dimensions level and the overall system level). Additional details about these two levels are provided in the next sections of this chapter. An e-learning system will be considered *effective* with respect to a characteristic (or dimension), when learners perceive its characteristics (or dimensions) as highly important and are highly satisfied by those same characteristics (or dimensions). Similarly, an e-learning system will be considered *ineffective* with respect to a characteristic (or dimension) when learners perceive its characteristics (or dimensions) as unimportant or as highly unsatisfied by such characteristics (or dimensions).

Based on the previously mentioned approach for learners' perceived system effectiveness, this study concentrates on defining, outlining, and developing measurements of the *satisfaction* and *value* constructs in the context of e-learning systems based on existing validated instruments. Although, *attitude* and *behavior* (or use) constructs are significant, such constructs are proposed by prior research as intermediate constructs. For elaborated reviews of relationships, rationale, and justification on this subject, see the value theory review in Chapter II. Accordingly, Figure 1 represents the overall conceptual

Figure 1. General conceptual model for effectiveness of e-learning systems

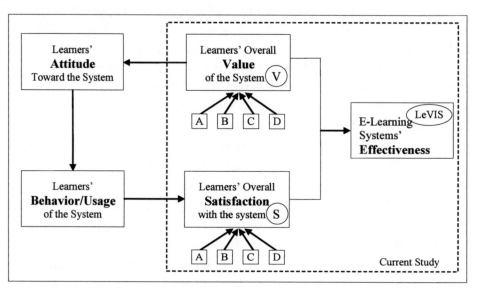

model proposed by this study. The model provides a general conceptual framework including the *learners' overall perceived satisfaction* with e-learning systems, *learners' overall perceived value* of e-learning systems, *learners' attitude* towards e-learning systems, learners' *behavior* (or use) with respect to e-learning systems, and implications for learners' perceived e-learning systems effectiveness. As suggested before, the intermediate constructs and the associated implications are not the aim of this study. Therefore, the approach is to provide a framework for the *normative measurement* of e-learning systems effectiveness, utilizing the key constructs: value of e-learning systems and satisfaction with e-learning systems. The next section will provide an overview of the proposed research model and will suggest more specific research questions as the framework is built. The rationale for each of the specific research questions is provided prior to each of the question's statements. Additional specific research questions are provided in Chapters V and VI.

Proposed E-Learning
System Characteristics

Based on the comprehensive literature covered in Chapters II and III from the Technology Mediated Learning (TML) theory and other theories such as information systems satisfaction, information systems effectiveness, and value theory, this study proposes a set of characteristics that learners may find important, or value, when using e-learning systems. In the context of this study, e-learning systems characteristics are defined as "the attributes (or features) associated with e-learning systems." The list of e-learning systems characteristics will be built primarily from literature and subsequently through exploratory focus groups, as well as the qualitative questionnaire. Some e-learning systems characteristics were specifically proposed in literature with direct links to a specific survey item, whereas other e-learning systems characteristics were only noted vaguely and were never fully empirically investigated. Since the aim of this study is to provide a comprehensive list of e-learning systems characteristics, all suggested characteristics will be explored. Examples of e-learning systems characteristics include quality of technical support, network availability, quality of course content, quality of student-professor interactions, user comfort with technology, and so on.

Consequently, the first research question of this study (RQ1) is:

RQ1:   What characteristics of e-learning systems are important for learners?

As the first step, a list of e-learning systems characteristics from literature will be created. Table 1 provides a preliminary set of 48 characteristics based on the literature. The table also provides sample items (questions) from literature used to measure these or similar characteristics in prior studies and documents other literature indicating similar characteristics without a specific survey item on how to measure each one. An asterisk denotes a characteristic that was found to be significant in a given study, although level of significance varies and is not documented here. This preliminary set of 48 e-learning systems characteristics will be subjected to focus groups in order to validate their potential relevance and to augment the current list. This will be accomplished in Phase I of the study to confirm relevance of the individual characteristics' and to augment to the existing list. Additional information of the study phases and the validation of such lists is provided in Chapter VII.

Table 1. Proposed characteristics of e-learning systems from literature

No.	Propose E-Learning Systems Characteristics from Literature	Item Source	Item Text from Literature	Other Literature
1.	Quick answer from technical support via phone	Ives, Olson, & Baroudi, 1983 (Q30*)	Communication with support staff	Baroudi & Orlikowski, 1988*; Keeney, 1999; Pitt, Watson, & Kavan, 1995*
2.	Quick answer from technical support after-hours via e-mail	Webster & Hackley, 1997 (Q86)	There was little need for technical support for this technology	Keeney, 1999; Moore & Kearsley 1996, pp. 169-170; Pitt et al. 1995*
3.	Quality of technical support	Baroudi & Orlikowski, 1988 (BO6*) ; Ives et al., 1983 (Q11*)	Expectation of computer support (Q11*); Attitude of support staff (BO6*)	Keeney, 1999; Moore & Kearsley, 1996, pp. 76, 163 ; Pitt et al., 1995*
4.	System operation time (up-time)	Hiltz, 1996 (H36); Webster & Hackley, 1997 (Q85)	The system was always reliable and ready for use when needed (Q85); The system was being "down" a lot (H36)	Bailey & Pearson, 1983*; DeLone & McLean, 1992; Doll & Torkzadeh, 1988*; Hiltz & Johnson, 1990*; Piccoli, Ahmad, & Ives, 2001, p. 407; Srinivasan, 1985*
5.	Reduced system errors	Ives et al., 1983 (H12*); King & Epstein, 1983 (KE16*); Webster & Hackley, 1997 (Q62)	The technology was subject to frequent problems and crashes (Q62); Corrections of errors (H12); Minimization of errors (KE16*)	Bailey & Pearson, 1983*; Doll & Torkzadeh, 1988*; DeLone & McLean, 1992; Leidner & Jarvenpaa, 1993; Piccoli et al., 2001, p. 407; Srinivasan, 1985*
6.	System security (discourages hacking, secure access, etc.)	Ives & Jarvenpaa, 1996	Greater security	Keeney, 1999
7.	Access to courses from anywhere in the world (via the Internet)	Ives et al., 1983 (Q24*); Ives & Jarvenpaa, 1996	Convenience of access (Q24*); Accessible throughout the world	Piccoli et al., 2001, p. 407; Srinivasan, 1985*; Webster & Hackley, 1997
8.	High network availability & low network congestion	Hiltz, 1996 (H33)	Access to online class was a problem for me (H33)	Bailey & Pearson, 1983*; Hiltz & Johnson, 1990*; King & Epstein, 1983*; Piccoli et al., 2001, p. 407; Srinivasan, 1985*; Webster & Hackley, 1997;
9.	Learning at anytime of the day (schedule flexibility)	Webster & Hackley, 1997 (Q30); Ives et al., 1983 (I38*)	This type of multi-media technology provide little flexibility in the delivery of the course (Q30); Flexibility of system (I38)	King & Epstein, 1983*; Leidner & Jarvenpaa, 1993; Moore & Kearsley, 1996, pp. 134-136, 168
10.	Submit assignments from anywhere (via the Internet)	Ives & Jarvenpaa, 1996 (IJ); Piccoli et al., 2001 (P) p. 414	Ability to submit assignments while ignoring time differences and geographic distances (IJ); Students complete their homework at home, work, or school computer	Carswell, Thomas, Petre, Price, & Richards, 1999
11.	Different system tools (chat, bulletin-board or discussion forums, etc.)	Piccoli et al., 2001	Collection of tools used to deliver the learning material and to facilitate communication among participants	
12.	Access of all courses from one area (portal)	Hiltz & Johnson, 1990*	Access via terminal	
13.	Taking quizzes remotely (off-campus)			Leidner & Jarvenpaa, 1993

Table 1. Proposed characteristics of e-learning systems from literature (cont.)

No.	Propose E-Learning Systems Characteristics from Literature	Item Source	Item Text from Literature	Other Literature
14.	Review course audios	Ives & Jarvenpaa, 1996	Ability to review recorded classes	
15.	Availability of course content	Doll & Torkzadeh, 1988 (C2*)	Does the information content meet your needs (C2*)	Baroudi & Orlikowski 1988*; Ives et al., 1983*; Ives & Jarvenpaa, 1996; King & Epstein, 1983*; Moore & Kearsley, 1996 pp. 102-123; Srinivasan, 1985*; Swan, 2002, p. 5
16.	Amount of material in courses	Doll & Torkzadeh, 1988 (C4*)	Does the system provide sufficient information (C4*)	Bailey & Pearson, 1983 (*); Ives et al., 1983*; Ives & Jarvenpaa, 1996; King & Epstein, 1983*
17.	Interesting subject matter	Hiltz, 1996 (A1); Hiltz et al., 2000 (H9); Marks, 2000 (C18); Webster & Hackley, 1997 (Q5, Q8)	The subject matter of this course is ambiguous (Q5); The subject matter of this course is easy to understand (Q8); As a result of taking this course, I have more positive feeling toward this field of study (C18); The course content was interesting to me (A1); I gained more interest in the subject (H9)	Bailey & Pearson, 1983 (*); Baroudi & Orlikowski, 1988*; Doll & Torkzadeh, 1988*; Ives et al., 1983*; Hiltz & Johnson, 1990*; Leidner & Jarvenpaa, 1993; Moore & Kearsley, 1996, p. 162; Piccoli et al., 2001, p. 403;
18.	Difficulty of subject matter	Marks, 2000 (C5, C26)	How difficult has this course been for you? (C5); For me, this is the most demanding course that I have taken (C26)	King & Epstein, 1983*; Marks, 2000; Moore & Kearsley, 1996, pp. 162-163
19.	Availability of other content (syllabus, objectives, assignments, schedule)	Bures, Abrami, & Amundsen, 2000 (T3); Hiltz, 1996 (A3, A4) ; Webster & Hackley, 1997 (Q64)	There was a good balance between presentation and interaction (Q64); CMC was an effective way to learn the course content (T3); Course goals were clear to me (A2); Work requirements and grading system were clear from the beginning (A3)	Moore & Kearsley, 1996, pp. 107-108
20.	Enjoyment from the courses/lessons	Alavi, 1994 (GE3); Webster & Hackley, 1997 (Q38, Q81)	This type of multi-media technology is fun (Q38); I found the course to be a good learning experience (Q81); Group work was fun (GE3)	Doll & Torkzadeh, 1988*; Hiltz & Johnson, 1990*; Moore & Kearsley, 1996, p. 162
21.	Quality content of courses	Doll & Torkzadeh, 1988 (F1*, F2*); Hiltz, 1996 (A7); Webster & Hackley, 1997 (Q82; Q83)	The quality of information (videos, audios, graphics) was high (Q82); The activities for the classes were carefully planned (Q83); Do you think the output is presented in a useful format? (F1*); Is the information clear? (F2*); The lecture material is poor (A7)	Alavi, Yoo, & Vogel, 1997; Baroudi & Orlikowski, 1988*; DeLone & McLean, 1992; Hiltz & Johnson, 1990*; Ives et al., 1983*; Ives & Jarvenpaa, 1996; Keeney, 1999; King & Epstein, 1983*; Piccoli et al., 2001, p. 404; Srinivasan, 1985*; Webster & Hackley, 1997
22.	Ease-of-use (with course content, navigation, interface, etc.)	Bures et al., 2000 (T1); Doll & Torkzadeh, (E1*, E2*)	Learning to use computer-mediated communication (CMC) was easy (T1); Is the system user friendly? (E1*); Is the system easy to use? (E2*)	Bailey & Pearson, 1983; Carswell et. al., 1999, Hiltz & Johnson, 1990*; Keeney 1999; King & Epstein, 1983*; Yuthas & Eining, 1995*
23.	Similar of interface across all online courses	Swan et al., 2000*, p. 517	"Transparent Interface"	Leidner & Jarvenpaa, 1993; 1995; Piccoli et al., 2001, p. 420
24.	Gathering information quickly	Doll & Torkzadeh, 1988 (Timeliness) (T1*, T2*)	Do you get the information you need in time? (T1*); Does the system provide up-to-date information? (T2*)	Baroudi & Orlikowski, 1988*; Hiltz & Johnson, 1990*; Ives et al., 1983*; Keeney, 1999; King & Epstein, 1983*

Table 1. Proposed characteristics of e-learning systems from literature (cont.)

No.	Propose E-Learning Systems Characteristics from Literature	Item Source	Item Text from Literature	Other Literature
25.	Organization of courses (content of courses, organization of assignments, etc. across all courses)	Webster & Hackley, 1997 (Q97); Marks, 2000 (C14)	The course is well organized	Doll & Torkzadeh, 1988*; Ives & Jarvenpaa, 1996; Keeney, 1999; King & Epstein 1983*; Marks, 2000
26.	Taking practice tests prior to graded test			Moore & Kearsley, 1996, p. 108; Ives & Jarvenpaa, 1996
27.	Amount of professor-to-student interaction	Alavi et al, 1997; Carswell et. al., 1999; Hiltz, 1996 (B9); Swan, 2002, p. 10; Swan et al., 2000, p. 27 (*)	Professor was not available for help and consultation (B9)	Alavi, 1994; Ives et al., 1983*; Leidner & Jarvenpaa, 1993; Moore & Kearsley, 1996, pp. 76, 127-132, 163; Piccoli et al., 2001 p. 404
28.	Professor's attitude (across all professors)	Marks, 2000 (C32); Webster & Hackley, 1997 (Q67)	The instructor was actively helpful when students had difficulty (C32); The instructor encouraged questions from students (Q67)	Ives et al., 1983*; Leidner & Jarvenpaa, 1993; Marks, 2000; Moore & Kearsley, 1996, p. 162; Piccoli et al., 2001
29.	Learning a lot from the professor (across all courses)	Hiltz & Johnson, 1990*	Expected productivity from course*	Alavi, 1994; King & Epstein, 1983 (practicality*)
30.	Quality of professor-to-student interaction			Ives et al., 1983*; Leidner & Jarvenpaa, 1993; 1995; Piccoli et al., 2001, p. 404; Yuthas & Eining, 1995*
31.	Freedom of learning (selective seeking and processing of information)	Ahmad, 1999 (Q4 p.126); Webster & Hackley, 1997 (Q28); Piccoli et al., 2001 (P), p. 414	In this class I was able to learn at my own pace (Q4 p.126); This type of multi-media technology allows the instructor to maintain control over the direction of the course (Q28); Students are free to review or skip any lecture or components of it (P)	Ives et al., 1983*; Ives & Jarvenpaa, 1996; Leidner & Jarvenpaa, 1993, 1995; Moore & Kearsley, 1996, pp. 76, 107, 163;
32.	Submission time window for assignments and quizzes			Moore & Kearsley, 1996, pp. 107, 163
33.	Online workload of courses	Marks, 2000 (C24)	In relations to other courses, this course's workload was heavy	Marks, 2000
34.	Learning a lot in these classes	Marks, 2000 (C17); Hiltz, 1996 (C2)	I am learning a lot in this class (like C1); I learned a great deal in this course (C2)	Alavi, 1994; Alavi et al., 1995; Marks, 2000
35.	Amount of interaction with classmates	Bures et al. 2000 (T8); Webster & Hackley, 1997 (Q72)	I felt comfortable interacting with other students (Q72); Using CMC facilitated my work with other students in the course (T8)	Alavi et al., 1995; Baroudi & Orlikowski, 1988*; Hiltz & Johnson, 1990*; Ives et al., 1983*; Leidner & Jarvenpaa, 1993; Piccoli et al., 2001 p. 404; Swan, 2002, p. 13
36.	Quality of interaction with classmates	Alavi, 1994 (CE4); Hiltz, 1996 (E15)	The help I got from other students was useless (E15); Student comments were useful to me (CE4)	Alavi et al., 1995; Baroudi & Orlikowski, 1988*; Hiltz & Johnson, 1990*; Ives et al., 1983*; Leidner & Jarvenpaa, 1993; Piccoli et al., 2001, p. 404 ; Swan et al., 2000, p. 517 "valued and dynamic interactions" (*)

Table 1. Proposed characteristics of e-learning systems from literature (cont.)

No.	Propose E-Learning Systems Characteristics from Literature	Item Source	Item Text from Literature	Other Literature
37.	Classmates' attitude (across all courses)	Hiltz, 1996 (E16, K10)	Students in my class tend to be corporative (E16); I found comments made by other students to be useful (K 10)	Alavi, 1994; Alavi et al., 1995 ; Hiltz & Johnson, 1990*; Ives et al., 1983; Leidner & Jarvenpaa, 1993
38.	Being part of a "class" although it was online	Webster & Hackley, 1997 (Q69)	I felt like I was part of the entire class even though it was online	Alavi et al., 1995; Baroudi & Orlikowski, 1988*; Hiltz & Johnson, 1990*; Ives et al., 1983*; Keeney, 1999; Moore & Kearsley, 1996, p. 162; Piccoli et al., 2001, p.403; Swan, 2002, p. 14; Swan et al., 2000, p. 517
39.	Your comfort with online learning and technology	Bures et al., 2000 (T2, T9, & T13) ; Hiltz et al., 2000 (H6) ; Webster & Hackley, 1997 (Q56, Q57, Q58, Q77, Q 79, Q80, & Q91)	I believe that I will be able to use this technology easily in the future (Q56); I believe that my communications skills will improve substantially using this type of technology in the future (Q57); I was comfortable when interacting in this type of Distance Education classroom (Q58); I learned as well in this type of Distance Education course as I do in traditional course (Q77); I would recommend this type of distance learning course to someone else (Q79); This distance education classroom was suitable for learning (Q80); I was very satisfied with the use of this technology for the course (Q91); Using CMC was frustrating (T2); I learned a great deal more because of the use of CMC (T9); I will not voluntarily take another course utilizing CMC (T13); I would not take another online course (H6)	Alavi et al., 1995; Baroudi & Orlikowski, 1988*; Carswell et. al, 1999 ; Hiltz & Johnson, 1990*; Ives et al., 1983*; Piccoli et al., 2001, p. 405; Webster & Hackley, 1997
40.	Your Internet and computer skills	Bures et al. 2000 (T2) ; Webster & Hackley, 1997 (Q56, Q57,Q91)	I believe that I will be able to use this technology easily in the future (Q56); I believe that my communications skills will improve substantially using this type of technology in the future (Q57); I was very satisfied with the use of this technology for the course (Q91); Using CMC was frustrating (T2);	Alavi et al., 1995; Carswell et. al, 1999; Hiltz & Johnson, 1990*; Leidner & Jarvenpaa, 1993, 1995; Piccoli et al., 2001; Webster & Hackley, 1997
41.	Self-discipline and time management			Hiltz, 1988; Leidner & Jarvenpaa, 1993, 1995; Piccoli et al., 2001
42.	Cost of courses	Hiltz & Johnson, 1990*	Cost to use the system*	Alavi, 1994; Alavi et al., 1995; Ives & Jarvenpaa, 1996; Keeney, 1999; King & Epstein, 1983*; Moore & Kearsley, 1996, p. 74
43.	Cost of ISP and Internet access	Hiltz 1996 (I37, I38); Hiltz & Johnson, 1990*	The cost of telephone access has been a problem for me (I37); The cost of Internet Service Provider has been a problem for me (I38); Cost to reach the system*	Keeney, 1999
44.	Reduced travel cost/time (to and from campus)	Hiltz & Johnson, 1990*	Expected time saving*	Keeney, 1999

Table 1. Proposed characteristics of e-learning systems from literature (cont.)

No.	Propose E-Learning Systems Characteristics from Literature	Item Source	Item Text from Literature	Other Literature
45.	Ability to travel while taking online courses (for business or other)	Ives & Jarvenpaa, 1996 (IJ); Piccoli et al., 2001, (P) p. 405	Ability to travel while attending MBA program (IJ); Work constrains (P)	Piccoli et al., 2001, p. 405
46.	Employer support and your ability to work while learning	Ives & Jarvenpaa, 1996	Ability to work full time while attending MBA program	Moore & Kearsley, 1996, p. 162; Piccoli et al., 2001, p. 405
47.	Attendance to family responsibilities	Piccoli et al., 2001, p. 405	Family constrains	Moore & Kearsley, 1996, p. 162
48.	Family support			Moore & Kearsley, 1996, p. 162

Proposed E-Learning System Dimensions

Due to the heterogeneity nature of the e-learning system characteristics proposed in the previous section, it will be appropriate to group the characteristics according to the four dimensions proposed by Webster and Hackley (1997). The four dimensions are named technology and support, course, professor, and learner. Table 2 proposes a categorization of the set of 48 proposed characteristics found in literature grouped into the four dimensions following Webster and Hackley (1997). The e-learning systems characteristics grouping to one of the four e-learning system dimensions was done based on two judgments. The first judgment for allocation of a specific e-learning systems characteristic to an e-learning system dimension was done following prior literature. An e-learning system characteristic was assigned to a specific e-learning system dimension if it was suggested in literature as part of that particular e-learning system dimension. For example, Webster and Hackley (1997) suggest that "system reliability" is a characteristic that should be grouped with the technology and support dimension. Moreover, Marks (2000) suggests that "course organization" is a characteristic that should be grouped with the course dimension. If no grouping suggestion was to be found in prior

Table 2. Proposed e-learning system characteristics assigned to Webster and Hackley's (1997) dimensions

A.	Technology & Support Dimension	B.	Course Dimension	C.	Professor Dimension	D.	Learner Dimension
A1	Quick answer from technical support via phone	B1	Availability of course content	C1	Amount of professor-to-student interaction	D1	Learning a lot in these classes
A2	Quick answer from technical support after-hours via e-mail	B2	Amount of material in courses	C2	Professor's attitude (across all professors)	D2	Amount of interaction with classmates
A3.	Quality of technical support	B3	Interesting subject matter	C3	Learning a lot from the professor (across all courses)	D3	Quality of interaction with classmates·
A4	System operation time (up-time)	B4	Difficulty of subject matter	C4	Quality of professor-to-student interaction	D4	Classmates' attitude (across all courses)
A5	Reduced system errors	B5	Availability of other content (syllabus, objectives, assignments, schedule)	C5	Freedom of learning (selective seeking and processing of information)	D5	Being part of a 'class' although it was online
A6	System security (discourage hacking, secure access, etc.)	B6	Enjoyment from the courses/lessons	C6	Submission time window for assignments and quizzes	D6	Comfort with online learning and technology
A7	Access to courses from anywhere in the world (via the Internet)	B7	Quality content of courses	C7	Online workload of courses	D7	Internet and computer skills
A8	High network availability & low network congestion	B8	Ease-of-use (with course content, navigation, interface, etc.)			D8	Self-discipline and time management
A9	Learning at anytime of the day (schedule flexibility)	B9	Similar of interface across all online courses			D9	Cost of courses
A10	Submit assignments from anywhere (via the Internet)	B10	Gathering information quickly			D10	Cost of ISP and Internet access
A11	Different system tools (chat, bulletin-board or discussion forums, etc.)	B11	Organization of courses (content of courses, organization of assignments, etc. across all courses)			D11	Reduced travel cost/time (to and from campus)
A12	Access of all courses from one area (portal)	B12	Taking practice tests prior to graded test			D12	Ability to travel while taking online courses (for business or other)
A13	Taking quizzes remotely (off-campus)					D13	Employer support and your ability to work while learning
A14	Review course audios					D14	Attendance to family responsibilities
						D15	Family support

literature, a second judgment of allocating was used based on the name of the e-learning system characteristics and its similarity to other e-learning system characteristics within a particular e-learning system dimension. For example, "family support" was not suggested in prior literature as part of a particular e-learning system dimension, however similar e-learning system characteristics such as "employer support" was suggested by Ives and Jarvenpaa (1996) as part of the learner dimension. Therefore, due to the similarities in meaning, "family support" was suggested to be assigned to the learner dimension. Consequently, 14 e-learning system characteristics are grouped under dimension A or the *technology and support* dimension. Twelve e-learning system characteristics are grouped under dimension B or the *course* dimension. Seven e-learning system characteristics are grouped under dimension C or the *professor* dimension. Additionally, 15 e-learning system characteristics are grouped under dimension D or the *learner* dimension. Validation of such groupings and allocations is part of this research study and will be documented in Chapter VII.

Previous studies in technology mediated learning (TML) concentrated on various types of distance learning. However this study investigates specifically web based online learning systems or e-learning systems. As part of the exploratory process of this study it will be fruitful to investigate how the e-learning system characteristics load onto factors in general (exploratory factor analysis). Furthermore, it will be appropriate to report how the results of the exploratory analysis correspond to the proposed Webster and Hackley's (1997) dimensions as well as the categories proposed here.

A survey instrument will be developed based on the results of Phase I of this study and on previously validated instruments. The survey instrument will include two items (questions) for each e-learning system characteristic measuring the *perceived satisfaction* level with e-learning system and the *perceived value* learners express of e-learning system. In Phase II of the study, the survey instrument will be used to collect pilot data from a group of students attending courses using e-learning systems. Additional information on the development of the survey instrument, data collection methodology, and results is provided in Chapter VII.

As part of Phase II, an exploratory factor analysis will be used to analyze the empirical pilot data quantitatively in order to clean and adjust the survey instrument. The major data collection effort will take part in Phase III. This data will again be analyzed using an exploratory factor analysis in order to validate the reliability of the proposed e-learning system characteristics and e-learning system dimensions. Based on the results of the analysis in Phase III, a revised survey instrument will be provided for future studies. Further details about the process of validating the reliability of the survey instrument will be provided in Chapter VII.

The factors found as a result of Phase III may be different from the proposed dimensions and also may be different for value and for satisfaction measures.

Consequently, the second and third research questions (RQ2 and RQ3) are:

RQ2:   What are the significant factors for learners' perceived *value* of e-learning systems?

RQ3:   What are the significant factors for learners' perceived *satisfaction* of e-learning systems?

Prediction of Values

Multi-Criteria Decision Aid (MCDA)

To date, most IS studies, in particular IS behavioral studies and IS satisfaction studies, were mathematically modeled by assuming linearity. Some researchers suggest that there is an indication from various fields that behavioral and IS satisfaction phenomena might be better explained with non-linear models (Sethi & King, 1999, p.87). Sethi and King (1999) suggest to measure IS user satisfaction via linear and nonlinear techniques in order to see which will provide better predictions. Their results show that analysis of nonlinear, noncompensatory models performed "at par or better than the linear model" (p. 87). Consequently, it was appropriate to investigate non-linear models in the context of this study. Hence, this dissertation study also proposes looking at non-linear models of learners' perceived satisfaction and value of e-learning systems.

Keeney and Raiffa (1993) suggested that *value* construct is best explained by an additive utility function. Consequently, they named such functions as *additive value functions* (Keeney, 1999, p. 539). The additive value function is a utility function where attributes' preferences for the consequences (the values) depend solely on the individual levels of the separate attributes rather than on the manner in which the levels of the different attributes are combined (Keeney, 1994, p. 796).

In the section to follow, a review of several data mining and knowledge discovery techniques, namely multi-criteria decision aid (MCDA) approaches, is provided. MCDA provides a variety of techniques in construction of utility functions. Such techniques were applied to develop linear and non-linear models for predicting learners' dimension value and satisfaction measures, as well as the learners' overall value and satisfaction measures of the e-learning system under study. The review here includes four main streams of data mining and knowledge discovery techniques from the field of decision sciences, namely additive utility (UTA and UTADIS), multigroup hierarchical discrimination (MHDIS), and multicriteria satisfaction analysis (MUSA).

Additive Utility (UTA and UTADIS)

The UTA method (UTilités Additive) proposed by Jacquet-Lagreze and Siskos (1982) is based on an additive utility function proposed by Keeney and Raiffa (1993). However, UTA method deals with a set of additive utility functions rather than a single one, whereby all such functions are based on the user's a-priori preferences. Keeney and Raiffa (1993) propose an approach to assess a model of individual's preference that leads to the aggregation of all criteria into a unique criterion called a utility function. The UTA method is grounded in such an approach and is based on an ordinal regression technique that develops additive utility methods. Such a method (UTA) can be used to rank a set of alternatives from the most preferred (high value) to the least preferred (low value). Using linear programming techniques, the UTA method adjusts optimally additive non-linear utility functions to fit the data based on the subjective preferences made by the user. The method can also be used interactively in order to reduce the set of assessed utility functions to a single overall function (Jacquet-Lagreze & Siskos, 1982, p. 152).

The UTA method suggests that a utility function can be based upon the observation of a set of preferences by several individuals. Furthermore, the UTA method proposes an indirect estimation of the additive utility function that is "as consistent as possible with the observed choices or known subjective preferences" (p. 153). Such estimation is done in a piecewise linear fashion (see Figure 2). The evaluation criteria (g_i) interval is divided into equal intervals $(\alpha-1)$ provided by the researcher to indicate the number of estimated points (α) of the utility function (i.e. in Figure 2, $\alpha = 4$ where it is divided into three equal intervals).

The solution of the optimization computer program provides the marginal utility $u_i(g_i) \in [0, p_i]$ based on the users' preferences. The estimation of $u_i(g_i)$ provides the weights or importance of the criterion (p_i) which is the upper bound of $u_i(g_i)$. The great benefit of such an approach is that once a method that relates to a set of preferences is being developed and validated, it can be used to support future decision situations.

Figure 2. UTA method — Piecewise linear approximation of utility function

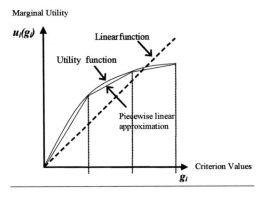

Source: Zopounidis, Doumpos, and Zanakis, 1999, Figure 1, p. 317

Following the recommendation of Sethi and King (1999), this study was set to investigate the relationships between learners' perceived satisfaction and value also in a non-linear approach. Whereas the learners' perceived satisfaction was the evaluative criteria, and the learners' perceived value was the weights of the evaluative criteria. Such an approach utilizes the UTA method to develop piecewise linear approximation models and compare such results with traditional linear models. Furthermore, it used the UTA method to develop similar models for the overall measures and comparing the imputed results to the ones elicited from learners.

Zopounidis, Doumpos, and Zanakis (1999) used a new model called UTADIS (utilités additive discriminantes), which is built on the UTA method. As stated earlier, the UTA method is suitable for developing additive utility models in ranking problems. However, it is evident from prior literature that during surveys it is much more convenient for the respondents to specify their preferences as a rating, rather than as a ranking. Therefore, survey analysis can be most often considered in the form of a classification context. Within this context, the UTADIS method is an important extension of the UTA method and a useful tool for developing appropriate classification models in the form of additive utility functions. Furthermore, the UTADIS method provides a better indirect estimation for additive utility functions by an exploration process that includes evaluation and classification of any new alternatives (preferences) into one of the several user-predefined groups (p. 313). One assumption of the UTADIS method is that the preferences of the user are monotone (increase or decrease) functions on the evaluation criteria scale (p. 316). Similarly to UTA, the piecewise linear approximation of the additive utility function is developed by UTADIS through division of the preference scale into predefined intervals. However unlike the UTA method where the predefined intervals were equal, the UTADIS method uses an exploration process to predict the appropriate intervals to better estimate the additive utility function. For each such interval, an end of the interval point is estimated by the UTADIS method, which in turn estimates the level of the utility function for that given point. The UTADIS method estimates the level of the additive utility function for such point by minimizing the misclassification error. The misclassification errors are considered using two error functions, representing over and under deviations (see Figure 3) (Zopounidis et al., 1999, p. 316). If an alternative a is classified by the user in a given class C_k, and according to its global utility it should be classified in class $C_{k+i} (i > 0)$, then the misclassification error represents the amount of utility that should be *added* (over deviation) to the global utility of alternative a so that it can be correctly classified. Likewise, if an alternative a is classified by the user in a given class C_k, and according to its global utility it should be classified in class $C_{k-i} (i > 0)$, then the misclassification error represents the amount of utility that should be *subtracted* (under deviation) to the global utility of alternative a so that it can be correctly classified (see Figure 3). Consequently, the UTADIS method uses linear programming in order to develop a piecewise linear approximation of the additive utility function by estimating the utility function in each of the end-of-interval point while minimizing errors (Zopounidis et al., 1999, p. 316).

Zopounidis et al. (1999) also used a new variation of the UTADIS method, UTADIS I, that is compared to the original UTADIS method using a case study. The minimization of the misclassification error in the UTADIS method is achieved by comparing the misclassified alternatives from the utility threshold at the end-of-interval point using the two error functions. The utility threshold defines the lower bound for each predefined class or preference. Therefore, the utility threshold distinguishes between such classes or preferences. It was observed by the authors that the objective of minimizing a misclassification error may not be sufficient as it may place some correctly classified alternatives "very close to the utility threshold, resulting in poor predictions given by the model" (Zopounidis et al., 1999, p. 320). Therefore, UTADIS I method provides a more precise indirect estimation by minimizing misclassification errors and at the same time maximizing the distances of the global utility point currently estimated, from the utility threshold (see Figure 4). Such distance

Figure 3. UTADIS method — The classification error (two-group case)

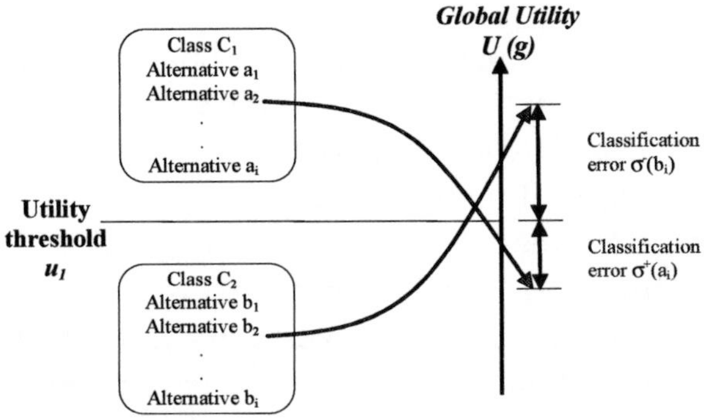

Source: Doumpos, Zanakis, and Zopounidis, 2001, Figure 1, p. 342

maximization is similar to the maximization of the among-groups variance in traditional discriminant analysis (DA) (Doumpos, Zanakis, & Zopounidis, 2001, p. 341).

The UTADIS and UTADIS I methods were then explored in a case study of 98 stocks from the Athens stock exchange, using 15 criteria of evaluation. Stocks were evaluated in order to provide assistance to portfolio managers so they can make recommendations to their clients (investors) concerning stocks that are more valuable to pursue (Zopounidis et al., 1999, p. 314). Stocks were evaluated both on UTADIS and the revised UTADIS I methods. Their results obtained from the UTADIS I method are similar to the results obtained by the UTADIS method. There were only changes in the global utilities of stocks. Such results indicate that the UTADIS I method provides the same classification as the UTADIS method even though the distance from utility threshold maximization constrain was imposed (Zopounidis et al., 1999, p. 328).

In a later paper, Doumpos et al. (2001) used two more methods in the UTADIS family, namely UTADIS II and UTADIS III. The UTADIS II method is built on the first UTADIS method, however it "incorporate[s] a more direct measures to estimate the quality of the resulting classification, leading to [a better] minimization of the number of misclassification" (Doumpos et al., 2001, p. 341). The UTADIS III method combines both the newer method of minimization of the number of misclassification offered by UTADIS II with the constrain of maximizing the distances of the global utility point estimated from the utility threshold offered by UTADIS I.

Multigroup Hierarchical Discrimination (MHDIS)

In yet another paper, Doumpos et al. (2001) propose a new method based on the UTADIS method family named MHDIS (Multigroup Hierarchical DIScrimination). The MHDIS method has great similarities to the UTADIS method family. However, it employs a hierarchical procedure in the classification process of the alternatives into predefined classes. The hierarchical procedure used in the MHDIS method enables the classification of alternatives by examining if it can be assigned to the best class, if not, then the method tries to classify it into the second best class, and so on. During the first stage, all alternatives are assessed against the best class. All alternatives found to belong to such best class (correctly or incorrectly) are excluded from future consideration. During the second stage all remaining alternatives are assessed against the second best class. Similarly, all alternatives found to belong to such second best class (correctly or incorrectly) are excluded from future consideration. The same process continues *q-1* times (where *q* is the predetermined number of classes), where all alternatives are classified into the predefined classes (Doumpos et al., 2001, p. 343).

MHDIS method includes an analysis procedure comparing two classification alternatives (utility functions). One utility function is constructed as an increasing function on the criterion's scale suggesting classifying the alternative into a class C_k. The other utility function is constructed as a decreasing function criterion's scale suggesting not to classify the alternative *a* into a class C_k. Both functions are then compared in order to determine whether an alternative belongs to group C_k or not. If the level of the increasing utility function is higher than the level of the decreasing function, then alternative *a* is classified into the group C_k and the procedure will stop. Otherwise, if the decreasing utility function is higher than the level of the increasing function, then alternative *a* is not classified into the group C_k and the procedure continues to the next pair of utility functions. The same process is repeated for the next two utility functions until the classification of the alternative is achieved (Doumpos et al., 2001, p. 351). The MHDIS method provides even more precise indirect estimation than all UTADIS methods by combining two linear programs (LP1, LP2) and one mixed-integer program (MIP) that are solved for each stage of the hierarchical classification process (Doumpos et al., 2001, p. 348). The first linear program (LP1) attempts to minimize the overall classification error measured in distance terms similar to the UTADIS method, whereas the second linear program (LP2) attempts to maximize the distances of the global utility point currently

Figure 4. Doumpos et al. (2001) — Six methods mean classification accuracy

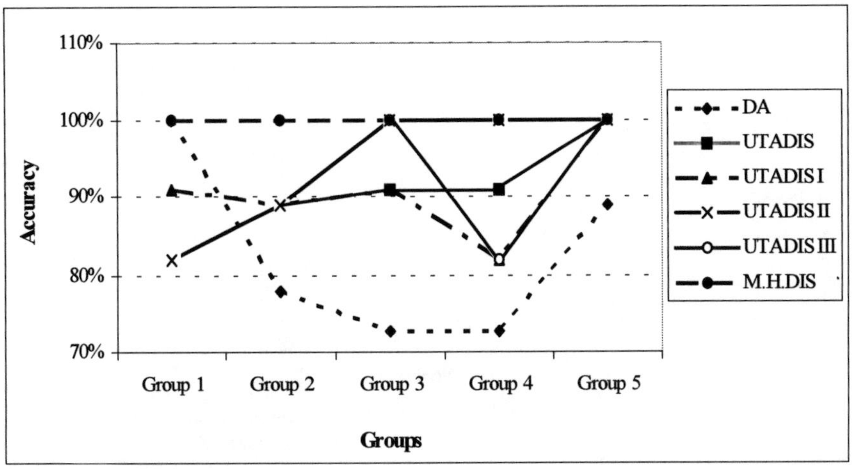

Source: Doumpos, Zanakis, & Zopounidis, 2001, Figure 14, p. 375

estimated, from the utility threshold. The third program, mixed-integer (MIP), attempts to minimize the number of misclassification errors. The three programs are run sequentially starting with LP1 and then proceeding with MIP and LP2 in order to estimate the optimal approximation (Doumpos et al., 2001, p. 349).

To validate the new MHDIS method, a comparison of the UTADIS family method, MHDIS, and standard discriminant analysis (DA) was done by assessing investment risks in 51 countries that have stock exchanges according to 27 evaluation criteria. The classification results from six methods (UTADIS, UTADIS I, UTADIS II, UTADIS III, MHDIS, and DA method) were compared to the results suggested by a group of international investments experts commissioned by *The Wall Street Journal*. Among the evaluation methods, MHDIS provided the most accurate results (see Figure 4), essentially reproducing the classification done by the group of experts (Doumpos et al., 2001, p. 333). Table 3 provides an overview of all five MCDA methods comparing the main objectives and associated constrains.

Consequently, this study seeks to assess learners' perceived value from the satisfaction scores by utilizing the MHDIS method. Such an approach enabled the development of piecewise linear approximation models proposed by each method. Comparisons between the all methods were evaluated in the context of learners' perceived satisfaction and value of e-learning systems.

Table 3. UTADIS family and MHDIS methods objectives and constrains

Method	Objective and main features	Constrains
UTA	Provides an indirect piecewise linear estimation of additive utility functions in ranking problems	Does not consider the number of inconsistencies between the model's results and the pre-defined ranking
UTADIS	Provides an indirect piecewise linear estimation of additive utility functions in classification problems	Does not consider the number of misclassifications
UTADIS I	Extends UTADIS I considering not only the magnitude of the classification errors (goodness of fit) but also the clarity of the classification (badness of fit)	The trade-off between the goodness and badness of fit must be carefully analyzed
UTADIS II	Provides an indirect piecewise linear estimation of additive utility functions in classification problems with a direct optimization of the quality of the model (number of misclassifications)	May require increased computational effort, even for small data sets
UTADIS III	Combines UTADIS I and II considering the quality of the model and the clarity of the classification	The trade-off between the goodness and badness of fit must be analyzed. May require increased computational effort, even for small data sets
MHDIS	Development of set of additive utility functions for classification problems. Hierarchical classification scheme, which is well-suited to multi-class problems. Lexicographic optimization of both the quality of the model (number of misclassifications) and the clarity of the classification.	May require increased computational effort for large data sets with significant group-overlap

Multicriteria Satisfaction Analysis (MUSA)

The multicriteria method MUSA (Multicriteria Satisfaction Analysis) was proposed by Grigoroudis and Siskos (2002) based on the UTA method. The method is based on additive utility functions and satisfaction functions based on individual judgments (e.g., satisfaction with e-learning systems). The main objective of the MUSA method is to develop models to aggregate the individual judgments into a collective value function assuming that the individual's overall satisfaction (e.g., overall satisfaction with e-learning systems) depends on a set of *n* criteria or variables representing service level of *n* characteristics (Grigoroudis & Siskos, 2002, p. 149). Another objective of the MUSA method is to impute values (weights) of each characteristic based on the satisfaction level and the overall satisfaction level provided by the users. The method enables analysis in nested satisfaction layout (see Figure 5) where an overall satisfaction depends on the level of satisfaction of several dimensions of the system or service. In turn each of the dimension satisfaction level depends

Figure 5. Nested satisfaction levels

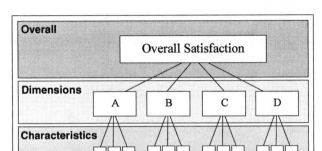

on the level of satisfaction of several characteristics of that system or service dimension. Such nested analysis is especially important for this study as the e-learning system dimensions are suggested by prior scholars to be heterogeneous (Webster & Hackley, 1997).

The MUSA method also provides guidelines on the development of value-satisfaction action and improvement grids. Additional information about such grids and the development of the grids will be provided in Chapter V. Table 4 presents the major findings and contributions found in the literature studies reviewed in this section, which are related to MCDA models for classification and ranking problems.

Part of the aim of this study is to investigate different linear and non-linear models in order to predict the value scores based on the satisfaction scores. Thus, it is applicable to develop predictive models for the overall and four e-learning systems' dimensions measures. Using data from one level above a given level it will be feasible to impute the satisfaction and value measures. Consequently, overall measures (S_o and V_o) and e-learning systems' dimension measures (S_a, S_b, S_c, S_d and V_a, V_b, V_c, V_d) can be calculated using statistical models (e.g., linear models) based on the data from the level mentioned previously. This study investigates both linear, multiple linear regression, non-linear, ordinal logistic regression, and MCDA techniques. Additional information is provided in Chapter VII. The overall measures can be derived based on the four e-learning systems' dimensions data, whereas each e-learning systems' dimension measure can be derived based on the e-learning system characteristics data.

As suggested from the literature in Chapters II and III, values are criteria of desirability; they represent what individuals consider important (King &

Table 4. Summary of MCDA studies of models for classification and ranking problems

Study	Methodology	Technique	Instrument/Constructs	Main findings or contribution
Jacquet-Lagreze & Siskos, 1982	Theoretical & Survey	UTA	Based on additive utility function proposed by Keeney and Raiffa (1993)	- The method can also be used interactively in order to **reduce** the **set** of assessed utility functions **to a single overall function.** - The UTA computer program develops a **piecewise linear approximation** of the additive utility function.
Zopounidis, Doumpos, & Zanakis, 1999	Theoretical, Case study, & Survey	UTADIS & UTADIS I	UTADIS – Minimizing misclassification error UTADIS I – based on UTADIS, considers minimizing misclassification errors, BUT at the same time maximizing the distances of the global utility point currently estimated, from the utility threshold (See Figure 12 in Chapter II).	UTADIS I method is a **more appropriate** approach.
Doumpos, Zanakis, & Zopounidis, 2001	Theoretical, Case study, & Survey	UTADIS II, UTADIS III, & MHDIS	MHDIS is based on UTADIS family methods Using hierarchical procedure Analysis procedure comparing two classification alternatives: 1. Increasing utility function 2. Decreasing utility function	Among the evaluation methods, **MHDIS provided the most accurate results** (See Figure 16 in Chapter II), essentially reproducing the classification done by the group of WSJ experts.
Grigoroudis & Siskos, 2002	Theoretical & Case study	MUSA	Based on UTA and MHDIS	Allow the development of nested satisfaction models. Provide guidelines for the development of Value-Satisfaction action grids and improvements grids.

Epstein, 1983, p. 34; Posner & Munson, 1979, p. 10; Williams, 1979, p. 28). King and Epstein (1983) proposed a linear combination of the satisfaction measures where the value scores are the "relative importance weights" attached to the system characteristic (p. 35). Following King and Epstein's

(1983) approach, this study will seek to impute such values, or "relative importance weights," using linear combinations of the satisfaction measures when developing the predictive models (one model for each dimension and one for the overall system). Hence, the linear model that is developed to predict the *overall satisfaction* measure (the dependent variable) provides weight for each of the four e-learning systems' *dimension satisfaction* measures (the independent variables). At the same time, the linear model that is developed to predict each of the four e-learning systems' *dimension satisfaction* measures (the dependent variables) provides weight for each of the e-learning system characteristics *satisfaction* measures included in that dimension (the independent variables). As theory suggests, these weights correspond to the values of the e-learning system characteristics or e-learning systems' dimensions. As the aim of this study is to investigate thoroughly the *value* construct, it is fruitful to investigate the similarities (or lack thereof) of these weights generated by the linear and non-linear models with the values elicited from the learners. Additional information on the linear and non-linear formulation and the development of these measures is provided in Chapter VII.

Many studies of IS satisfaction have constructed mathematical models to predict overall system satisfaction using linear models. Chapter III provided an overview of these studies as well as some critiques. Such criticisms were based mainly on the notion that some psychological constructs (such as *satisfaction*, *attitude*, *behavior*, and *value*) are better explained by non-linear models (Sethi & King, 1999, p.87). One study that developed models to predict overall system satisfaction via linear and non-linear techniques (Sethi & King, 1999) indicated that nonlinear models performed better than linear models. Furthermore, King and Epstein (1983) mentioned that values may be better modeled using non-linear techniques (p. 40). Consequently, it is also appropriate to investigate non-linear models when attempting to predict the overall and e-learning systems' dimensions measures. This study also looks at the weights generated by these non-linear models and compares these with the values elicited from the learners as well as the weights generated by the linear models suggested previously. Ordinal logistic regression and MCDA techniques were proposed to impute the weights that correspond to the values elicited from the learners. Furthermore, these techniques are proposed to develop non-linear models for predicting e-learning systems' dimension value and satisfaction, as well as the overall value and satisfaction measures of e-learning systems similarly to the linear models suggested previously.

Consequently, the fourth research question (RQ4) is:

RQ4:   How well do the actual value measures elicited from learners fit the imputed value measures derived via data mining techniques? Which data mining technique provides the best fit and how does it compare with statistical estimation procedures?

Perceived Learning in E-Learning Systems

Several studies in Technology Mediated Learning (TML) theory address the pedagogical or learning perspective, comparing the learning outcomes of online learning courses with that of on-campus courses (Alavi et al., 1997; Hiltz, 1993; Hiltz & Johnson, 1990; Leidner & Jarvenpaa, 1993; Piccoli, Ahmad, & Ives, 2001). The aim of this study is, in part, to investigate the level of *satisfaction* and level of the *value* learners find with e-learning systems and how such measures (satisfaction and value) can be utilized to indicate *learners' perceived effectiveness* of e-learning systems. Moreover, Cook and Campbell (1979) suggest measuring other constructs, ones not under the focus of the study proposed, in order to provide added validation for the constructs under study (p. 69). Consequently, due to the nature of the type of system under study, the e-learning systems, it was fruitful to explore how such constructs (*satisfaction*, *value*, and *effectiveness*) are associated to learners' overall perceived learning.

Consequently, the fifth research question (RQ5) is:

RQ5:   How is the overall perceived learning measure related to the overall value, satisfaction and perceived effectiveness of an e-learning system?

Chapter Summary

This chapter provided an overview of the proposed conceptual model and the first three specific research questions. The proposed conceptual model is grounded in the literature reviewed in Chapters II and III. It starts by providing a theoretical overview of the constructs related to this study and continues with some suggested steps on gathering the values associated with e-learning systems. Definitions of e-learning system characteristics and e-learning system dimensions are also provided. The e-learning systems characteristics are proposed and categorized to the e-learning systems dimensions based on literature. Additionally, each characteristic is linked to specific questions or survey items from literature. This comprehensive list of the e-learning systems characteristics will serve as the ground for the development of the survey in this study. Additionally, this chapter provides the rationale for the development of measurements of value in order to develop linear and non-linear predictive models for the overall and four e-learning systems' dimensions measures. Moreover, as the nature of the type of information systems in this study is learning systems, perceived learning is assessed to validate the construct validity of value, satisfaction, and effectiveness constructs in this type of system.

Chapter V

Value-Satisfaction Grid of E-Learning Systems

Introduction

This chapter provides the rationale of the first of three tools suggested in this book to assess value and satisfaction of e-learning systems in order to provide an assessment of the effectiveness of such systems. The other two tools are presented in the following chapter. The first tool proposed by the conceptual model is the Value-Satisfaction grid which aggregates the learners' value and satisfaction with e-learning systems in order to indicate the learners' perceived effectiveness of e-learning systems. The Value-Satisfaction grid also helps indicate the action and improvement priorities that are needed for the characteristics and dimensions of an e-learning system under study. A proposed method of aggregation of learners' perceived value of e-learning systems and satisfaction with e-learning systems to construct the Value-Satisfaction grid and the two tools presented in the following chapter is also presented in this chapter.

The understanding of the Value-Satisfaction grid provides the first building block toward a complete set of assessment tools of learners' perceived effectiveness of e-learning systems. The development of this set of tools is a significant achievement as scholars have suggested that prior research in technology mediated learning (TML) lacked the overall system approach and concentrated only on one or two dimensions at a time (Alavi & Leidner, 2001a, p. 9).

The Value-Satisfaction Grid
of E-Learning Systems

Galletta and Lederer (1989) suggested practitioners are interested in tools "as a mechanism to uncover user perception of strength and weaknesses [of system characteristics]" (p. 421). Valentin (2001) suggests that marketing scholars (e.g., Andrews, 1987; Ansoff, 1965; Mintzberg, Ahlstrand, & Lampel, 1998; and Porter, 1991) propose using Strengths-Weaknesses-Opportunities-Threats (SWOT) grids framework to assess companies' or products' performance. Such grids provide positioning of companies or products on a 2×2 matrix to indicate success and suggest improvements, modification, fundamental changes or elimination needed to improve such a company or product in the marketplace. Following the SWOT method in the context of e-learning systems, the Value-Satisfaction grid is developed to provide actions and improvement priorities for e-learning system characteristics and dimensions.

Due to the heterogeneous nature of the e-learning system dimensions, it is appropriate to develop a grid for each of the four dimensions defined earlier as well as for the overall system. The Value-Satisfaction grid is developed to indicate the learners' perceived e-learning system effectiveness and the improvements priorities for e-learning system characteristics and dimensions. The grid is developed for each of the four dimensions and includes the e-learning system characteristics as points in that grid. The grid developed for the overall system level includes the four e-learning system dimensions as points in that grid. This results in total of five grids, one for each dimension (noted as *dimension grid*) and one for the overall (noted as *overall grid*). Additional information about the grid development as well as the implications of e-learning system characteristics and e-learning system dimensions positioned in the grids is presented in subsequent paragraphs.

It is assumed that the learners' satisfaction with e-learning systems measured on a specific dimension, defined as *learners' dimension perceived satisfac-*

tion, is a function of all the *learners' perceived satisfaction* with e-learning system characteristics within that dimension. Similarly learners' value of e-learning systems measured on a specific dimension, or *learners' dimension value*, is a function of all the *learners' perceived value* of e-learning system characteristics within that dimension. Therefore, the location of the corresponding e-learning system characteristics is used to indicate learners' perceived effectiveness for that dimension using the grid. Similarly, it is assumed that the learners' satisfaction with the whole e-learning system, defined as *learners' overall perceived satisfaction*, is a function of all the *learners' perceived satisfaction* with e-learning system dimensions within that system. Learners' value of the whole e-learning system, or *learners' overall value*, is also a function of all the *learners' perceived value* of e-learning systems' dimensions. Therefore, the location of the corresponding e-learning system dimensions is used to indicate learners' perceived effectiveness for the whole system using the grid.

In order to develop such grids, a single score of value and satisfaction is needed for each e-learning system characteristic and dimension. The survey instrument includes a question measuring the *perceived satisfaction* and *perceived value* at the characteristics and dimension level. Results of the data collected of the e-learning system characteristics and e-learning system dimensions were then aggregated across all learners. These aggregated measures resulted in two scores (value and satisfaction) for each e-learning system characteristic and two scores for each e-learning system dimension (value and satisfaction).

A common aggregation method is arithmetic mean (or average) which is the average of all scores noted by the learners. However, another aggregation method, geometric mean, is suggested as a better method providing superior results over arithmetic mean in particular when aggregating evaluations from multiple decision-makers or aggregation over individuals' judgments (Aczel & Saaty, 1983; Sampson, 1999, p. 426; Sun, 2001). Geometric mean is an aggregation method to measure the central tendency; however, unlike arithmetic mean that uses addition to summarize data, geometric mean uses multiplication to summarize data that provides a lower score than arithmetic mean. Consequently, this study uses geometric mean as the method to aggregate all learners' perceptions in the development of the aggregated value and satisfaction mean scores for each e-learning system characteristic and e-learning system dimension.

The proposed method of aggregation was by using geometric mean averaging all responses to calculate the *mean characteristic satisfaction* for each e-learning system characteristic ($\overline{S}_{a1}$,..., $\overline{S}_{a14}$, $\overline{S}_{b1}$,..., $\overline{S}_{b12}$, $\overline{S}_{c1}$,..., $\overline{S}_{c7}$, and $\overline{S}_{d1}$,...$\overline{S}_{d15}$). Similarly, an aggregation was made by using geometric mean averaging all responses to calculate the *mean characteristic value* for each e-learning system characteristic ($\overline{V}_{a1}$,..., $\overline{V}_{a14}$, $\overline{V}_{b1}$,..., $\overline{V}_{b12}$, $\overline{V}_{c1}$,..., $\overline{V}_{c7}$, and $\overline{V}_{d1}$,...$\overline{V}_{d15}$). The aggregated satisfaction score for e-learning system dimensions is the *mean dimension satisfaction* for each dimension ($\overline{S}_a$, $\overline{S}_b$, $\overline{S}_c$, and $\overline{S}_d$). Additionally, the aggregated value score for e-learning system dimensions is the *mean dimension value* for each dimension ($\overline{V}_a$, $\overline{V}_b$, $\overline{V}_c$, and $\overline{V}_d$). All aggregated scores are calculated over all respondents in order to provide accurate measure that reflects the average satisfaction and value of the system under study.

The Value-Satisfaction grid is developed in a similar manner to that of the SWOT grid as proposed by marketing scholars (Andrews, 1987; Ansoff, 1965; Mintzberg et al., 1998; Porter, 1991). It is based on aggregated learner-elicited perceived satisfaction with e-learning system, and the value of e-learning system characteristics and dimensions. The Value-Satisfaction grid is constructed by positioning the *mean satisfaction* score on one axis and the *mean value* score on the other axis. Each score range is divided into two intervals representing *low* and *high*. Hence, the *mean satisfaction* score with e-learning system is divided into a *low satisfaction* interval and a *high satisfaction* interval respectively. Similarly, *mean value* scores of an e-learning system are also divided into a *low value* interval and a *high value* interval respectively. EBI (2002) suggests positioning of the cut-off-point between the low and the high range at 75% of the maximum scale. Additional information will be provided in Chapter VII.

The Value-Satisfaction grid provides 2×2 matrix resulting in four quadrants for each grid (see Figure 1). The first quadrant of *low-satisfaction* and *high-value* (Q1) is called *improvement*. E-learning system dimensions positioned in this quadrant (Q1) of the *overall grid* provide the top opportunity for improvement in order to avoid learners' attrition. E-learning system characteristics positioned in this quadrant (Q1) in each of the four *dimension grids* are first in the improvement priority. Improvement in such e-learning system characteristics could occur by providing more resources to increase learners' satisfaction with the characteristics that are valued highly, hence help avoid learners' attrition (see Figure 2).

The second quadrant of *high-satisfaction* and *high-value* (Q2) is called *effective*. E-learning system dimensions positioned in this quadrant of the *overall grid* are effective and show the competitive advantage of the online

Figure 1. Value-satisfaction grid for e-learning systems

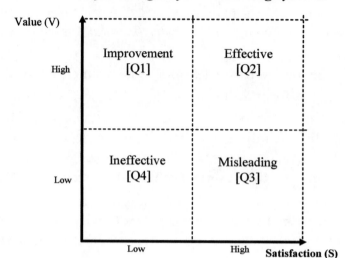

learning initiative as learners are both highly satisfied with and highly value these e-learning system dimensions. E-learning system characteristics positioned in this quadrant (Q2) in each of the four *dimension grids* are effective and show the characteristics contributing to the strengths of the e-learning system dimension. These e-learning system characteristics can be used in advertising campaigns as they feature the key strengths of the initiative. E-learning system dimensions and e-learning system characteristics in this quadrant (Q2) are second in the priority for improvement (see Figure 2).

The third quadrant of *high-satisfaction* and *low-value* (Q3) is called *misleading*. E-learning system dimensions positioned in this quadrant of the *overall grid* suggest that the institution is doing well in the associated dimensions that are simply not as important. This suggests that resources that are provided to e-learning system dimensions in this quadrant should be closely investigated as some of these resources may be more appropriately utilized if transferred to other dimensions located in the "improvement" (Q1) quadrant. Similarly to the overall e-learning system characteristics positioned in this quadrant in each of the four *dimension grids* indicating that the institution is doing well in the associated characteristics that are simply not as important to the learners. E-learning system dimensions and characteristics in this quadrant (Q3) are third in the priority for improvement (see Figure 2).

Figure 2. Summary of value-satisfaction grid quadrants for e-learning systems

Quadrant		Improvement Priority Level	Dimension grid	Overall grid
Improvement	Q1	1st	E-learning system characteristics needs **improvement**, which could occur by providing more resources to increase learners' satisfaction with the characteristics that are valued highly	E-learning system dimensions provide opportunity for **improvement** in order to avoid learners' attrition
Effective	Q2	2nd	E-learning system characteristics are **effective** and showing the characteristics contributing to the strengths of online learning initiative Can be featured in ad campaigns.	E-learning system dimensions are **effective** and show the competitive advantage of the online learning initiative
Misleading	Q3	3rd	The institution is doing well in the associated characteristics that are simply not as important to the learners. **Resources** invested in maintaining these e-learning systems characteristics maybe more appropriately utilized if **transferred** to other characteristics located in "action opportunity" or "improvement" quadrant	The institution is doing well in the associated dimensions that are simply not as important. **Resources** provided to these e-learning system dimensions maybe more appropriately utilized if **transferred** to other dimensions located in "action opportunity" or "improvement" quadrant
Ineffective	Q4	4th	E-learning system characteristics are **ineffective** and may be disregarded. However, closer investigation of these e-learning systems characteristics may be needed!	E-learning system dimensions are at a stage of status quo and generally no action is needed

Finally, the fourth quadrant of *low-satisfaction* and *low-value* (Q4) is called *ineffective*. E-learning system dimensions positioned in this quadrant (Q4) of the *overall grid* are at a stage of status quo and generally no action is needed. Although learners' may perceive e-learning system dimensions in this quadrant as both low on satisfaction and low on value, these e-learning system dimensions may be needed for the operation of the program, hence "status-quo". E-learning system characteristics positioned in this quadrant (Q4) in each of the four *dimension grids* are not needed and may be disregarded. However, closer investigation of these e-learning system characteristics may be needed. This investigation should explore the possibility for future increase in value. For example, future increase in value may result by changes in accreditation standards or anticipation of increase learners' interest (increase in value) in the future. If the investigation resulted in some e-learning system characteristics in the "status quo" or "discard" quadrant that are expected to have an increase in value in the future, these e-learning system characteristics may need improvement or further consideration. These e-learning system characteristics may shift in the future to the "improvement" (Q1) quadrant, resulting in an increased interest in it for the organization. E-learning system dimensions and characteristics in this quadrant (Q4) are last in the priority for improvement (see Figure 2).

Consequently, the sixth research question of this study (RQ6) is:

RQ6: How are aggregated learners' perceptions of the overall value and overall satisfaction of the e-learning system under this study positioned in the Value-Satisfaction grid (Overall and separately for each of the four e-learning system dimensions)?

Chapter Summary

This chapter provided the theoretical rationale for the development of the Value-Satisfaction grid of e-learning systems. The Value-Satisfaction grid of e-learning system is proposed in order to provide action and improvement priorities for e-learning systems characteristics and e-learning system dimensions. Although the Value-Satisfaction grid is a great mapping tool to indicate general effectiveness as well as providing action and improvement priorities, it does not provide a precise measure of the perceived effectiveness. Therefore, another tool is needed to provide such a precise measure. Additionally, a third tool that combines both the map and the precise measure is needed. However, a review of the Value-Satisfaction grid proposed in this chapter is needed as a theoretical base for the development of the two new tools. The following chapter is building upon the Value-Satisfaction grid reviewed in this chapter. It proposes the Learners' Value Index of Satisfaction (LeVIS) and the effectiveness grid in the pursuit of a precise measure and mapping of the learners' perceived effectiveness of e-learning systems utilizing aggregated scores of value and satisfaction as discussed in this chapter.

Chapter VI

Learners' Value Index of Satisfaction (LeVIS)

Introduction

The previous chapter provided a review of the first tool (Value-Satisfaction grid of e-learning systems) to assess the effectiveness of e-learning systems using learners' perceived value of e-learning systems and learners' perceived satisfaction with such systems. The second tool, which is proposed in this chapter, is the Learners' Value Index of Satisfaction (LeVIS) that is developed in order to provide a precise numeric score for the learners' perceived effectiveness of e-learning systems. The Value-Satisfaction grid proposed in the previous chapter provides a key tool to indicate action and improvement priorities for e-learning systems as well as an overall map to indicate the learners' perceived effectiveness of e-learning systems. However, the Value-Satisfaction grid cannot provide a precise indication of the level or specific score of the learners' perceived effectiveness of such systems. Consequently, an index (i.e., the LeVIS index) would be useful to provide a measure of the magnitude of the learners' perceived effectiveness of e-learning systems utilizing the aggregated value and satisfaction scores. By the definition of the LeVIS index, it provides the ability to look at constant levels of the learners' perceived effectiveness within the Value-Satisfaction grid that are called *effectiveness curves*. The combination of such effectiveness curves and the Value-Satisfaction grid yields the development of the third tool suggested by this framework. The third tool is called the *effectiveness grid* which will be defined and proposed in this chapter. The effectiveness grid provides an overall map and an indication of the specific effectiveness level under one tool; in essence, it combines both the Value-Satisfaction grid as well as the LeVIS index into one tool. The four quadrants of the Value-Satisfaction grid proposed in the previous chapter are divided by the effectiveness curves resulting in two segments per quadrant or a total of eight segments indicating various levels of effectiveness proposed in the effectiveness grid. Clearly, prior to the review of the effectiveness grid, a clear understanding of the LeVIS index is needed in conjunction with the understanding of the Value-Satisfaction grid proposed in the previous chapter.

The LeVIS Index

The Learners' Value Index of Satisfaction (LeVIS) is proposed as a benchmarking tool combining the learners' perceived value and satisfaction in order to indicate the magnitude of learners' perceived effectiveness of e-learning systems. The LeVIS index combines the e-learning systems *value* measures and e-learning systems *satisfaction* measures in order to provide an overall index of the effectiveness of such systems. Prior literature concentrated mainly on the measurement and improvement priorities of IS satisfaction. However, as noted in literature that was reviewed in Chapter III, the investigation of value of e-learning systems in conjunction with satisfaction with e-learning systems will provide fruitful information regarding learners' perceived effectiveness of e-learning systems. Figure 1 provides an overview of the benefits provided by measuring satisfaction with e-learning systems, value of e-learning systems, and the resulted benefits provided by measuring both satisfaction with e-learning systems and value of e-learning systems together (see column "Learners' Perceived Effectiveness").

The proposed framework in this study is based on three levels (overall, four e-learning systems dimensions, and 48 e-learning systems characteristics). As part of the survey instrument, users were asked to rate both value of e-learning

Figure 1. Learners' perceived value, satisfaction, and effectiveness of e-learning systems

The Institution's Perspective	Learners' Perceived Satisfaction	Learners' Perceived Value	Learners' Perceived Effectiveness
What is asked?	Rate the performance of the system	Rate the performance you desire	The extent to which the system's performance correspond to the performance learners desire
What perspective the institution gets from respondents?	Post-experience feeling	Enduring core beliefs & importance	Normative perspective
What is the time duration of the measure?	Short time	Long time or Lifetime	Relative measure!
What is measured?	Are the learners satisfied with the e-learning system characteristics and e-learning system Dimensions?	How important are the e-learning system characteristics and e-learning system Dimensions for learners?	What is the extent that learners are more satisfied by the e-learning system characteristics and e-learning system Dimensions they find as important
How is it measured?	Satisfaction level (Based on UIS & EUCS)	Importance level (Based on King & Epstein 1983; Keeney 1999)	Multiplication of satisfaction & value (LeVIS)
What is desired by the institution?	High satisfaction in all e-learning system characteristics and e-learning system dimensions	Knowing which e-learning system characteristics and e-learning system dimensions are important (high value)	High satisfaction in e-learning system characteristics and e-learning system dimensions in which the user indicates high value
How is the institution going to improve?	Improve e-learning system characteristics and dimensions that perceived with low satisfaction	Concentrate on e-learning system characteristics and dimensions that perceived with high value	See Value-Satisfaction grid for action and improvement priorities

systems and satisfaction with e-learning systems in all three levels. Theory suggests that satisfaction measures the perceived performance level of each system characteristic (Doll & Torkzadeh, 1991, p. 6; Kim, 1989, p. 7). Theory also suggests that value measures the perceived importance level of each system characteristic (Rokeach, 1969, p. 160). Following Grover et al.'s (1996) normative approach and in the context of this study, an e-learning system is considered effective when learners value its characteristics as highly important and are highly satisfied by those same characteristics. Consequently, the LeVIS index integrates both value of e-learning systems and satisfaction with e-learning systems to indicate the users' perceived IS effectiveness in the context of e-learning systems.

As defined in the Value-Satisfaction grid in the previous chapter, it is not only sufficient for value or only for satisfaction measures to be high, rather the combination or multiplication of both value and satisfaction in order to ensure high learners' perceived effectiveness. Consequently, the proposed LeVIS index multiplies the *overall satisfaction* (S_o) by the *overall value* (V_o) to provide a score of the overall magnitude of the learners' perceived effectiveness of e-learning systems. Several methods of aggregation of data, all using the geometric mean as suggested in the previous chapter, are proposed to address the one that best matches the actual data elicited from the learners. The two measures (S_o and V_o) are measured on a scale of 1 to 6. Bailey and Pearson (1983) suggested calibrating the overall score by dividing the actual score by the maximum possible score in the evaluating scale (p. 534). Therefore, the multiplication of the two measures was calibrated to provide the LeVIS index on a scale from 0 to 1 by dividing by 36. When LeVIS is near 0, this indicates a very low learners' perceived e-learning systems effectiveness. When LeVIS is near 1, this indicates a very high learners' perceived e-learning systems effectiveness. This measure provides that if only one of the two measures (S_o or V_o) is high, the overall system measure (LeVIS) score is not high. As indicated by the "effective" quadrant (Q2) of the Value-Satisfaction grid, it is the combination of both high-value and high-satisfaction that indicate high effectiveness of e-learning systems.

Whereas the LeVIS index is developed for the overall system level, it is also possible to develop a similar effectiveness index for each of the four e-learning systems dimensions. As stated previously, the developed instrument also includes two general questions for each of the four dimensions, the dimension satisfaction (S_a, S_b, S_c, and S_d) and dimension value (V_a, V_b, V_c, and V_d) measures (see Figure 2). Users were asked to rate the dimension satisfaction and the dimension value for each of the four dimensions. Based on these eight measures (four dimension satisfaction measures and four dimension value measures) similar indices of effectiveness can be made in each of the four e-learning systems' dimensions. These indices were noted as E_a, E_b, E_c, and E_d (see Figure 2) and these four effectiveness indices are calculated as the multiplication

Figure 2. Overview of Learners' Value Index of Satisfaction (LeVIS)

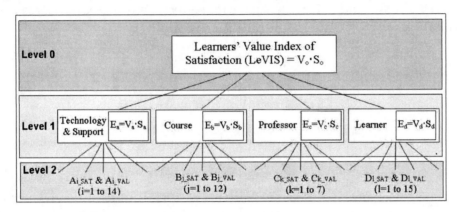

$$LeVIS =^{1}\left(\frac{1}{36}\right)\cdot V_{o}\cdot S_{o} \quad \Rightarrow \quad 0\leq LeVIS\leq 1 \qquad (2)$$

Ledger:

Level 0 (Overall)	LeVIS	Learners' Value Index of Satisfaction for overall e-learning systems effectiveness	
Level 1 (dimensions)	$E_a^2 -$	Dimension *effectiveness* related to technology and support	
	$E_b^2 -$	Dimension *effectiveness* related to the course	
	$E_c^2 -$	Dimension *effectiveness* related to the professor	
	$E_d^2 -$	Dimension *effectiveness* related to the learner	
	$V_a^2 -$	Dimension *value* measure related to technology and support	
	$V_b^2 -$	Dimension *value* measure related to the course	
	$V_c^2 -$	Dimension *value* measure related to the professor	
	$V_d^2 -$	Dimension *value* measure related to the learner	
	$S_a^2 -$	Dimension *satisfaction* measure related to technology and support	
	$S_b^2 -$	Dimension *satisfaction* measure related to the course	
	$S_c^2 -$	Dimension *satisfaction* measure related to the professor	
	$S_d^2 -$	Dimension *satisfaction* measure related to the learner	
Level 2 (characteristics)	Ai_{VAL}	*Value* items related to the technology and support characteristics	*(i = 1 to 14)*
	Bi_{VAL}	*Value* items related to the course characteristics	*(j = 1 to 12)*
	Ci_{VAL}	*Value* items related to the professor characteristics	*(k = 1 to 7)*
	Di_{VAL}	*Value* items related to the learner characteristics	*(l = 1 to 15)*
	Ai_{SAT}	*Satisfaction* items related to the technology and support characteristics	*(i = 1 to 14)*
	Bi_{SAT}	*Satisfaction* items related to the course characteristics	*(j = 1 to 12)*
	Ci_{SAT}	*Satisfaction* items related to the professor characteristics	*(k = 1 to 7)*
	Di_{SAT}	*Satisfaction* items related to the learner characteristics	*(l = 1 to 15)*

[1] Assumes linearity. [2] Actual and Imputed. Actual results elicited from learners and imputed results predicted via various linear and non-linear models.

of the dimension satisfaction (S_a, S_b, S_c, and S_d) by the corresponding dimension value (V_a, V_b, V_c, and V_d) for each of the four dimensions. These measures were also calibrated by dividing by 36 resulting in a scale from 0 to 1.

Effectiveness Curves and Effectiveness Grid

The effectiveness grid combines the Value-Satisfaction grid and the LeVIS index under one roof. Since the LeVIS index is a multiplication of learners' perceived value and satisfaction of e-learning systems, looking at a given constant level of LeVIS within the Value-Satisfaction grid provides a curve along the Value-Satisfaction grid of equal effectiveness. Increase of such a constant enables the identification of a family of such curves of multiple effectiveness levels that are termed *effectiveness curves*. These curves are hyperbola graphs by nature, and result from the equation: $V = LeVIS_{(Constant)} / S$, where LeVIS is constant for each effectiveness curve. Since the original value-satisfaction graph does not starts at the origin (0, 0), but rather at (0.5, 0.5) there is no issue of asymptotes of the hyperbola graphs or effectiveness curves. Additional information and rationale for the shift in the graph's origin was provided in the previous chapter. Figure 3 illustrates the effectiveness curves and the gradient of improvement towards the high-value and high-satisfaction area. Figure 4 provides the *effectiveness grid* of e-learning systems by combining the effectiveness curves and the Value-Satisfaction grid under one graph. Combining the two provides a very clear representation of both the areas of increased effectiveness and the improvement priorities. The resultant effectiveness grid presents eight segments, two for each of the quadrants of the Value-Satisfaction grid. Figure 4 also indicates the eight names of such segments and their relationship to the quadrants proposed in the previous chapter.

Consequently, the seventh and final research question of this study (RQ7) is:

RQ7:   What is the learners' perceived effectiveness of e-learning systems (as measured by LeVIS) for each of the e-learning system's dimension (technology and support, course, professor, and learners' dimension) and overall?

Figure 3. Effectiveness curves of e-learning systems

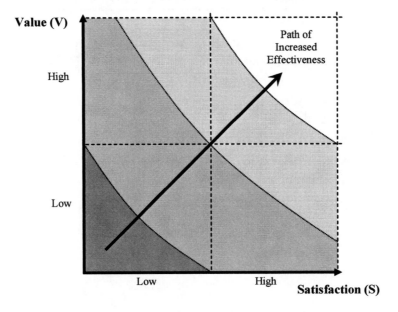

Figure 4. Effectiveness grid of e-learning systems

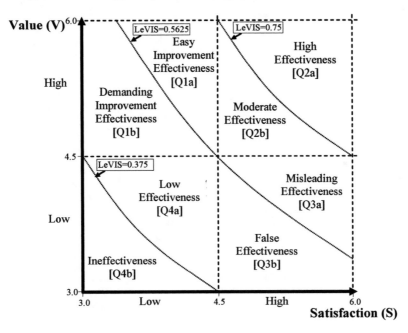

Chapter Summary

This chapter provided an overview of Learners' Value Index of Satisfaction (LeVIS), effectiveness curves, and effectiveness grids. The LeVIS index is defined and proposed in order to provide a benchmarking tool to suggest precise magnitude of effectiveness of e-learning systems as perceived by learners. Based on such a definition, effectiveness curves are proposed and superpose in the Value-Satisfaction grid to produce the effectiveness grid. The resulting effectiveness grid provides eight segments of various levels of effectiveness and improvement priority level.

Chapter VII

The Case Study: Methodology and Results

Introduction

This chapter provides details on the case study that was conducted in order to validate the research model and framework proposed in Chapter IV. Additionally, it seeks to validate the three tools proposed in Chapters V and VI. This chapter is guided by the seven research questions proposed in the previous three chapters and presents both the methodology used as well as the results of each section of this study.

Straub (1989) suggested a three-phase method for valid and sound results of survey instruments in IS research. The first phase that he proposed included a qualitative technique of exploring the phenomena and developing a theoretical framework grounded in previous theories. The second phase includes quantitative empirical techniques in order to explore the proposed theory. The third and last phase includes conceptual refinements based on the findings in the previous phases. The methodology proposed in this study follows closely these three phases for the development of valid and sound instruments to assess the value and satisfaction of e-learning systems.

Figure 1. Overview of the research design process

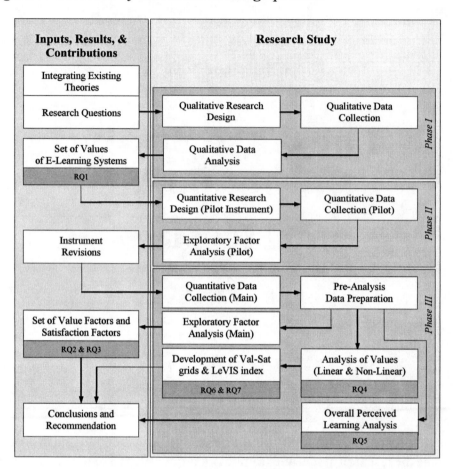

Phase I (see Figure 1) includes a qualitative assessment of characteristics that learners' value and express satisfaction (or dissatisfaction) when learning online. The findings of this phase were added to the findings previously reported in literature. Phase II of the study is noted as the "pilot study" and includes the development of a survey instrument based on all the characteristics found in literature as well as those newly uncovered in Phase I of this study. Pilot data collected in Phase II was analyzed via exploratory factor analysis using principal components analysis (PCA) to identify the distinct factors resulting from the data. This was done in order to provide initial validation of the instrument and to help clean items that do not add to the overall validity. Adjustments were made to the developed instrument based on preliminary results, and these were incorporated in the phase that followed. Phase III of the study repeats the data collection using the revised instrument over a larger group of online learners and is noted as the "main study." Exploratory analysis of the main study data was made in order to clean any irregularities such as multivariate outliers. This was followed by the principal components analysis (PCA) to identify the significant factors and provide the final validation of the instrument.

Exploratory Qualitative Research (Phase I)

The first phase of this study included qualitative research, following Keeney's (1999) methodology, in the pursuit of e-learning systems characteristics to which learners attribute value when learning online. It is important to note that due to the nature of technology and the extensive progress made in the past decade in Internet technologies for learning systems, existing literature lacks some of the characteristics for which learners hold value associated with new technologies. Consequently, the purpose of this part of the study was to augment the characteristics found in prior literature.

To augment the set of e-learning system characteristics found in literature, a qualitative questionnaire was developed following Keeney's (1999) methodology. Such a qualitative questionnaire starts with open-ended questions to asking learners about characteristics they value when learning online. Appendix B includes the open-ended questionnaire. Keeney (1999) suggests first guiding users to think generally about what they find valuable and only later guiding them to think in a more detailed manner. Following this methodology, the open-ended questionnaire is divided into two main sections. Initially, learners were provided with the first section only and were instructed to think about *all* characteristics they find important when learning online. The first section included general open-ended questions to capture such general characteristics responses. This section is completely open allowing respondents the opportunity to express any and all possible characteristics they value when learning online. Subsequently, learners were provided with the second section and were instructed to focus on more specific characteristics associated with each of the four dimensions (technology and support, content of courses, instructors, and learners' dimension). The second section of the questionnaire included open-ended questions to capture responses along these special dimensions. This was done in order to obtain more structured results focused on the four main dimensions.

The open-ended questionnaire was delivered in a computer lab via the Web to learners that were taking online and online-assisted business courses. These students were provided with instructions on answering the questionnaire. The instructions guided the students on how to answer the open-ended question-naire as well as the process that is to be followed. To eliminate duplications and insure the integrity of the data, the questionnaire was administered on a server that allowed access to registered learners only. To provide anonymity and spot duplicated submissions, the questionnaire was set to gather only the Internet protocol (IP) number of the computer used by the learner who submitted the data.

Data collected from this step was analyzed following Keeney's (1999) meth-odology. Responses from the learners were grouped based on their similarities and categorized based on each of the four main dimensions proposed by Webster and Hackley (1997). Due to the nature of qualitative exploratory work, responses from learners are most likely to differ in terminology. There-fore, similar terminology was converted and matched with similar characteris-tics and compared with the characteristics found in literature. For example, if one learner suggested that *system uptime* is an important characteristic and another learner suggested that *availability of the system* is important, then these two responses were grouped under the same one characteristic: *system availability*. Once similar responses were converted to common terms, these characteristics were assigned to one of the four literature dimensions that matched most closely. If a response cannot be assigned to an existing characteristic found in literature, a new characteristic was added to the list for further analysis and validation. The same process was repeated by another researcher and results were compared for validation purposes. The results of this phase of the study addressed research question one (RQ1) by providing a list of characteristics of e-learning systems that are important to learners.

Following this methodology, learners were surveyed on this list of e-learning systems characteristics in order to assess their perception of the value and satisfaction level for each of these characteristics. The preliminary survey instrument was developed in Phase II based on the findings from this qualitative phase (Phase I) and the prior literature.

Results of the Exploratory Qualitative Research (Phase I)

The first phase of this study was conducted during the 2001-2002 academic year following the methodology proposed by Keeney (1999) in order to provide initial insight into the list of e-learning system characteristics that learners' value when learning online. Following a proposed list of e-learning system characteristics from literature, an open-ended qualitative questionnaire was developed following Keeney's (1999) approach (see Appendix B). Four groups of students enrolled in courses utilizing e-learning systems in the college of business at a state university in southeastern United States, participated in this phase of the study. Two graduate and two undergraduate groups were used. The first graduate group included students attending an online master's degree during the summer of 2001 using the e-learning system under study, and the second graduate group included students attending an on-campus master's degree during the spring 2002 using the same e-learning system to supplement their on-campus class activities. Additionally, the third group included undergraduate students attending online courses using the e-learning system under study during the spring of 2002, and the fourth group included undergraduate students attending an on-campus course using the e-learning system to supplement their on-campus class activities. The data collection was facilitated by the same instructor.

For each group, the instructor first asked the students to access the first section of the open-ended questionnaire and think, in general, about all the e-learning system characteristics that are important for them when using the e-learning system. Then, the instructor asked the students to access the second section of the open-ended questionnaire and provide the names of the e-learning system dimensions (technology and support, course, instructor, learner), asking participants to think about more specific e-learning system characteristics associated with these dimensions (See Appendix B). Data was captured using a Web-based system as described previously. Responses to the questionnaire were nine out of 11 students (or a response rate of about 82%) for the first graduate group, 34 out of 39 students (or a response rate of about 87%) for the second graduate group. Additionally, five out of 19 students (or response rate of about 32%) of the first undergraduate course and 27 out of 46 students (or response rate of about 59%) of the second undergraduate course responded to the questionnaire. Overall, there were 75 out of 115 students' responses (an overall response rate of over 65%).

Subsequently, the qualitative date was analyzed following Keeney's (1999) methodology. Responses from learners were grouped based on their similarities and categorized based on each of the four main dimensions proposed by Webster and Hackley (1997). Due to the nature of qualitative exploratory work, responses differed widely in terminology. Similar terminologies were converted to one e-learning system characteristic and compared with the characteristics found in literature. Some of the terms did not correspond to existing e-learning system characteristics found in literature. As a result, the following six new characteristics were added to the list: taking quizzes remotely (off-campus), taking practice tests prior to a graded test, quality of professor-to-student interaction, submission time window for assignments and quizzes, self-discipline and time management, and family support. Results of the qualitative process are presented in Table 1. E-learning systems characteristics noted with "*" refer to new ones not specifically noted in literature, however noted by the learners as important characteristics when learning online. Out of the 48 e-learning systems characteristics, four were selected to be worded in a negative term (noted with "**"), one in each e-learning system dimension, as suggested previously. Thus, Table 1 addresses the first research question (RQ1) by providing a list of characteristics of e-learning system that are important for learners.

Pilot Quantitative Research (Phase II)

The purpose of this phase is to develop a preliminary survey instrument based on the previous qualitative phase and test its validity on a pilot group of students attending online courses. Developing the survey instrument based on the framework proposed in the literature and qualitative work in Phase I provides the robustness for the foundation of this research. Furthermore, the approach in this phase is to develop an instrument that has content validity, construct validity, and reliability as well as providing preliminary empirical testing to ensure its overall validity as discussed later on in this chapter. Following the development of the preliminary instrument, it was submitted to two focus groups. The first focus group included faculty teaching online courses. Feedback and suggestions were incorporated. Subsequently, the revised preliminary instrument was submitted to a second focus group of learners attending online courses. Again, feedback and suggestions were incorporated. Once the

Table 1. Resulted e-learning systems characteristics from literature and Phase I

	E-Learning Systems Characteristics
A1	Quick answer from technical support via phone
A2	Quick answer from technical support after-hours via e-mail
A3	Quality of technical support
A4	System operation time (up-time)
A5	Reduced system errors
A6	System security (discourage hacking, secure access, etc.)
A7	Access to courses from anywhere in the world (via the Internet)
A8**	High network availability & low network congestion
A9	Learning at anytime of the day (schedule flexibility)
A10	Submit assignments from anywhere (via the Internet)
A11	Different system tools (chat, bulletin-board or discussion forums, etc.)
A12	Access of all courses from one area (My WebCT)
A13*	Taking quizzes remotely (off-campus)
A14	Review course audios
B1	Availability of course content
B2	Quality content of courses
B3	Amount of material in courses
B4	Interesting subject matter
B5	Difficulty of subject matter
B6**	Availability of other content (syllabus, objectives, assignments, schedule)
B7	Enjoyment from the courses/lessons
B8	Ease-of-use (with course content, navigation, interface, etc.)
B9	Similar of interface across all online courses
B10	Gathering information quickly
B11	Organization of courses (content of courses, organization of assignments, etc. across all courses)
B12*	Taking practice tests prior to graded test
C1	Amount of professor-to-student interaction
C2	Professor's attitude (across all professors)
C3**	Learning a lot from the professor (across all courses)
C4*	Quality of professor-to-student interaction
C5	Freedom of learning (selective seeking and processing of information)
C6*	Submission time window for assignments and quizzes
C7	Online workload of courses
D1	Learning a lot in these classes
D2	Amount of interaction with classmates
D3	Quality of interaction with classmates
D4	Classmates' attitude (across all courses)
D5	Being part of a "class" although it was online
D6	Your comfort with online learning and technology
D7	Your Internet and computer skills
D8*/**	Self-discipline and time management
D9	Cost of courses
D10	Cost of ISP and Internet access
D11	Reduced travel cost/time (to and from campus)
D12	Ability to travel while taking online courses (for business or other)
D13	Employer support and your ability to work while learning
D14	Attendance to family responsibilities
D15*	Family support

preliminary instrument was revised based on comments from both focus groups, it was adopted to a Web-based survey format. Specific information about the instrument development is provided in the *Instrument Development* section. After these two revisions, the instrument was given to a group of students attending online courses via an e-learning system. Additional information about the data collection is provided in the *Pilot Study Data Collection* section. A preliminary data analysis was done using the principal components analysis (PCA) to explore the initial validity and reliability of the instrument as well as providing guidelines for necessary adjustments of the instrument. Subsequently, the adjusted instrument was used in phase III of the study to gather data on a larger group of learners attending online courses. Additional information about the main study data collection is provided in the *Main Study Data Collection* section.

Instrument Development

Straub (1989, p.150) suggested that "an instrument valid in content is one that has drawn representative questions from a universal pool." Leidner and Jarvenpaa (1995, p.280) pointed out that "IS researchers should find it useful to draw upon well-established variables from education research rather than creating new variables as they pursue research in the area." Consequently, this study develops an instrument by drawing representative characteristics from the following validated research pool:

1. Alavi, Yoo, and Vogel (1997)
2. Bures, Abrami, and Amundsen (2000)
3. Doll and Torkzadeh (1988, 1991)
4. Hiltz (1993)
5. Hiltz and Johnson (1990)
6. Ives, Olson, and Baroudi (1983)
7. Marks (2000)
8. Piccoli, Ahmed, and Ives (2001)
9. Torkzadeh and Doll (1991)
10. Webster and Hackley (1997)

Baroudi and Orlikowski (1988) suggested using survey questions (items) in a minimal verbal format to eliminate user confusion with feeling or other uncertainties of the exact measure. They proposed stating the characteristics' name only, rather than as a question type statement (p. 55). Fowler (1995) also favors the use of words in the scales (e.g., satisfied, very satisfied, extremely satisfied, etc.) rather than numeric scale (e.g., 1, 2, 3, etc.) as "all of the points are more consistently calibrated by the use of words" (p. 53). Fowler (1995) also suggested that in many occasions the use of adjectival scales provided more consistent results and therefore more reliable measurements (p. 55). Following this recommendation, the developed instrument provided respondents with the names of the characteristics rather than question type statements. For example, the proposed instrument asks learners to state their satisfaction level from extremely unsatisfied to extremely satisfied with "amount of interaction" rather than asking them to state their satisfaction level on a statement such as, "I felt comfortable using the system to interact with other people."

Initial assessment of value construct was done by asking users to rank characteristics based on their level of importance (Feather, 1967, 1975; Rokeach, 1969, 1973, 1975). Subsequent work on value construct suggested that such an approach is a major burden to respondents as well as researchers by limiting the analysis techniques that can be used on the collected data (Brown, 1976, pp. 20-21; Chapman, Blackburn, & Austin, 1983, p. 419; Kahle & Kennedy, 1988, p. 53; Thompson, Levitov, & Miederhoff, 1982, p. 902). Furthermore, value ranking instruments provide major limitation due to the fact that once a respondent ranked an item as the most important (or ranked it as number 1) by default, all other items are ranked lower. Some researchers assert that individuals may find different characteristics almost equally important but cannot rate them as equally important due to the same rank nature of the instruments (Thompson et al., 1982, p. 903). Moreover, an additional disadvantage of ranking measures over rating measures is that the distance between any two consecutive ranks is exactly one, whereas the differences of their rating measure can vary widely (Kahle & Kennedy, 1988, p. 54).

From literature reviewed in Chapter III, it is evident that rating value items seems more appropriate when measuring value perceptions (Thompson et al., 1982, p. 903). It was also suggested in prior literature that rating value items are more suitable than and at least as valid as a ranking procedure (Chapman et al., 1983, p. 421; Kahle et al., 1986, p. 406; Ng, 1982; Payne 1988, p. 275). King and Epstein (1983) noted a high correlation (0.969, n = 236) between the results drawn from ranking and rating items (p. 40). They concluded that there

Figure 2. Proposed survey instrument items scales

Quality of Technical Support	Level of Satisfaction						Level of Importance					
	○	○	○	○	○	○	○	○	○	○	○	○
	Extremely Unsatisfied	Very Unsatisfied	Unsatisfied	Satisfied	Very Satisfied	Extremely Satisfied	Not Important	Not so Important	Slightly Important	Important	Very Important	Extremely Important

is little added benefit from using a "cumbersome procedure" such as ranking for the measurement of values (pp. 41-42). Consequently, a rating measure of value items was proposed in this instrument.

Fowler (1995) also suggested that survey items associated with feelings, such as satisfaction, should be rated on a positive to negative scale (p.46). Additionally, other researchers suggested that the rating of survey items associated with value should indicate the degree to which the objective is met (Keeney, 1994, p. 795). Kahle and Kennedy (1988) suggested that value items in a rating format should vary on a zero-to-positive scale (p. 53). Fowler (1995) also suggested that five to seven categories of the evaluative scale for each item are the ultimate in rating survey instruments (p. 53). He also argued that the use of an odd number of scales provides ambiguity for survey instruments. The middle point can pose a major dilemma for respondents as it can either be interpreted as *neutral point* or *not applicable*. As a result, Fowler (1995) suggested using an even number, preferably six (p. 54). He also mentioned that it is difficult to generate more than six adjectives that respondents can reliably remember and use. Consequently, the proposed survey instrument used one scale of six adjectives for measuring satisfaction (level of satisfaction) and another six to measure value (level of importance) (see Figure 2). This scale is also similar to the dual scale suggested by Bailey and Pearson (1983) (see Figure 6 in Chapter III).

IS satisfaction literature defines items in a survey instrument as questions that seek to measure users' perceptions of certain characteristics (Bailey & Pearson, 1983; Doll & Torkzadeh, 1988, 1991; Ives et al., 1983; Galletta & Lederer, 1989; Torkzadeh & Doll, 1991). Drawing from IS satisfaction literature (Doll & Torkzadeh, 1991, p. 6; Kim, 1989, p. 7), learners' satisfaction items are the measures of the perceived performance level that learners find at a post-experience point of time with each e-learning system characteristic. Whereas, drawn from psychology and behavioral science literature (Allport, Vernon, & Lindzey, 1951, p. 6; Posner & Munson, 1979,

p. 10; Rokeach, 1969, 1973, 1979), learners' value items will be defined in the context of this study as measures of the importance of enduring core beliefs concerning each characteristic of an e-learning system when learning online. Furthermore, *learners' dimension satisfaction measure* is defined as the aggregation of all perceived learners' satisfaction items with each dimension. Similarly, *learners' dimension value measure* is defined as the aggregation of all perceived learners' value items with each dimension. Additionally, *learners' overall satisfaction* is defined as the aggregation of all four dimension satisfaction measures, whereas *learners' overall value* is defined as the aggregation of all four learners' dimension value.

In order to detect problems where respondents answer all items the same (i.e., response-set), Fowler (1995) suggested adding several items in a negative form for each survey (p. 92). As the instrument uses short item description rather than long question as discussed previously, it was feasible to incorporate only one negative question for each of the four e-learning system dimensions. Therefore, each of the four dimensions included one item that was set in a negative form. Example of a negative item includes: *low network availability and high network congestion*. Additional information on data recoding and reflection of scores needed due to these negative questions are provided under the *Item Analysis* section in this chapter.

Galletta and Lederer's (1989) user information satisfaction (UIS) instrument added three overall satisfaction items to the original Ives et al. (1982) 13-item UIS instrument. The items ask respondents to answer their overall satisfaction level with each of the three main satisfaction dimensions of their study (IS product, IS support, and user involvement). A fourth item provides an overall measure of satisfaction with the entire IS environment (overall satisfaction). Similarly, the proposed instrument in this study included two overall items for each of the four dimensions. One item asks learners to rate their overall level of satisfaction with each dimension (known as dimension satisfaction measure), while the other item asks learners to rate overall how important all characteristics in each dimension are for them when learning online (dimension value measure). Also similar to Galletta and Lederer (1989), three overall items were added to measure the overall satisfaction with e-learning systems, overall value of e-learning systems, and overall perceived learning, taking into account all e-learning system characteristics from all four dimensions. A copy of the revised survey instrument is available in Appendix E.

Instrument Validity and Reliability

The main objective of this study was to provide an investigative process into the question "Is there a relationship between learners' perceived *satisfaction* with e-learning systems and learners' perceived *value* in order to indicate learners' perceived effectiveness of e-learning systems?" As such, this study did not intend to test hypotheses or to use strict experimental design, rather it was intended to develop new theory grounded in the theories covered in Chapters II and III, as well as the model proposed in Chapter IV. In this case, the validity and reliability of the instrument proposed must be demonstrated. Traditionally, three different categories of validity were examined. They are internal validity, predictive or external validity, and instrument validation (including content and construct validity). Therefore, the following sections provide an overview and justification for the validity and reliability issues associated with the instrument proposed following the methodology suggested by Straub (1989). It includes the following subsections: *Internal Validity*, *External Validity*, and *Instrument Validation*. Subsequently, the instrument reliability section is presented.

Internal Validity

Internal validity refers to "whether the observed effects could have been caused by or correlated with a set of non-hypothesized and/or unmeasured variables" (Straub, 1989). Straub (1989) suggested that internal validity in MIS research can be maximized by an investigation of all the appropriate constructs and variables related to the studied phenomenon (p. 151). As a result, this study utilizes the qualitative phase (Phase I) in order to gather all values from learners prior to the development of the instrument. The use of the qualitative data collection and analysis minimizes the internal validity threats when developing the instrument. Moreover, since the instrument was subjected to subsequent analysis, the validity of the instrument was further tested. Furthermore, since the goal of this study was not to test hypotheses or rigid experimental design, it was more appropriate to address the issues related to internal validity at the level of construct validity which is reviewed under the *Instrument Validation* section.

External Validity

External validity refers to "how the results of a study can be generalized" (Cook & Campbell, 1979, p. 70). Cook and Campbell (1979) suggested that results of studies can be generalized via two approaches: "(1) generalized to particular target of persons, settings, and times, and (2) generalizing across types of persons, settings, and times" (p. 71). The aim of this study was to develop a general framework for the relationship between learners' perceived *satisfaction* with e-learning systems and learners' perceived *value* of e-learning systems and to propose how this relationship can be used for learners' perceived effectiveness of e-learning systems. Consequently, on one hand the results of this study can be generalized to new learners using the same e-learning system in order to predict the learners' perceived effectiveness of the e-learning system under study based on the learners' perceived *satisfaction* with e-learning systems and learners' perceived *value*, corresponding with approach (1). On the other hand, the process used in this study to gather values and develop the instrument to measure them can be generalized to other information systems, corresponding with this approach (2). Examples for generalizing the process used in this study to other types of information systems are presented in the *Suggestions for Future Research* section in Chapter VIII.

Instrument Validation

Instrument validation includes two measures: content validity and construct validity. Content validity refers to the question: "are the instrument measures drawn from all possible measures of the properties under investigation" (Straub, 1989, p.150)? An instrument that has content validity refers to one that uses representative validated questions from a wide pool of appropriate questions (Straub, 1989, p.150). The instrument proposed in this study uses items from a variety of validated sources as suggested in the *Instrument Development* section. Furthermore as discussed in chapter four, the list of e-learning systems characteristics is based on a wide variety of sources as presented in Table 1 in Chapter IV.

Construct validity refers to "whether the measures chosen are true constructs describing the event or merely artifact of the methodology itself" (Straub, 1989, p. 150). High validity is achieved when there is high correlation between measures that represent the same construct and low correlation between measures that represent different constructs (Straub, 1989, p. 150). Kerlinger and Lee (2000) suggested two methods of construct validity: one is the examination of the correlations between the total score and item scores and the second is by examining the results of factor analysis. Others also suggest that the extent to which an item correlates with the total score is indicative of construct validity for the item (Ives et al., 1983, p. 789). However, this is an appropriate measure only in the event of linearity. If a non-linear relationship may exist, such a measure is not appropriate. Consequently, this study suggests using both linear measures of correlation (Pearson correlation) as well as non-linear measures of correlations (Eta, η, correlation).

The second method of construct validation is factor analysis. Baroudi and Orlikowski (1988) noted that "factors resulted from factor analysis are an important method of construct validity" (p. 48). Consequently, this study suggests using factor analysis in order to investigate the validity of the e-learning system dimensions. At the same time, this study suggests using factor analysis to assess the e-learning system characteristics in order to provide strong evidence for the construct validity of the instrument. Additional information is provided later on in this chapter.

Reliability

Instrument reliability refers to the extent to which its measurement error is minimized and provides "an evaluation of measurement accuracy" (Straub, 1989, p. 150). Galletta and Lederer (1989) suggested that scholars should be aware of "instrument reliability." Straub (1989) suggested that the reliability of an instrument is generally measured by Cronbach's α. High correlation between alternative survey items or large Cronbach's α (> 0.70), are usually indications that the survey items are reliable (Straub, 1989, p. 150). This study proposes to evaluate the reliability of both the e-learning system dimensions as well as the e-learning system characteristics. Additional information on the process to establish the reliability tests for each is provided in the sections *E-Learning System Dimension Analysis* and *E-Learning System Characteristics and Instrument Adjustments*.

Another common reliability issue associated with survey instruments is that it is self-administered. Fowler (1993) suggested that self-administered surveys require careful design with clear and precise instructions, text of questions or items, and the measurement scale (e.g., Likert scale) (p. 66). Consequently, the instructions and text of items proposed for this instrument were reviewed by two focus groups (faculty focus group and student focus group) for clarity, as suggested previously. Revisions were made following the comments from the two focus groups prior to the pilot data collection. Fowler (1993) also suggested that respondents are required to have good reading skills, otherwise the reliability of results are questionable. It was assumed that undergraduate business students attending online courses in an accredited state university have sufficient reading skills to answer the survey proposed in this study. Finally, Fowler (1993) claimed that self-administered surveys actually provide an advantage over interviewer-administered surveys (phone or face-to-face) by "the fact that the respondent does not have to share answers with an interviewer" and thus, increasing the reliability of the results (p. 66).

Pilot Study Data Collection

Fowler (1993) suggested that a use of computer-assisted data collection can greatly improve the reliability of the data as it eliminates the human data entry step that includes some natural human errors (p. 63). Consequently, the survey was delivered via the web to undergraduate learners who attend business courses via an e-learning system. The Web-based survey system collected responses via the Internet and Web browser, where learners submitted a Web form to the MS® FrontPage® server that collected the data and submitted it to a centralized database. During the submission process, each selection by the user was translated automatically to a numeric score. For *satisfaction* measures, the database entries were 1 for *extremely unsatisfied* to 6 for *extremely satisfied*. For *value* measures, the database entries were 1 for *not important* to 6 for *extremely important*.

Three types of requests were made to all students taking online courses, asking them to submit the survey. The first request was sent via e-mail during the last week of the term asking them to submit the survey with a direct link from the e-mail message to the survey Web site. A second request was done via a message that was posted during the last week of the term in the homepages of all fully online courses asking students to submit their survey. A third request was made as a pop-up window to all students taking fully online courses when accessing the e-learning system (see Figure 3).

To eliminate duplications and insure the integrity of the data, respondents were asked to use their *online-course evaluation code* sent by the university's

Figure 3. Pop-up survey request

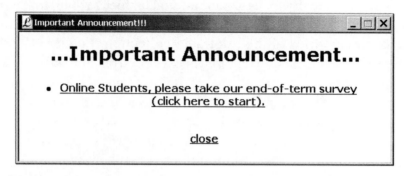

continuing and professional education department. The code is unique and each student receives a different code every term for each course they have been taking in order to perform the end-of-term course evaluation. The code is unknown to anyone, including the researcher, except to the university's continuing and professional education department, a separate department within the university. The sole purpose of the use of such code in this study was to detect multiple submissions. Moreover, the survey was administered on a server that captures the Internet protocol (IP) number of the computer used by the learner to submit the data. Using both the unique *online-course evaluation code* and the IP numbers allowed elimination of duplications in the data submitted.

Pilot Data Analysis

The pilot data was subjected to exploratory factor analysis using principal components analysis (PCA) with the anticipation of loading onto various factors done separately for satisfaction measures and value measures. Results provided *satisfaction factors* and *value factors* separately. Initially, PCA was set to allow the extraction of as many factors as suggested by the data. The number of needed principal components, or main factors, for satisfaction and for value was determined by both the cumulative variance explained by the factors (also using the scree-plot) and by the level of eigenvalue each factor has. Results of this process allowed the selection of a fixed number of factors that were further explored for validity and reliability.

These *satisfaction factors* and *value factors* may or may not be similar to the four dimensions specified in Table 2 in Chapter IV. Cronbach's α reliability tests were done to check the reliability of the instrument and help spot items that may reduce the Cronbach's α of each factor. Items that load below 0.7 on a factor (both for *satisfaction factors* and *value factors*) were subjected to future investigation. As part of this investigation, a review was done to spot items that may load between 0.4 and 0.6 on more than one factor. This investigation was also done by plotting the items' factor scores on two graphs: scores on factor 1 vs. scores on factor 2, and scores on factor 3 vs. scores on factor 4. This generated two graphs for *satisfaction* factor scores and two graphs for *value* factor scores. In each graph, the whole factor score scale was divided into low and high using the factor score mean as the cut-off-point between the low and high intervals. An observation was made on items that may load on the high-high quadrant of the factor scores space. This identified the items that load highly on both factors, indicating the need for further review. Such items were closely reviewed for the clarity of the text of the e-learning system characteristic. Revisions of the instrument were recommended as a result of this phase to improve the clarity of the instrument instructions as well as the text used for the e-learning systems characteristics.

Results of the Pilot Quantitative Research (Phase II)

The purpose of this phase was to develop a preliminary survey instrument based on the previous qualitative phase and help establish the reliability of such instrument on a pilot group of students attending online courses. Following the development of the preliminary instrument, it was submitted to two focus groups. The first focus group included nine faculty teaching online courses. Feedback and suggestions such as minor textual changes were incorporated. Subsequently, the revised preliminary instrument was submitted to a second focus group of learners attending an online course. The sample was limited to an undergraduate online MIS course and included 26 students. Again, feedback and suggestions were incorporated. Subsequently, the preliminary instrument was revised based on comments from both focus groups and was developed in a Web-based survey format.

The pilot data collection was conducted during the fall of 2002. The sample included all undergraduate students taking online courses during the fall of 2002. Three types of requests were used asking students to submit the survey, as noted previously. The first request was sent via e-mail during the last week of the term asking them to submit the survey with a direct link from the e-mail message to the survey Web site. A second request was done via a message that was posted during the last week of the term in the homepages of all online courses asking students to submit the survey. A third request was made as a pop-up window to all undergraduate students taking online courses when accessing the e-learning system's portal. One hundred and forty-one responses were submitted to the database representing nearly 27% of undergraduate students taking online courses during the fall of 2002, out of a total of 523 individuals. The data collection was done using a web-based system and the survey was set to ensure all items are answered prior to submission of the survey, resulting in no missing values across all respondents.

The pilot data was subjected to exploratory factor analysis using principal components analysis (PCA) using varimax rotation and allowed the extractions of as many factors as possible under the constrain of eigenvalue larger than one. Nine *satisfaction factors* were resulted with cumulative variability explained of nearly 76% and high Cronbach's α (see Appendix C). Ives et al. (1983) noted that Cronbach's α is an acceptable measure of instrument reliability. Moreover, they noted that Cronbach's α reliability score of .80 is considered satisfactory (Ives et al., 1983, p. 788). Moreover, 10 *value factors* resulted with cumulative variability of nearly 73% and high Cronbach's α (see Appendix D). Using the factor loading on both analyses, survey items were closely looked for low loading (< 0.4) or for medium to high loading (~ 0.4 to 0.6) on more than one factor. Results suggested six items (A_6, A_9, A_{14}, B_2, D_1, and D_6) that required some minor changes to the item text. As the main goal of this phase was to provide initial validity and reliability for the instrument, no further analyses were done on the pilot data. Results of this phase contributed to the minor changes to the six items addressed earlier resulting in the revised survey instrument (see Appendix E).

Main Quantitative Research (Phase III)

The purpose of this phase is to use the revised survey instrument based on changes made in Phase II and collect data on a larger group of students (noted as "main study") that were attending online courses. Data from this study was analyzed to further explore and confirm the factors using PCA. Factors resulting from the main study were compared to the results found in the pilot study and add to the reliability and validity of the instrument. The principal factors resulted from this analysis were suggested as new e-learning system dimensions for future studies. Furthermore, e-learning system characteristics were examined for elimination from the original instrument based on the *item analysis* described in this section. Results of this process provided a new revised instrument that is suggested for future studies. This research phase also includes the development of the Value-Satisfaction grids and the LeVIS index to suggest learners' perceived effectiveness of the e-learning system under study. Moreover, analyses of the values resulting from linear and non-linear models was done and compared with the actual values elicited from users. Additional information about the steps of these analyses is provided in subsequent paragraphs.

Main Study Data Collection

The main survey was delivered via the Web to undergraduate learners who attended business courses using an e-learning system. Similarly to the pilot data collection, the main study data collection was done using the same three types of requests (e-mail request, message to fully-online course homepages, and the pop-up window). The main study also included an e-mail reminder a week after classes ended to encourage students who did not submit the survey instrument to do so. Such technique was proposed by Fowler (1995) as a method to increase the overall response rate.

To eliminate duplications and insure the integrity of the data, the main data collection was implemented by asking respondents to use their *professor evaluation code* sent by the university's continuing and professional education department and was administered on the same server to capture the Internet protocol (IP) number of the computer used by the learner to submit the data. Similar to the pilot data collection, using both the unique professor evaluation code and the IP numbers allowed the elimination of duplications in the main study data submitted and at the same time provide anonymity for the learners.

Results of the Main Quantitative Research (Phase III)

The main data collection was conducted during the spring of 2003 using the revised survey instrument (see Appendix E). The sample included all under-graduate students taking online courses during the spring of 2003. Similarly to the pilot data collection, three types of requests were used to ask all students taking online courses to submit the survey including the e-mail request during the last week of the term, the message that was posted during the last week of the term in the homepages of all online courses, and the pop-up window on the e-learning system's portal homepage.

Two hundred and seven responses were submitted to the database representing a little over 32% of undergraduate students taking online courses at the college of business during the spring of 2003, out of a total of 644 individuals. After the responses were submitted, an extensive pre-analysis data preparation was conducted to ensure the reliability of the results. Seven value/satisfaction response-sets and eight multivariate outliers on both satisfaction and value measures were observed in the data resulting in a total of 192 cases available for final analyses.

Data Analyses and Results

This section includes detailed descriptions on the statistical analyses proposed for the main data. Prior to data analyses, a process to identify irregularities in the main study data was proposed. This process is called *pre-analysis data preparation* and includes several steps needed to adjust or clean the data prior to the final analyses. Following the pre-analysis data preparation, a review of the principal component analysis is provided. Detailed descriptions on the process to develop the Value-Satisfaction grids and LeVIS index are provided.

Pre-Analysis Data Preparation

Pre-analysis data preparation deals with the process of detecting irregularities or problems with the collected data. This process is required prior to the major data analysis to provide assurance that the results and conclusions will be valid (Mertler & Vannatta, 2001, p. 25). There are four main reasons to conduct the data preparation prior to the final analysis. The first reason deals with the accuracy of the data collected. Clearly, if the data collected is not accurate, the analysis will not be valid either. For example, data entry errors can occur when inputting data from a paper-and-pencil instrument to a computer database. Another example for inaccurate data collection is due to errors in the script used to input the data from a Web-based survey into the computer database. As the data collection for this study was done via Web-based survey, the survey and script to submit the survey responses were tested by several technicians to assure it is error free. Submitted survey responses were noted as *cases*, to be consistent with literature. Furthermore, the data collected was subjected to frequency distribution, descriptive statistics, and outlier examination to detect any irregularities in the data as suggested by Mertler and Vannatta (2001, p. 25).

The second reason for pre-analysis data preparation addresses the issue of response-set. *Response-set* refers to cases where respondents submitted the same score for all items. Kerlinger and Lee (2000) noted that "response-set can be considered a mild threat to valid measures" (p. 713). They suggested observing the data collected for response-sets and, if applicable, to consider eliminating them from the final analysis. Accordingly, the data collected in this study was subjected to a response-set test. One way to detect such a response-set was by using negatively worded questions embedded into each dimension. Learners who provided the same answer for all items including the negatively worded items will be subject to further investigation. As part of that investigation, cases that were initially observed as a response-set was further analyzed by comparing the responses submitted on all satisfaction measures with the responses submitted on all value measures. If a given case yielded as both a response-set for satisfaction measures and a response-set for value measures, the case was eliminated from the final analysis. If the response-sets were equal in both scores, they were eliminated. For example, if a given case in the data included marks of 6 for all the satisfaction measures as well as 6 for all the value measures, this case was eliminated from the final analysis. However, if a given case in the data included marks of numbers other than 6 for all the satisfaction measures and marks of 6 for all the value measures (or vise versa), the case was not eliminated from the final analysis since it did not constitute a full response-set across value and satisfaction items.

The third reason for pre-analysis data preparation deals with missing data. When respondents fail to answer an item or when there is a flaw in the data collection, the result is missing data. The amount of missing data can significantly effect the validity of the data collected and the results drawn from it (Mertler & Vannatta, 2001, p. 25). As the data collection in this study was done using a Web-based system, the survey was set to ensure all items were answered prior to the submission of the survey. Several technicians reviewed the survey to ensure all questions were required for submission. This prevented the occurrence of missing data. Consequently, due to the nature of the data collection technique used in this study, no missing data was expected. However, the collected data was scanned to ensure no missing data exists.

Finally, the fourth reason for pre-analysis data preparation deals with the effects of extreme cases (i.e., outliers). Extreme cases or outliers analysis is required as it is inadequate to draw conclusions from data that is skewed by a number of extreme cases. Mertler and Vannatta (2001) suggested that "an outlier can cause a result to be insignificant when, without the outlier, it would have been significant" (p. 27). As this study was based on multiple variables, it was appropriate to analyze the main study data for multivariate outliers. Multivariate outliers are "cases with unusual combination of scores on two or more variables" (Mertler & Vannatta, 2001, p. 27). Two criteria were used to identify multivariate outliers. If cases were found to be outliers in both criteria they were removed from future analyses. The first method is based on the results of the *Mahalanobis distance* which evaluates the distance of each case from the centroid of the remaining cases, where the centroid is created by the means of all the variables in that analysis. The test is done using χ^2 statistics with degrees of freedom equal to the number of variables in the analysis (Mertler & Vannatta, 2001, p. 27). The Mahalanobis distance analysis was done separately for the 48 satisfaction measures and for the 48 value measures. Results were summarized in a table to identify cases that are outliers on both satisfaction measures and value measures as cases that were eliminated must have been eliminated on both measures and not only one. The second criterion to identify multivariate outliers was utilizing the PCA factor score bi-plots for each of the cases. The bi-plots were computed by plotting the PCA factor scores of all cases in the main study data in the first and second factor scores space as well as in the third and fourth factor scores space respectively. This resulted in four scatter plots with two bi-plots for satisfaction measures and two bi-plots for value measures. Three ellipsoids were graphed for each of the bi-plots representing 99.9%, 99%, and 95% confidence curves. Cases that fell outside these confidence interval ellipsoids were observed and noted in the same summary table proposed earlier. As suggested by Mertler and Vannatta (2001, p. 29), cases that were found to be outliers via Mahalanobis distance and the ones that fell outside the 99% confidence ellipsoids of both the satisfaction and value measures, were eliminated from the final analysis. It is important to note that although the extreme case analysis proposes case elimination prior to the final analysis, Stevens (found in Mertler & Vannatta, 2001, p. 29) suggested to perform two sets of analysis, one with the outliers and one without and then compare the results. Therefore, this study performed the final analysis once with the outliers and once without.

Results of the Pre-Analysis Data Preparation

As noted previously, pre-analysis data preparation deals with the process of detecting irregularities or problems with the collected data. Seven cases were observed in the main data as full response-sets (cases number: 12, 36, 77, 106, 158, 195, and 196) and were eliminated from further analyses (see Appendix F). Similar to the pilot data, the main data collection was done using a Web-based system ensuring that no data entry errors occurred in the submission process. Moreover, the survey was set to ensure all items were answered prior to the submission of the survey resulting in no missing values across all respondents. However, extreme cases analysis was performed to identify outliers. The Mahalanobis distance was conducted separately for the 48 satisfaction measures and for the 48 value measures. Results were summarized in a table to identify cases that were observed as outliers on both satisfaction and value measures (see Appendix F). These cases were subjected for further investigation. The second criterion to identify multivariate outliers was done using the PCA factor score bi-plots of the cases. The bi-plots were done by plotting the PCA factor scores of all cases of the main study data in the first and second factor scores space as well as in the third and fourth factor scores space respectively. This resulted in scatter plots, and two separate bi-plots for satisfaction measures and two bi-plots for value measures. Three ellipsoids were graphed for each of the bi-plots representing 99.9%, 99%, and 95% confidence curves (see Appendix G). Cases that fell outside these confidence intervals ellipsoids were observed and noted in the summary table (see Appendix F). As a result, eight cases (cases number: 28, 56, 87, 125, 155, 163, 179, and 184) were observed as outliers via Mahalanobis distance as well as fell outside the confidence curves of both satisfaction measures and value measures were eliminated from the final analyses.

Another irregularity was observed in the data regarding contradictory responses in learners' elicited scores for the overall measures (the four dimensions and overall measures). The contradiction resulted when learners marked various scores on the satisfaction measures (S_{o_act}, S_{a_act}, S_{b_act}, S_{c_act}, and S_{d_act}) or value measures (V_{o_act}, V_{a_act}, V_{b_act}, V_{c_act}, and V_{d_act}) and their dimension or overall scores were set outside the range (below the minimum of all lower level

Table 2. Results of the internal contradictory overall scores' check

Satisfaction (n = 192)			Value (n = 192)		
Variable	No. of Scores Out of Range		Variable	No. of Scores Out of Range	
So_act	7		Vo_act	12	
Sa_act	2		Va_act	9	
Sb_act	10		Vb_act	20	
Sc_act	7		Vc_act	25	
Sd_act	2		Vd_act	3	
Total:	28	14.6%	Total:	69	35.9%

scores or above the maximum of all lower level scores) of all lower level scores. For example, if a learner marked 4 for all satisfaction measures in Dimension A and at the same time he or she marked 6 for the *dimension A satisfaction* measure, this constituted an "internal contradictory overall scores" as the overall score (6 in this example) is above the maximum of all lower level scores (4 in this example). Therefore, an analysis was done to locate such "internal contradictory overall scores" and suggested modification for the overall score based on other cases that have the same scores for the lower level measures. Results of the satisfaction "internal contradictory overall scores" check are presented in Appendix H. (For example, see case number 57 internal contradictory overall scores and the decision of changing its overall score.) This analysis was done 10 times, five for satisfaction and five for value, whereas the five for each construct included once for each of the e-learning system dimension and once for each of the overall scores (Satisfaction and Value). The results of all 10 analyses suggested adjustments to a total of 28 cases for satisfaction measures (dimensions satisfaction and overall satisfaction) and a total of 69 cases for value measures (dimensions value and overall value) (see Table 2). Cases were adjusted accordingly.

Value and Satisfaction Correlation Analysis and Results

Prior to the main statistical analyses of this study, an investigation was made of the correlation between the value and satisfaction constructs. This analysis included Pearson correlation, an indicator for linear association between two variables. Additionally, this analysis also included Eta (η) correlation, an indicator for non-linear association between two variables. Results of such analysis are provided in Table 3. These results suggest that there are no correlations (linear

Table 3. Eta and Pearson correlations for dimensions and overall measures

Var 1 (Y) * Var 2 (X)	Eta	Pearson	Relationship
Sa_Act * Va_Act	0.228	0.228	No observed relationship
Va_Act * Sa_Act	0.390	0.228	No observed relationship
Sb_Act * Vb_Act	0.345	0.339	No observed relationship
Vb_Act * Sb_Act	0.499	0.339	No observed relationship
Sc_Act * Vc_Act	0.239	0.224	No observed relationship
Vc_Act * Sc_Act	0.434	0.224	No observed relationship
Sd_Act * Vd_Act	0.438	0.407	No observed relationship
Vd_Act * Sd_Act	0.486	0.407	No observed relationship
So_Act * Vo_Act	0.359	0.308	No observed relationship
Vo_Act * So_Act	0.419	0.308	No observed relationship

or non-linear) observed between value and satisfaction measures. The results are quite profound as they suggest that value and satisfaction are two distinct uncorrelated constructs. This adds to the overall validity of the current study as the approach was to suggest learners' perceived effectiveness using two distinct components. Hence, it also adds to the validity of the Value-Satisfaction grids and the LeVIS index by indicating that these tools use two distinct measures. Additional information on the results of the Value-Satisfaction grids and the LeVIS index are provided further on in this chapter.

Factor Analysis and Results

Exploratory factor analysis was accomplished by using the PCA, which was used for two main purposes. The first was to help improve the instrument by eliminating e-learning systems characteristics that were not significant or not valid in the analysis of learners' perceived satisfaction with and value of e-learning systems. Detailed information on the methodology used is provided under the section *E-Learning System Characteristics and Instrument Adjustments*. Moreover, Cronbach's α reliability tests were done to check the reliability of the instrument and to help spot items that may reduce the Cronbach's α of each factor. The second was to help explore the main principal components resulted from the data and suggest new e-learning system dimensions based on such components for future studies. Detailed information on the methodology used is provided under the section *E-learning System Dimensions Analysis*.

The exploratory factor analysis was done using the PCA method for two main purposes. The first was in improving the instrument by eliminating e-learning system characteristics that were not significant or not valid in the analysis of learners' perceived satisfaction with e-learning systems and value of e-learning systems. Results of this analysis are provided in the section *E-Learning System Characteristics Analysis and Instrument Adjustments*. Moreover, Cronbach's α reliability tests were done to check the reliability of the instrument and help spot items that reduced the Cronbach's α of each factor. The second purpose of using PCA was in exploring the main principal components resulted from the data and suggest new e-learning system dimensions based on such components for future studies. Results of this analysis are provided under the section *E-Learning System Dimensions Analysis*.

E-Learning System Characteristics Analysis and Instrument Adjustments

The survey instrument includes two items for each e-learning system characteristic. One measuring the satisfaction with a given e-learning system characteristic, noted as *satisfaction item*, and the other measuring the value of a given e-learning system characteristic, noted as *value item* (See Figure 2). As suggested earlier, there were four e-learning system characteristics that were worded in a negative term to detect response set, one for each of the e-learning system dimensions (A_8, B_6, C_3, and D_8). Therefore, the survey instrument included eight items that were required reversal of the negative scores, four satisfaction items (A_{8_SAT}, B_{6_SAT}, C_{3_SAT}, and D_{8_SAT}) and four value items (A_{8_VAL}, B_{6_VAL}, C_{3_VAL}, and D_{8_VAL}). As these items provided assessment of the negative measure (negatively stated), it was necessary to recode the scores of those items prior to the full analysis, that is noted as *recode*. This recoding was done using a transformation of 7-(rated score) converting scores to a positive scale (1 to 6, 2 to 5, etc.). All responses were recoded. Furthermore, a second analysis was required to detect learners (cases in the data) that unintentionally marked the negative measures as positive however their overall responses are not constituted as a "response set." These cases were required a reflection back to the original negative score, that is noted as *reflected*. This reflection was done using a transformation of 7 — (recoded score) converting recoded scores back to the original scale (6 to 1, 5 to 4, etc.). This analysis utilized the Kolmogorov-Smirnov (KS) test in order to detect cases for reflection. The KS test was done separately for the satisfaction measures and for the value measures. Each KS test was comparing the scores on the four negatively worded items to the other 44 items in the survey. Cases were marked in four levels of the KS test on the satisfaction items and value items using difference equal 0, or between 0 and 0.05, 0.05 and 0.10, or 0.10 and 0.15. Four reflection levels were suggested for cases observed at these four difference levels of the KS tests. Following the recommendation made by Stevens (found in Mertler & Vannatta, 2001, p. 29) for outliers' analysis, it was also appropriate here to perform an additional four sets of PCA factor analysis for satisfaction and four for value, besides the two done (one for satisfaction measures and one for value measures) without any negatively worded reflection. The eight PCA factor analyses include two for each of the main data with reflected scores detected at the four difference levels by the KS tests (one for satisfaction measures and one for value measures at each of the four difference levels). A comparison was made between the five sets of results. The first one was done without reflection, noted as *no negative items*. The second one was done with reflection at a difference equal to 0, noted as *reflected no. 1*. The third one was done with reflection at difference between 0 and 0.05, noted as *reflected no. 2*. The fourth one was done with reflection at a difference between 0.05 and 0.10, noted as *reflected no. 3*. Finally, the fifth one was done with reflection at a difference between 0.10 and 0.15, noted as *reflected no. 4*. Based on the results of these five PCA factor analyses, a decision was made on what level of reflection should be considered as part of the final results based on the reliability test using Cronbach's α if deleted for the negatively worded items. Additional information about such methods is provided in subsequent paragraphs.

In an effort to improve the survey instrument, each e-learning system characteristic measure (noted as satisfaction item or value item) was examined using three criteria in order to consider it for elimination from or inclusion in the final proposed instrument. A separate analysis was done for all satisfaction items and another one was done for all value items. The first criterion includes an analysis of the PCA factor loading each item has when it loads into its principal component and how it was compared with the loadings of this item with the rest of the components. Items that load below 0.7 on a factor (separately on *satisfaction factors* and on *value factors*) were subjected to future investigation. As part of this investigation, a review of the first criterion was done to spot items that may load between 0.4 and 0.6 on more than the primary factor originally loaded. This investigation was done by plotting the items' factor loadings on two graphs: loadings on factor 1 vs. loadings on factor 2, and loadings on factor 3 vs. loadings on factor 4. This will generate two graphs for *satisfaction* factor loadings and two graphs for *value* factor loadings. In each graph the whole factor loading scale was divided into low and high. An observation was made on items that may load on the high-high quadrant of the factor loading space. This identified the items that load highly on two factors, indicating the need for further review. Such items were closely reviewed for the clarity of the text of the e-learning system characteristic. Revisions of the instrument were recommended as a result of this phase to improve the clarity of the instrument instructions as well as the text used for the e-learning system characteristics.

The second criterion includes the Cronbach α of the principal factor if that given item is not included in the principal factor. Each factor of the final results was subjected to Cronbach α analysis. As part of this analysis a total reliability measure for all the items in the factor is provided by the Cronbach α measure. Moreover, this analysis also provides Cronbach α reliability scores for each item in the event that it is deleted or eliminated from the factor. The resulted Cronbach α score is an indication of the reliability of the factor without the item. Consequently, if the resulting Cronbach α reliability score without the item was lower than the one with the item, this suggests that the item is a reliable measure and needed to increase the overall Cronbach α reliability score for that factor (Kerlinger & Lee, 2000, p. 655). However, if the resulting Cronbach α reliability score without the item was considerably higher (>0.10) than the one with the item, this suggests that the item may not be a reliable measure and needs further consideration by the other criteria for elimination from the revised instrument.

The third criterion includes an observation of similar vectors pointed by two (or more) items in the PCA factor loading bi-plots. New PCA factor loading bi-plots were done, similarly to the bi-plots shown previously using the absolute factor loadings, however these graphs also included lines plotted from the origin to each of the items. This resulted in scatter plot type graphs with vector lines from the origin for each item. The resulted plots helped spot items that coincide on two factors loading at a time, hence noted as *similar vector analysis*. This may suggest that the two items provide similar measure. Hence, a consideration can be made to eliminate the one with the shorter vector. This similar vectors criterion was not the only indicator for item elimination, but an additional indicator added to the Cronbach α proposed previously.

Each item was a candidate for inclusion in or elimination from the final survey instrument based on all the previously-mentioned criteria. However, the analysis of such items should have also taken into consideration the results of all three criteria of its counterpart item from the *satisfaction factors* or *value factors*. For example, if item A1_SAT (Item measuring *satisfaction* with e-learning systems characteristic *1* in e-learning systems Dimension *A*, hence *A1_SAT*) loaded between 0.4 and 0.6 on more than the primary *satisfaction factor* originally loaded, it was appropriate to investigate the loading of the counterpart item A1_VAL (Item measuring *value* with e-learning systems characteristic *1* in e-learning systems Dimension *A*, hence *A1_VAL*). In that case, if the counterpart item A1_VAL also loaded between 0.4 and 0.6 on more than the primary *value factor* originally loaded, this e-learning systems characteristic (A1) was subjected to second and third criteria investigation on both SAT and VAL analyses. In this case, if both items (A1_SAT and A1_VAL) also reduce the overall Cronbach's α reliability score for the factors they are a part of, and there is another item identified for each in the "similar vector analysis" with a better vector, this e-learning system characteristic (A1) was eliminated from the revised instrument. However, if the second and third criteria for both SAT and VAL measures did not suggest violations of such criteria (e.g., not decreasing the overall Cronbach's α reliability score for the factors or does not have a better vector in the "similar vector analysis"), the e-learning systems characteristics under investigation was not be eliminated from the revised instrument.

Results of the E-Learning System Characteristics Analysis

The main data was subject to exploratory factor analysis using PCA with varimax rotation done separately for satisfaction and value measures. Using the factor loading on both analyses, survey items were closely looked at for low loading (<0.4) or for medium to high loading (~ 0.4 to 0.6) on more than one factor. Additionally, the four e-learning systems characteristics (A_8, B_6, C_3, and D_8) expressed in negative terms required further analyses. As these items provided assessment of the negative measure (negatively worded), it was required to recode the scores of those items back to a positive scale, noted as *recode*. This recoding was done using a transformation of 7 — (rated score) converting scores to a positive scale (1 to 6, 2 to 5, etc.). All cases were recoded. Furthermore, another analysis was needed to detect learners (cases in the data) that unintentionally marked the negative measures as positive however their overall responses did not constitute a "response set." These cases required a reflection back to the original negative score, noted as *reflected*. This analysis utilized the Kolmogorov-Smirnov (KS) test in order to detect cases for reflection. Cases were marked in four levels of the KS test on the satisfaction items and value items using differences equal to 0, or between 0 and 0.05, 0.05 and 0.10, or 0.10 and 0.15. Four adjustment levels were suggested for the negatively worded measures at these four difference level of the KS tests. Results of the KS test and priority for case adjustments are noted in Appendix F. The additional four sets of PCA factor analysis for satisfaction and four for value besides the two already done (one for SAT and one for VAL) without any negative worded reflection were performed. The eight PCA factor analyses included two for each of the main data with reflected scores detected at the four difference level by the KS tests (one for SAT and one for VAL on the four difference levels) (see Appendices M and N). Results for satisfaction analyses indicate that reflected items group together and form a separate factor with no theoretical rationale supporting such grouping besides the reflection process (see Appendix M). Moreover, results for value analyses indicate that reflected items group together and form a separate factor, also with no theoretical rationale supporting such grouping besides the reflection process (see Appendix N). As a result, all four negatively worded e-learning systems characteristics (A_8, B_6, C_3, and D_8) were dropped from further analyses.

Another criterion was used to investigate reliability and validity of survey items, namely the Cronbach α of the principal factor if that given item is not included in the principal factor. Each resulted factor was subjected to Cronbach α analysis. As part of this analysis, a total reliability measure for all the items in the factor was provided by the Cronbach α measure and the reliability scores for each item in the event that it was deleted or eliminated from the factor (see Appendices M and N). As suggested earlier, these analyses must also consider the results of the satisfaction item as well as the value item. Only items that were observed as reducing the overall Cronbach α for the factor in both satisfaction and value are valid to be eliminated from the instrument. Results of this analysis suggested only one e-learning system characteristic (B12) to be dropped from further analyses.

As mentioned previously, an observation of similar vectors pointed by two (or more) items in the PCA factor loading bi-plots was done to suggest other items that were not eliminated from further analyses and provide similar measure to the ones eliminated (see Appendices O and P). Results of this *similar vector analysis* indicate that all 10 items (five satisfaction items: A_{8_SAT}, B_{6_SAT}, C_{3_SAT}, D_{8_SAT}, and B_{12_SAT}; as well as five value items: A_{8_VAL}, B_{6_VAL}, C_{3_VAL}, D_{8_VAL}, and B_{12_VAL}) had other items with a similar vector or a higher vector on the same path indicating that all 10 items can be eliminated from further analyses without losing their contribution to the overall factors. Consequently, the final analyses included only 43 out of the initial 48 e-learning systems characteristics.

E-Learning System Dimension Analysis

PCA was used on the data cleaned by the pre-analysis data preparation procedures. As suggested by the theories reviewed in chapter three, satisfaction measures and value measures are fundamentally different and represent different constructs. As a result, one PCA analysis was done for satisfaction measures, noted as *SAT*, and another PCA analysis was done for value measures, noted as *VAL*. Similarly to the preliminary PCA analysis done on the pilot data, this PCA analysis was expected to provide *satisfaction factors* and *value factors* separately. In the initial stage, PCA was allowed to extract as many significant factors as are suggested by the data. Based on both the accumulative variance added by the factors (through the use of the scree-plot), the eigenvalue for each factor, and by the Cronbach α for the factors, a decision was made on the number of factors that was appropriate. A second PCA analysis was done forcing the number of factors as suggested by the previous step. Moreover, the Cronbach α of each of the new factors proposed was retested to provide further evidence for validity and reliability of the factors. The *satisfaction factors* and *value factors* resulted were also compared with the four dimensions proposed in Table 2 in Chapter IV. New e-learning systems dimensions were then named and proposed based on the *satisfaction factors* and *value factors* resulted from this analysis. This analysis seeks to address research questions two and three (RQ2 & RQ3) by providing the relevant factors for learners' perceived *value* of e-learning systems and the relevant factors for learners' perceived *satisfaction* of e-learning systems.

Results of the E-Learning System Dimension Analysis

PCA was performed on the data remaining after the pre-analysis data preparation procedures. The first step of the PCA process as discussed earlier, provided nine *satisfaction factors* with cumulative variability of nearly 76% and quite high Cronbach's α (see Appendix I). Moreover, 10 *value factors* were resulted with cumulative variability of nearly 73% and relatively high

Cronbach's α (see Appendix J). The cumulative variance added by the factors and through the use of the scree-plot four *satisfaction factors* and four *value factors* were deemed appropriate (see Appendices K and L).

A second PCA analysis was done forcing the number of factors to four as suggested by the cumulative variance and by the scree-plot for the satisfaction measures and to four for the value measures separately using the 43 e-learning system characteristics. This resulted in four forced factors for satisfaction and four forced factors for value. The Cronbach α of each of the new factors resulted was retested to provide further evidence for reliability of the factors proposed.

Final results for the satisfaction PCA analysis are provided in Table 4. Four *satisfaction factors* were extracted with a total cumulative variance explained of nearly 60% with high Cronbach's α for the first three factors (0.946, 0.940, and 0.897 respectively) and a moderate Cronbach's α for the forth factor (0.571). The four new *satisfaction factors* were named: (1) course and professor; (2) technology and support; (3) learner and interface support; and (4) cost. Similarly, final results for the value PCA analysis are provided in Table 5. Four *value factors* were extracted with a total cumulative variance explained of nearly 61% with high Cronbach's α for all four factors (0.961, 0.857, 0.943, and 0.837 respectively). The four new *value factors* were named: (1) course, professor, and technology; (2) learners' environmental support; (3) classmates; and (4) technical support. These results address research questions two and three (RQ2 & RQ3) by providing the relevant factors for learners' perceived *value* of e-learning systems and the relevant factors for learners' perceived *satisfaction* of e-learning systems.

Results of the satisfaction PCA analysis show that two out of the four e-learning system dimensions suggested by prior literature (course and professor) were grouped together to form a new factor. This is an interesting result as it appears that for online learning students, e-learning systems characteristics related to the course and professor appears as integrated in respect to satisfaction with e-learning systems. The second factor resulted from the satisfaction PCA analysis (technology and support) is consistent with e-learning system dimension suggested by prior literature. However, the two other factors resulted from this analysis (cost and learner and interface support) are different than the e-learning system dimensions suggested previously by literature (Webster & Hackley, 1997). Some explanations for such deviance may lie in the fact that the current student population using the e-learning system under study is

Table 4. Satisfaction factors resulted from PCA analysis

PCA Varimax Rotated Component Matrix (Satisfaction)
Main Study (n=192) After eight outliers and five items eliminated

Factor Name	Item	1	2	3	4	Alpha if deleted	Characteristics
Course & Professor	C4_SAT	0.836	0.070	-0.024	0.098	0.9429	Quality of professor-to-student interaction
	C2_SAT	0.805	0.122	-0.015	-0.016	0.9436	Professor's attitude (across all professors)
	B7_SAT	0.794	0.185	0.183	0.079	0.941	Enjoyment from the courses/lessons
	C1_SAT	0.768	0.121	0.035	0.039	0.9436	Amount of professor-to-student interaction
	D1_SAT	0.728	0.125	0.251	-0.019	0.9423	Learning a lot in these classes
	C5_SAT	0.692	0.189	0.368	0.050	0.9421	Freedom of learning (selective seeking and processing of information)
	B2_SAT	0.677	0.327	0.314	-0.025	0.9419	Quality content of courses
	D5_SAT	0.654	0.079	0.342	0.221	0.9426	Being part of a 'class' although it was online
	B4_SAT	0.652	0.183	0.300	0.012	0.943	Interesting subject matter
	B3_SAT	0.652	0.179	0.285	0.022	0.9429	Amount of material in courses
	B11_SAT	0.621	0.331	0.368	0.101	0.9421	Organization of courses (content of courses, organization of assignments, etc. across all courses)
	D3_SAT	0.616	0.053	0.268	0.161	0.9438	Quality of interaction with classmates
	D2_SAT	0.606	0.038	0.296	0.147	0.944	Amount of interaction with classmates
	C7_SAT	0.577	0.217	0.172	0.367	0.9441	Online workload of courses
	B5_SAT	0.570	0.180	0.274	0.014	0.9443	Difficulty of subject matter
	C6_SAT	0.557	0.281	0.121	0.340	0.9454	Submission time window for assignments and quizzes
	B10_SAT	0.493	0.377	0.466	0.098	0.9435	Gathering information quickly
	D4_SAT	0.416	0.044	0.397	0.067	**0.9465**	Classmates' attitude (across all courses)
Technology & Support	A10_SAT	0.037	0.810	0.281	0.049	0.9322	Submit assignments from anywhere (via the Internet)
	A12_SAT	0.080	0.808	0.212	-0.035	0.9327	Access of all courses from one area (My WebCT)
	A7_SAT	-0.079	0.797	0.281	0.012	0.9337	Access to courses from anywhere in the world (via the Internet)
	A4_SAT	0.179	0.765	0.083	-0.069	0.934	System operation time (up-time)
	A6_SAT	0.052	0.741	0.271	0.061	0.9342	System security (discourage hacking, secure access, etc.)
	A9_SAT	0.203	0.739	0.241	-0.099	0.9345	Learning at anytime of the day (schedule flexibility)
	A13_SAT	0.233	0.730	0.234	0.062	0.9346	Taking quizzes remotely (off-campus)
	A11_SAT	0.180	0.716	0.123	0.151	0.9354	Different system tools (chat, bulletin-board or discussion forums, etc.)
	A5_SAT	0.230	0.710	0.000	-0.022	0.936	Reduced system errors
	A3_SAT	0.264	0.675	0.045	-0.041	0.936	Quality of technical support
	A2_SAT	0.189	0.672	0.072	0.053	0.9362	Quick answer from technical support after-hours via e-mail
	A14_SAT	0.074	0.670	0.064	0.225	0.938	Review course audios
	A1_SAT	0.180	0.655	0.016	-0.074	0.9374	Quick answer from technical support via phone
Learner & Interface Support	D12_SAT	0.147	0.156	0.751	0.050	0.8824	Ability to travel while taking online courses (for business or other)
	D14_SAT	0.260	0.154	0.717	0.248	0.8816	Attendance to family responsibilities
	D13_SAT	0.169	0.074	0.704	0.149	0.8856	Employer support and your ability to work while learning
	D11_SAT	0.233	0.088	0.666	0.110	0.8874	Reduced travel cost/time (to and from campus)
	D15_SAT	0.343	0.102	0.643	0.045	0.8848	Family support
	D7_SAT	0.046	0.298	0.625	-0.147	0.89	Your Internet and computer skills
	D6_SAT	0.362	0.232	0.589	0.024	0.8881	Your comfort with online learning and technology
	B9_SAT	0.268	0.296	0.538	-0.062	0.8899	Similar of interface across all online courses
	B8_SAT	0.395	0.353	0.522	-0.042	0.8869	Ease-of-use (with course content, navigation, interface, etc.)
	B1_SAT	0.415	0.380	0.431	-0.027	0.8912	Availability of course content
Cost	D9_SAT	0.271	-0.043	-0.039	0.845	-	Cost of courses
	D10_SAT	0.100	0.032	0.208	0.681	-	Cost of ISP and Internet access
	Cronbach	0.946	0.940	0.897	0.571		
	% of Var	36.43	12.52	5.49	4.75		
	Cumul %	36.43	48.95	54.44	59.20		

different than the student population used in the prior literature studies. It may well be that the current student population is mainly adults and working students, and thus making learner and interface support and cost factors that are more central for this changing student population in respect to satisfaction with e-learning systems. Moreover, although "cost" was suggested in prior literature as part of the learner dimensions, results of this analysis suggest that it appears as a factor by itself in respect to satisfaction with e-learning systems. This finding should be of great interest for universities and academic institutions

Table 5. Value factors resulted from PCA analysis

PCA Varimax Rotated Component Matrix (Value)
Main Study (n=192) After eight outliers and five items eliminated

Factor Name	Item	1	2	3	4	Alpha if deleted	Characteristics
Course, Professor & Technology	B2_VAL	0.745	0.198	0.224	0.191	0.9586	Availability of course content
	A10_VAL	0.710	0.254	-0.048	-0.015	0.9596	Submit assignments from anywhere (via the Internet)
	A9_VAL	0.702	0.168	-0.015	0.108	0.9596	Learning at anytime of the day (schedule flexibility)
	B1_VAL	0.694	0.201	0.131	0.188	0.9592	Availability of course content
	B3_VAL	0.693	0.096	0.392	0.007	0.9591	Amount of material in courses
	A5_VAL	0.691	0.177	-0.017	0.317	0.9593	Reduced system errors
	B4_VAL	0.690	0.227	0.347	0.032	0.9589	Interesting subject matter
	B11_VAL	0.683	0.267	0.168	0.214	0.9589	Organization of courses (content of courses, organization of assignments, etc. across all courses)
	B10_VAL	0.677	0.176	0.292	0.176	0.959	Gathering information quickly
	B8_VAL	0.670	0.282	0.084	0.239	0.9591	Ease-of-use (with course content, navigation, interface, etc.)
	C1_VAL	0.651	0.028	0.294	0.159	0.9595	Amount of professor-to-student interaction
	A11_VAL	0.637	0.177	0.083	0.146	0.9602	Different system tools (chat, bulletin-board or discussion forums, etc.)
	A12_VAL	0.635	0.310	0.050	0.143	0.9595	Access of all courses from one area (My WebCT)
	C6_VAL	0.624	0.284	0.163	0.182	0.9592	Submission time window for assignments and quizzes
	A6_VAL	0.623	0.179	0.116	0.296	0.9595	System security (discourage hacking, secure access, etc.)
	C2_VAL	0.602	0.222	0.325	0.168	0.9592	Professor's attitude (across all professors)
	B9_VAL	0.597	0.151	0.304	0.165	0.9596	Similar of interface across all online courses
	C4_VAL	0.594	0.117	0.288	0.226	0.9595	Quality of professor-to-student interaction
	B7_VAL	0.585	0.171	0.409	0.214	0.9593	Enjoyment from the courses/lessons
	A7_VAL	0.582	0.162	0.046	0.069	0.9605	Access to courses from anywhere in the world (via the Internet)
	D1_VAL	0.559	0.278	0.312	0.112	0.9595	Learning a lot in these classes
	B5_VAL	0.550	0.153	0.410	0.031	0.9599	Difficulty of subject matter
	A4_VAL	0.548	0.235	-0.021	0.315	0.9601	System operation time (up-time)
	D6_VAL	0.533	0.451	0.301	0.125	0.9592	Your comfort with online learning and technology
	C5_VAL	0.483	0.416	0.221	0.258	0.9595	Freedom of learning (selective seeking and processing of information)
	A13_VAL	0.483	0.331	0.040	0.241	0.9603	Taking quizzes remotely (off-campus)
	C7_VAL	0.480	0.258	0.157	0.197	0.9602	Online workload of courses
	D7_VAL	0.435	0.430	0.224	0.075	0.9602	Your Internet and computer skills
	D9_VAL	0.423	0.369	0.010	0.087	0.9609	Cost of courses
Learners' Environmental Support	D13_VAL	0.150	0.797	0.243	0.060	0.8182	Employer support and your ability to work while learning
	D15_VAL	0.197	0.787	0.222	0.113	0.8118	Family support
	D12_VAL	0.282	0.742	0.087	0.143	0.8236	Ability to travel while taking online courses (for business or other)
	D11_VAL	0.247	0.735	0.061	0.049	0.8349	Reduced travel cost/time (to and from campus)
	D14_VAL	0.343	0.664	0.163	0.108	0.8295	Attendance to family responsibilities
	D10_VAL	0.130	0.447	0.270	0.082	**0.876**	Cost of ISP and Internet access
Classmate	D3_VAL	0.157	0.149	0.902	0.036	0.9168	Quality of interaction with classmates
	D2_VAL	0.192	0.148	0.892	0.041	0.9194	Amount of interaction with classmates
	D4_VAL	0.132	0.246	0.882	0.053	0.9215	Classmates' attitude (across all courses)
	D5_VAL	0.167	0.271	0.822	0.126	**0.9449**	Being part of a 'class' although it was online
Technical Support	A1_VAL	0.138	0.139	0.128	0.890	0.7735	Quick answer from technical support via phone
	A2_VAL	0.284	0.069	0.031	0.886	0.7235	Quick answer from technical support after-hours via e-mail
	A3_VAL	0.432	0.143	0.075	0.733	0.7665	Quality of technical support
	A14_VAL	0.384	0.184	0.095	0.422	**0.8907**	Review course audios
	Cronbach	0.961	0.857	0.943	0.837		
	% of Var	39.66	9.44	6.35	5.08		
	Cumul %	39.66	49.10	55.46	60.54		

that offer online learning courses as students are sensitive to the costs related to taking online learning courses.

Results of the value PCA analysis show different factors. As suggested in Chapter III, no prior work was done in the development of factors related to value. Initially, it was the assumption that both satisfaction and value correspond to the same four e-learning systems dimensions. However, results of this analysis suggest that the two constructs have different factor structure. This is consistent with Rokeach's (1969) argument that *satisfaction* and *value* are two distinct constructs. Whereas one refers to the factors that appear significant in respect to satisfaction with e-learning systems, the other refers to different factors that appear significant in respect to value of e-learning systems.

The results suggest that in respect to the importance of e-learning system characteristics (or value), technology is considered by learners to be separate than the e-learning system characteristics associated with support. Furthermore, e-learning system characteristics related to technology were grouped with *course* and *professor* to form a new factor (*course, professor, and technology*). These results are intriguing as it implies that learners suggest that the importance of e-learning system characteristics related to *technology* are as important for them as e-learning system characteristics related to *course* and *professor* when learning online. The second factor suggested from the value PCA analysis results is the learners' support environment. This is consistent with prior literature suggesting that the support environment is significant in respect to the value of e-learning systems for online learners (Moore & Kearsley, 1996; Piccoli et al., 2001). Another factor suggested from this analysis is *classmates*. The results suggest that when learning online, e-learning system characteristics related to classmates appears to correlate and cluster together in respect to value of e-learning systems. Finally, the results suggest that e-learning system characteristics related to *technical support* appears to form a separate factor from e-learning system characteristics related to technology when learners consider the importance of such characteristics. One explanation for such results may be in the level of Internet and computer skills (D6) as well as learners' comfort with online learning (D7) suggested by the responses of this study. These results for the two measures (D6 and D7) suggest that the learners under study have relatively high technical skills. Consequently, it may be that these learners did not find technical support as important. Therefore, e-learning system characteristics related to technical support were separated to a new factor instead of being grouped with e-learning system characteristics related to technology as resulted in the satisfaction measures. Additionally, although these results suggest new factors for satisfaction and value, the remaining analyses of this study supports the four e-learning systems dimensions proposed by Webster and Hackley (1997). Future studies will utilize the new factors resulted from this work. Additional information about future research is provided in Chapter VIII.

Prediction of Values Analysis and Results

Another aim of this study was to investigate different linear and non-linear models in order to predict the value scores based on the satisfaction scores. As suggested previously, this study views value as the level of importance associated with each e-learning systems characteristic or each e-learning systems dimension. Thus, it is fruitful to compare the weights resulted from several techniques with the actual values elicited from learners. This can be done by developing predictive models using the satisfaction scores only and then compare the weights resulted with the actual values elicited from learners. As part of the development process, linear and non linear methods using conventional statistical techniques (such as ordinal logistic regression and multiple linear regression) as well as data mining techniques such as MCDA are explored to generate the outmost results. The next section contains three subsections that include detailed methodology for the development of the four types of imputed weights and the results of each of the methodologies conducted. The first subsection discusses methodology for imputing weights using multiple linear regression and the results of that analysis. The second subsection discusses methodology for imputing weights using ordinal logistic regression and the results of such an analysis. The third subsection discusses methodology for imputing weights using two non-linear models utilizing MHDIS and MUSA techniques as well as the results of both analyses. These three subsections are followed by a discussion of the methodology that was used in order to compare all four models with the actual values elicited from the user as well as the results of such a comprehensive comparison.

Results of the Prediction of Values Analysis

As suggested in Chapter IV, another aim of this study was to investigate different linear and non-linear models in order to predict the value scores based on the satisfaction scores elicited from learners. Consequently, linear and non-linear methods using conventional statistical techniques such as ordinal logistic regression and multiple linear regression as well as data mining techniques such as MUSA and MHDIS were employed in order to explore the method that generates the outmost results. The analysis was done using the methods mentioned previously to generate a predictive model on the satisfaction data, while the weights generated from such analyses, as suggested in literature, correspond to the value scores elicited from users. As discussed in Chapter IV, the ultimate goal is to impute the weights as accurately as possible that can then be transformed and compared to the actual values elicited from learners. An accurate imputation of the values can help by cutting in half the survey size in following data collections in the same settings and ultimately allows respondents to answer the survey in a shorter time. Additionally, the transformation of the weights is needed as the values elicited from users and the weights generated from some methods are not standardized nor in the same scale. The transformation is needed to normalize all scores (elicited values and weights generated from all four methods) in order to perform an adequate comparison. The additional three subsections provide the results of each of the methods conducted. Following, the *Comparison of Linear and Non-Linear Models to Predict Values* section provides additional information about such transformations and the results of the comparisons of all methods.

Multiple Linear Regression

As mentioned in Chapter III, previous literature indicated that values correspond to the level of importance. Ultimately, it is difficult to ask the learners to answer both the satisfaction level and importance level. The development of linear models to derive the value scores from the satisfaction scores is needed. As such, it is fruitful to develop models that can derive the value scores from the satisfaction scores elicited from the learners in order to reduce response time in future data collection of this setting and system. Therefore, the satisfaction scores elicited from users were used for the development of the predictive model. The value scores correspond to the learners assigned level of importance for each e-learning system characteristic or e-learning system dimension. Moreover, the standardized regression coefficients (SRCs) resulted from the analysis of the satisfaction scores that correspond to the level of importance that each variable has in regards to the overall measure. Consequently, a comparison was made between the values elicited from the user and the observed value of SRCs.

Webster and Hackley (1997) used multiple linear regression analysis in the development of their models. Following their approach, multiple linear regression analysis was used to develop five predictive models. The five models include one model for each of the four dimensions and one model for the overall measure. Results of each of the four models provided SRCs for each of the e-learning system characteristics when used to predict their associated e-learning system dimension. This was done for all four e-learning system dimensions.

Similarly, results of the overall model provided SRCs for each of the e-learning system dimensions when used to predict the overall measure.

The results of this analysis of the overall model provide the following equation:

$$S_o = \beta_{Sa} \cdot S_a + \beta_{Sb} \cdot S_b + \beta_{Sc} \cdot S_c + \beta_{Sd} \cdot S_d + c_{So}$$

Where $\beta_{Sa}, \beta_{Sb}, \beta_{Sc}, \beta_{Sd}$ are the SRC of S_a, S_b, S_c, S_d respectfully and c_{So} is the intercept coefficient for S_o. Similarly, results of dimensions A, B, C, and D provide the following equations:

$$S_a = \beta_{Sa1} \cdot A_{1\_SAT} + \beta_{Sa2} \cdot A_{2\_SAT} + ... + \beta_{Sa14} \cdot A_{14\_SAT} + c_{Sa}$$

Where $\beta_{Sa1}, \beta_{Sa2}, ..., \beta_{Sa14}$ are the SRC of $A_{1\_SAT}, A_{2\_SAT}, ..., A_{14\_SAT}$ respectfully and c_{Sa} is the intercept coefficient for S_o.

$$S_b = \beta_{Sb1} \cdot B_{1\_SAT} + \beta_{Sb2} \cdot B_{2\_SAT} + ... + \beta_{Sb12} \cdot B_{12\_SAT} + c_{Sb}$$

Where $\beta_{Sb1}, \beta_{Sb2}, ..., \beta_{Sb12}$ are the SRC of $B_{1\_SAT}, B_{2\_SAT}, ..., B_{12\_SAT}$ respectfully and c_{Sb} is the intercept coefficient for S_o.

$$S_c = \beta_{Sc1} \cdot C_{1\_SAT} + \beta_{Sc2} \cdot C_{2\_SAT} + ... + \beta_{Sc12} \cdot C_{7\_SAT} + c_{Sc}$$

Where $\beta_{Sc1}, \beta_{Sc2}, ..., \beta_{Sc7}$ are the SRC of $C_{1\_SAT}, C_{2\_SAT}, ..., C_{12\_SAT}$ respectfully and c_{Sc} is the intercept coefficient for S_o.

$$S_d = \beta_{Sd1} \cdot D_{1\_SAT} + \beta_{Sd2} \cdot D_{2\_SAT} + ... + \beta_{Sd15} \cdot D_{15\_SAT} + c_{Sd}$$

Where $\beta_{Sd1}, \beta_{Sd2}, ... \beta_{Sd7}$ are the SRC of $D_{1\_SAT}, D_{2\_SAT}, ..., D_{15\_SAT}$ respectfully and c_{Sd} is the intercept coefficient for S_o.

Results for each of the four models provide estimates (the weights, similar to SRCs in MLR) for each of the satisfaction measures when predicting their associated dimension satisfaction. This was done for all four e-learning system dimensions (A, B, C, and D). Similarly, results of the overall model provide estimates for each of the e-learning system dimension satisfaction measures (S_a, S_b, S_c, and S_d) when used to predict the overall satisfaction measure (S_o).

Multiple linear regression (MLR) analysis was used to develop five predictive models. The resulted SRCs from all five models were subjected to further transformations and analysis for the models comparison. Additional information is provided in the *Comparison of MLR and Ordinal Logistic Regression Models to Predict Values* section. Results of all five MLR analyses are presented in Figure 4.

MLR results for predicting the overall satisfaction (S_o) based on the four e-learning system dimension satisfaction measures (S_a, S_b, S_c, and S_d) indicate that all four predictors are significant ($p < 0.10$, marked with * in Figure 4) with an overall good prediction model:

$$R^2 = 0.724, R^2_{Adj} = 0.718, \quad F(df = 4, n = 192) = 122.53, p < 0.001.$$

MLR results for predicting the e-learning system dimension A satisfaction (S_a) based on the e-learning system characteristics satisfaction measures of that dimension ($A_{1\_SAT}, \ldots, A_{14\_SAT}$) indicate that seven of the thirteen predictors are significant ($p < 0.10$, marked with * in Figure 3) with an overall good prediction model:

$$R^2 = 0.784, R^2_{Adj} = 0.768, \quad F(df = 13, n = 192) = 49.55, p < 0.001.$$

Similarly, MLR results for predicting the e-learning system dimension B satisfaction (Sb) based on the e-learning system characteristics satisfaction measures of that dimension ($B_{1\_SAT}, \ldots, B_{11\_SAT}$) indicate that six of the 10 predictors are significant ($p < 0.10$, marked with * in Figure 4) with an overall good prediction model:

$$R^2 = 0.815, R^2_{Adj} = 0.805, \quad F(df = 10, n = 192) = 80.55, p < 0.001.$$

Figure 4. Results of multiple linear regression analysis

Multiple Linear Regression Coefficients
(n=192) After Internal Contradictory Overall Scores Adjustment
Satisfaction:

Overall (So)	Unst. Coeff	Stand. Coeff	Sig.	
(Constant)	-0.0407		0.863	
SA ACT	0.0948	0.1004	0.021	*
SB ACT	0.2518	0.2622	0.000	*
SC ACT	0.1829	0.2326	0.000	*
SD ACT	0.4802	0.4375	0.000	*

Model Summary

Overall (So)	
R Square	0.724
Adj R Sq	0.718
Std. Error	0.484
Sum of Squ	114.85
df	4
Mean Squar	28.71
F	122.53
Sig.	0.000

Dim. A (Sa)	Unst. Coeff	Stand. Coeff	Sig.	
(Constant)	-0.0437		0.826	
A1 SAT	0.0434	0.0460	0.389	
A2 SAT	0.0321	0.0320	0.583	
A3 SAT	0.2069	0.2090	0.000	*
A4 SAT	0.1778	0.1974	0.001	*
A5 SAT	0.1122	0.1270	0.034	*
A6 SAT	-0.0127	-0.0145	0.798	
A7 SAT	0.0407	0.0501	0.415	
A9 SAT	-0.0139	-0.0171	0.780	
A10 SAT	-0.0278	-0.0338	0.636	
A11 SAT	0.0987	0.1034	0.062	*
A12 SAT	0.1246	0.1405	0.031	*
A13 SAT	0.1044	0.1305	0.026	*
A14 SAT	0.1552	0.1754	0.000	*

Model Summary

Dim. A (Sa)	
R Square	0.784
Adj R Sq	0.768
Std. Error	0.465
Sum of Squ	139.53
df	13
Mean Squar	10.73
F	49.55
Sig.	0.000

Dim. B (Sb)	Unst. Coeff	Stand. Coeff	Sig.	
(Constant)	-0.1855		0.357	
B1 SAT	0.0966	0.0933	0.046	*
B2 SAT	0.1279	0.1338	0.027	*
B3 SAT	0.1239	0.1302	0.014	*
B4 SAT	0.0450	0.0486	0.368	
B5 SAT	0.0402	0.0382	0.387	
B7 SAT	0.2452	0.2780	0.000	*
B8 SAT	0.1498	0.1474	0.007	*
B9 SAT	-0.0061	-0.0056	0.910	
B10 SAT	0.0240	0.0230	0.671	
B11 SAT	0.1893	0.2162	0.000	*

Model Summary

Dim. B (Sb)	
R Square	0.815
Adj R Sq	0.805
Std. Error	0.417
Sum of Squ	140.28
df	10
Mean Squa	14.03
F	80.55
Sig.	0.000

Dim. C (Sc)	Unst. Coeff	Stand. Coeff	Sig.	
(Constant)	-0.5018		0.002	*
C1 SAT	0.0253	0.0256	0.615	
C2 SAT	0.2912	0.2988	0.000	*
C4 SAT	0.3390	0.3561	0.000	*
C5 SAT	0.2004	0.1685	0.000	*
C6 SAT	0.1640	0.1815	0.000	*
C7 SAT	0.0865	0.0881	0.015	*

Model Summary

Dim. C (Sc)	
R Square	0.864
Adj R Sq	0.859
Std. Error	0.432
Sum of Squ	221.61
df	6
Mean Squa	36.93
F	197.54
Sig.	0.000

Dim. D (Sd)	Unst. Coeff
(Constant)	0.3692
D1 SAT	0.1061
D2 SAT	0.1500
D3 SAT	-0.0274
D4 SAT	-0.0358
D5 SAT	0.1351
D6 SAT	-0.0146
D7 SAT	-0.0616
D9 SAT	0.0788
D10 SAT	0.0555
D11 SAT	0.1143
D12 SAT	0.0851
D13 SAT	0.1029
D14 SAT	0.0848
D15 SAT	0.1713

Model Summary

Dim. D (Sd)	
R Square	0.664
Adj R Sq	0.638
Std. Error	0.497
Sum of Squ	87.44
df	14
Mean Squa	6.25
F	25.25
Sig.	0.000

* - $p < .10$

Results of the MLR analysis for predicting the e-learning system dimension C satisfaction (S_c) based on the e-learning system characteristics satisfaction measures of that dimension ($C_{1\_SAT},...,C_{7\_SAT}$) indicate that five of the six predictors are significant ($p < 0.10$, marked with * in Figure 3) with an overall good prediction model:

$$R^2 = 0.864, R^2_{Adj} = 0.859, \ F(df = 6, n = 192) = 197.54, p < 0.001.$$

Finally, MLR results for predicting the e-learning system dimension D satisfaction (S_d) based on the e-learning system characteristics satisfaction measures of that dimension ($D_{1\_SAT},...,D_{15\_SAT}$) indicate that seven of the 14 predictors are significant ($p < 0.10$, marked with * in Figure 4) with an overall good prediction model:

$$R^2 = 0.664, R^2_{Adj} = 0.638, \ F(df = 14, n = 192) = 25.25, p < 0.001.$$

In summary, all five models provided good predictions with good Adjusted R^2 as noted in Figure 4. Further analysis, transformation, and comparison of the SRCs resulted from this analysis and the actual learners' elicited values will be done on the weights resulted from all five models. Additional information is provided in the *Comparison of Linear and Non-Linear Models to Predict Values* section.

Ordinal Logistic Regression

The current instrument includes both satisfaction and value measure. As suggested previously, answering both measures for each characteristic may be tedious for users. Consequently, the aim of this analysis was to impute the values from the satisfaction measures and cut by half of the survey size. In order to justify such action, an analysis of accuracy of the imputation of value scores is needed. However, the values imputed from these analyses are in a scale of 0 to 1, where the actual value scores from the current instrument are discrete in a scale of 1 to 6. As such, the results suggested from the multiple linear regression enjoy an unfair advantage when attempting to predict the dependent variable by allowing a non-integer predicted score. Since the variables in this study are ordinal $(6 > 5 > 4 > 3 > 2 > 1)$, ordinal logistic regression is also an appropriate analysis. Similar to multiple linear regression, the ordinal logistic regression analysis provided five models. These five models included one model for each of the four dimensions and one model for the overall measure. Results of each of the models provided weights (similar to the SRCs in MLR) for each e-learning system characteristic when used to predict their associated e-learning system dimension satisfaction measure. Additionally, it provided the weights for each of the e-learning system dimensions when used to predict the overall system satisfaction measure.

As just suggested, the dependent variables in these analyses are the satisfaction measures $(S_o, S_a, S_b, S_c,$ and $S_d)$. However, these measures are assessed by the instrument as discrete integer scores from 1 to 6. As such, the results suggested from the multiple linear regression enjoy an advantage when attempting to predict the dependent variable by allowing non-integer predicted scores. Since the variables in this study are ordinal $(6 > 5 > 4 > 3 > 2 > 1)$, ordinal logistic regression was also a viable appropriate. Similar to multiple linear regression, the ordinal logistic regression analysis was conducted five times, once for the overall, which used all four dimensions satisfaction as predictors and once for each of the dimensions that used all of the characteristic satisfaction measures for that associated dimension as predictors. Results of all five ordinal logistic regression analyses are presented in Figure 5.

Ordinal logistic regression results for predicting the overall satisfaction (S_o) based on the four e-learning system dimension satisfaction measures $(S_a, S_b, S_c,$ and $S_d)$ indicate that all four predictors are significant $(p < 0.10$, marked with * in Figure 5) with an overall reliable model:

$$-2 \text{ Log Likelihood} = 166.07, \chi^2(4) = 248.11, p < 0.001.$$

Ordinal logistic regression results for predicting the e-learning system dimension A satisfaction (S_a) based on the e-learning system characteristics satisfaction measures of that dimension $(A_{1\_SAT}, \ldots, A_{14\_SAT})$ indicate that six of the 13 predictors are significant $(p < 0.10$, marked with * in Figure 5) with an overall reliable model:

$$-2 \text{ Log Likelihood} = 227.62, \chi^2(13) = 268.18, p < 0.001.$$

Similarly, ordinal logistic regression results for predicting the e-learning system dimension B satisfaction (S_b) based on the e-learning system characteristics satisfaction measures of that dimension ($B_{1\_SAT},...,B_{11\_SAT}$) indicate that six of the 10 predictors are significant ($p < 0.10$, marked with * in Figure 5) with an overall reliable model:

$$-2 \text{ Log Likelihood} = 184.36, \chi^2(10) = 295.52, p < 0.001.$$

Results of the ordinal logistic regression analysis for predicting the e-learning system dimension C satisfaction (S_c) based on the e-learning system characteristics satisfaction measures of that dimension ($C_{1\_SAT},...,C_{7\_SAT}$) indicate that five of the six predictors are significant ($p < 0.10$, marked with * in Figure 5) with an overall reliable model:

$$-2 \text{ Log Likelihood} = 199.08, \chi^2(6) = 248.11, p < 0.001.$$

Finally, ordinal logistic regression results for predicting the e-learning system dimension D satisfaction (S_d) based on the e-learning system characteristics satisfaction measures of that dimension ($D_{1\_SAT},..., D_{15\_SAT}$) indicate that eight of the 14 predictors are significant ($p < 0.10$, marked with * in Figure 5) with an overall reliable model:

$$-2 \text{ Log Likelihood} = 243.23, \chi^2(14) = 204.55, p < 0.001.$$

The results of the ordinal logistic regression analysis are consistent with the results of the multiple linear regression analysis. Out of 29 significant variables found in the multiple linear regression analysis (see Figure 4), 28 variables were also found significant in the ordinal logistic regression analysis, which further confirms the validity of the results (see Figure 5). A_{12} is the only variable that was found to be significant by multiple linear regression analysis, whereas ordinal logistic regression analysis did not indicate it as significant although its p value is relatively small ($p_{A_{12}} = 0.112$). Moreover, D_{10} is the only variable found significant by ordinal logistic regression analysis, whereas multiple linear regression analysis did not indicate it as significant although its p value was also relatively small ($p = 0.131$).

In summary, all five models were statistically reliable as noted in Figure 5. Further analysis, transformation, and comparison of the estimates (or weights) resulted from these analyses and the actual learners' elicited values were done on the weights resulted from all five models. Additional information is provided in the *Comparison of Linear and Non-Linear Models to Predict Values* section.

Multi-Criteria Decision Aid (MCDA) Analysis

King and Epstein (1983) suggested that users' values of system characteristics may be better explained using nonlinear approaches (p. 40). Consequently, this study also attempted to explore the results of non-linear models and compare them with results of linear models as well as the actual values elicited from the learners. As discussed previously, there are several data mining techniques such as MCDA that were explored to provide weights of the satisfaction measures. These weights were then used in comparison with the SRCs from the linear models and the ordinal logistic regression and the actual values elicited from learners.

Multigroup hierarchical discrimination (MHDIS) method uses mixed integer linear programming to accurately estimate a piece-wise utility function of satisfaction (Doumpos, Zanakis, & Zopounidis, 2001), as shown in Figure 2 in Chapter IV. The MHDIS technique was used to develop five predictive models to estimate the four e-learning system dimension satisfaction scores and the overall satisfaction score based on a set of criteria (i.e., scores of the e-learning system characteristics satisfaction for each dimension and e-learning system dimension satisfaction). Hence, results of the analysis provide weights for each satisfaction item and dimension during each stage of the procedure. For each satisfaction measure, all weights resulted from the MHDIS sequential analysis were averaged to provide the associated weight for that given satisfaction measure. Therefore, the results of the overall model provide average weights $\overline{w}_a, \overline{w}_b, \overline{w}_c, \overline{w}_d$ corresponding to $S_a, S_b, S_c,$ and S_d respectfully. Similarly, results of the dimension A model provide average weights $\overline{w}_{a1}, \overline{w}_{a2}, ..., \overline{w}_{a14}$ corresponding to $A_{1\_SAT}, A_{2\_SAT}, ..., A_{14\_SAT}$ respectfully. Results of the dimension B model provide average weights $\overline{w}_{b1}, \overline{w}_{b2}, ..., \overline{w}_{b12}$ corresponding to $B_{1\_SAT}, B_{2\_SAT}, ..., B_{12\_SAT}$ respectfully. Results of the dimension C model provide average weights $\overline{w}_{c1}, \overline{w}_{c2}, ..., \overline{w}_{c7}$ corresponding to $C_{1\_SAT}, C_{2\_SAT}, ..., C_{7\_SAT}$ respectfully. Finally, results of the dimension D model will provide

Figure 5. Results of ordinal logistic regression analysis to predict satisfaction (overall and for each dimension)

Ordinal Logistic Regression

(n=192) After Internal Contradictory Overall Scores Adjustment

Satisfaction:

Overall (So)	Estimate	Sig.
SO ACT = 1	13.9388	0.000 *
SO ACT = 2	14.7408	0.000 *
SO ACT = 3	17.4733	0.000 *
SO ACT = 4	22.2525	0.000 *
SO ACT = 5	28.1331	0.000 *
SA ACT	0.3845	0.053 *
SB ACT	0.9173	0.001 *
SC ACT	1.0525	0.000 *
SD ACT	2.6974	0.000 *

Model Fitting Information

Overall (So)		
Model	Intercept Only	Final
-2 Log Likelihood	414.18	166.07
Chi-Square		248.11
df		4
Sig.		0.000

Dim. A (Sa)	Estimate	Sig.
SA ACT = 1	10.0659	0.000 *
SA ACT = 2	12.3496	0.000 *
SA ACT = 3	18.1542	0.000 *
SA ACT = 4	23.3704	0.000 *
SA ACT = 5	28.6850	0.000 *
A1 SAT	0.1749	0.499
A2 SAT	0.3278	0.279
A3 SAT	1.1164	0.000 *
A4 SAT	1.0292	0.000 *
A5 SAT	0.5485	0.035 *
A6 SAT	-0.0888	0.722
A7 SAT	0.2385	0.343
A9 SAT	-0.1050	0.682
A10 SAT	-0.1716	0.567
A11 SAT	0.5166	0.061 *
A12 SAT	0.4452	0.112
A13 SAT	0.5663	0.020 *
A14 SAT	0.8236	0.000 *

Model Fitting Information

Dim. A (Sa)		
Model	Intercept Only	Final
-2 Log Likelihood	495.79	227.62
Chi-Square		268.18
df		13
Sig.		0.000

Dim. B (Sb)	Estimate	Sig.
SB ACT = 1	13.0458	0.000 *
SB ACT = 2	17.2315	0.000 *
SB ACT = 3	20.2503	0.000 *
SB ACT = 4	27.2237	0.000 *
SB ACT = 5	32.9135	0.000 *
B1 SAT	0.5839	0.050 *
B2 SAT	0.7229	0.040 *
B3 SAT	0.6939	0.021 *
B4 SAT	0.2690	0.385
B5 SAT	0.2145	0.466
B7 SAT	1.4336	0.000 *
B8 SAT	0.7948	0.026 *
B9 SAT	0.0617	0.852
B10 SAT	0.0421	0.903
B11 SAT	1.1722	0.000 *

Model Fitting Information

Dim. B (Sb)		
Model	Intercept Only	Final
-2 Log Likelihood	479.88	184.36
Chi-Square		295.52
df		10
Sig.		0.000

Dim. C (Sc)	Estimate	Sig.
SC ACT = 1	11.5971	0.000 *
SC ACT = 2	16.3833	0.000 *
SC ACT = 3	20.8071	0.000 *
SC ACT = 4	26.6294	0.000 *
SC ACT = 5	31.5539	0.000 *
C1 SAT	0.2635	0.347
C2 SAT	1.4709	0.000 *
C4 SAT	1.8052	0.000 *
C5 SAT	1.0142	0.000 *
C6 SAT	0.8336	0.000 *
C7 SAT	0.4692	0.022 *

Model Fitting Information

Dim. C (Sc)		
Model	Intercept Only	Final
-2 Log Likelihood	562.30	199.08
Chi-Square		363.22
df		6
Sig.		0.000

Dim. D (Sd)	Estimate	Sig.
SD ACT = 1	8.8165	0.000 *
SD ACT = 2	10.2411	0.000 *
SD ACT = 3	13.4798	0.000 *
SD ACT = 4	19.4960	0.000 *
SD ACT = 5	23.5022	0.000 *
D1 SAT	0.4583	0.048 *
D2 SAT	0.6003	0.069 *
D3 SAT	0.0408	0.905
D4 SAT	-0.2383	0.293
D5 SAT	0.6253	0.027 *
D6 SAT	-0.0774	0.756
D7 SAT	-0.3534	0.199
D9 SAT	0.3618	0.009 *
D10 SAT	0.3128	0.073 *
D11 SAT	0.6129	0.016 *
D12 SAT	0.3397	0.234
D13 SAT	0.5611	0.028 *
D14 SAT	0.3702	0.213
D15 SAT	0.7905	0.006 *

Model Fitting Information

Dim. D (Sd)		
Model	Intercept Only	Final
-2 Log Likelihood	447.78	243.23
Chi-Square		204.55
df		14
Sig.		0.000

* - p<.10

average weights $\overline{w}_{d1}, \overline{w}_{d2}, ..., \overline{w}_{d15}$ corresponding to $D_{1\_SAT}, D_{2\_SAT}, ..., D_{15\_SAT}$ respectively. These results enabled a comparison between the values elicited from the learners and the average weights resulted from the MHDIS models. Additional information about the methodology of comparison is provided in the *Comparison of Linear and Non-Linear Models to Predict Values* section.

As suggested in the literature reviewed in Chapter IV, a second MCDA technique, Multcriteria satisfaction analysis (MUSA), was used. The MUSA method also uses piece-wise linear approximation in the development of additive utility functions based on a modified ordinal regression rather than linear programming as in MHDIS (Grigoroudis & Siskos, 2003). The other major difference between MHDIS and MUSA is in the development of the estimation of the utility functions. MHDIS generates piece-wise linear estimation for several utility functions for each variable (item) and finds the one that provides results as close as possible to the scores elicited from the learners. However, the MUSA model generates only one piece-wise linear estimation of the utility function. Moreover, due to the nested-satisfaction capabilities of the MUSA technique, this analysis was used to develop one predictive model to estimate the four e-learning system dimension satisfaction measures and the overall satisfaction measure based on a single set of all e-learning system characteristics satisfaction measures. Results of the MUSA analysis provided weights for each of the e-learning system characteristics satisfaction measure or e-learning system dimension satisfaction measure. Similarly to MHDIS's results, the results from the MUSA analysis enabled a comparison between the values elicited from the learners and the weights resulted from the MUSA models. Results of all five MHDIS analyses are presented in Figure 6.

MHDIS results for predicting the overall satisfaction (S_o) based on the four e-learning system dimension satisfaction measures $(S_a, S_b, S_c,$ and $S_d)$ indicate an overall good prediction model with 86.76% classification accuracy (n = 192). MHDIS results for predicting the e-learning system dimension A, B, C, and D satisfaction $(S_a, S_b, S_c,$ and $S_d)$ based on the associated e-learning system characteristics satisfaction measures of each dimension indicate very good models with 96.46%, 94.22%, 93.07%, and 92.40% classification accuracy respectively (n = 192).

The second MCDA technique used to develop predictive models and generate weights is the MUSA technique. As suggested previously, the main difference between MHDIS and MUSA is in the development of the estimation of the utility functions. MHDIS generates piece-wise linear estimation for several utility functions for each characteristic (or item) and finds the one that matches

Figure 6. Results of MHDIS analysis and weights

MHDIS Classification Models
(n=192) After Internal Contradictory Overall Scores Adjustment

Overall (So)	Ave Weight
SA	0.1700
SB	0.3533
SC	0.2400
SD	0.2367

Dim. A (Sa)	Ave Weight
A1	0.1447
A2	0.0873
A3	0.0595
A4	0.0805
A5	0.1081
A6	0.0500
A7	0.0343
A9	0.0084
A10	0.0563
A11	0.1028
A12	0.0623
A13	0.0583
A14	0.1474

Dim. B (Sb)	Ave Weight
B1	0.1138
B2	0.1519
B3	0.2083
B4	0.0547
B5	0.0306
B7	0.1356
B8	0.1116
B9	0.0331
B10	0.0627
B11	0.0976

Dim. C (Sc)	Ave Weight
C1	0.0936
C2	0.2772
C4	0.2072
C5	0.1271
C6	0.1367
C7	0.1582

Dim. D (Sd)	Ave Weight
D1	0.1030
D2	0.0166
D3	0.0487
D4	0.0649
D5	0.0631
D6	0.0181
D7	0.0546
D9	0.0727
D10	0.1543
D11	0.1122
D12	0.0794
D13	0.0489
D14	0.0259
D15	0.1378

Model Fitting Information

Overall (So)	
No. of Predictors	4
Total Classification Accuracy	86.76%

Model Fitting Information

Dim. A (Sa)	
No. of Predictors	13
Total Classification Accuracy	96.46%

Model Fitting Information

Dim. B (Sb)	
No. of Predictors	10
Total Classification Accuracy	94.22%

Model Fitting Information

Dim. C (Sc)	
No. of Predictors	6
Total Classification Accuracy	93.07%

Model Fitting Information

Dim. D (Sd)	
No. of Predictors	14
Total Classification Accuracy	92.40%

more accurately the scores elicited from the learners. However, the MUSA model generates only one piece-wise linear estimate of the utility function. Consequently, the MUSA technique provides a weight for each predictor (characteristic). Moreover, due to the nested-satisfaction capabilities of the MUSA technique, this analysis was used to develop one predictive model to estimate the four e-learning system dimension satisfaction measures and the overall satisfaction measure based on a set of all e-learning system characteristics satisfaction measures. Results of the MUSA analyses are presented in Figure 7.

MUSA results for predicting the overall satisfaction (S_o) based on the four e-learning system dimension satisfaction measures (S_a, S_b, S_c, and S_d) indicate a good overall prediction model with 67.19% classification accuracy (n = 192). Furthermore, results for predicting the overall satisfaction (S_o) based on the nested satisfaction of the four e-learning system dimension satisfaction measures (S_a, S_b, S_c, and S_d) and all 43 e-learning system characteristic satisfaction measures (13 As, 10 Bs, 6 Cs, and 14 Ds) with a total of 47 predictors, indicate an overall prediction model of 69.27% classification accuracy (n = 192).

In summary, all five MHDIS models indicated very good overall predictions with high (86.76%, 96.46%, 94.22%, 93.07%, and 92.40%) classification accuracy, whereas MUSA results indicated lower overall predictions with a classification accuracy of 67.19% for level 0 via level 1 dimension measures and a slight improvement to 69.27% for level 0 via nested satisfaction of both level 1 and level 2 predictors. Although MHDIS cannot accommodate nested satisfaction structure, results of MHDIS are much better. Further analyses, transformation, and comparison of the weights resulted from these analyses and the actual learners' elicited values was done on the weights resulted from all five models. Additional information is provided in the *Comparison of Linear and Non-Linear Models to Predict Values* section.

Comparison of Linear and Non-Linear Models to Predict Values

The main aim of this section of the study was to develop a reliable measure to impute the value scores from the satisfaction scores in order to cut down the size of the survey as noted in Chapter IV. Ultimately, a shorter survey may include satisfaction measures only, whereas the value scores can be imputed reliably. Consequently, it was appropriate to compare the weights resulted from the four methods (multiple linear regression, ordinal logistic regression, MHDIS, and

Figure 7. Results of MUSA analysis and weights

MUSA Classification Models
(n=192) After Internal Contradictory Overall Scores Adjustment

Overall (So)	Weight
SA	0.1326
SB	0.4900
SC	0.1468
SD	0.2305

Dim. A (Sa)	Weight
A1	0.0691
A2	0.0769
A3	0.0769
A4	0.0731
A5	0.0892
A6	0.0769
A7	0.0681
A9	0.0674
A10	0.0727
A11	0.0769
A12	0.0780
A13	0.0769
A14	0.0977

Dim. B (Sb)	Weight
B1	0.0644
B2	0.2153
B3	0.1030
B4	0.0794
B5	0.0789
B7	0.0879
B8	0.1000
B9	0.0692
B10	0.1000
B11	0.1020

Dim. C (Sc)	Weight
C1	0.0739
C2	0.6023
C4	0.1217
C5	0.0739
C6	0.0690
C7	0.0593

Dim. D (Sd)	Weight
D1	0.0714
D2	0.0714
D3	0.0682
D4	0.0714
D5	0.0714
D6	0.0714
D7	0.0714
D9	0.0548
D10	0.0588
D11	0.0729
D12	0.0714
D13	0.0990
D14	0.0714
D15	0.0750

Model Fitting Information

Overall (So)	
No. of Predictors	4
Total Classification Accuracy	67.19%

Model Fitting Information (Nested Satisfaction Predicting So via all L2 variables)

Overall (So)	
No. of Predictors	43 Char + 4 Dim =47
Total Classification Accuracy	69.27%

Figure 8. Value analysis: Performance measures results

Elicited Values vs. Weights from Four Methods

MEAN ABSOLUTE DIFFERRENCE				
Variable(s)	MLR (+)	MHDIS	MUSA	Ordinal
Level1	0.094	**0.053** *	0.121	0.156
Level 2 — A	0.049	0.035	**0.008** *	0.047
Level 2 — B	0.061	0.043	**0.023** *	0.062
Level 2 — C	0.083	**0.049** *	0.144	0.080
Level 2 — D	0.030	0.032	**0.008** *	0.037
OVERALL (#)	0.054	**0.039** *	**0.038** *	0.061

MEAN SQUARE DIFFERRENCE				
Variable(s)	MLR (+)	MHDIS	MUSA	Ordinal
Level1	0.015	**0.005** *	0.021	0.035
Level 2 — A	0.003	0.002	**0.000** *	0.003
Level 2 — B	0.005	0.003	**0.002** *	0.006
Level 2 — C	0.010	**0.003** *	0.038	0.008
Level 2 — D	0.001	0.002	**0.000** *	0.002
OVERALL (#)	0.005	**0.002** *	0.007	0.007

STD ERROR OF DIFFERRENCE				
Variable(s)	MLR (+)	MHDIS	MUSA	Ordinal
Level1	0.123	**0.069** *	0.146	0.188
Level 2 — A	0.055	0.043	**0.011** *	0.059
Level 2 — B	0.074	0.052	**0.040** *	0.077
Level 2 — C	0.100	**0.059** *	0.194	0.091
Level 2 — D	0.036	0.041	**0.011** *	0.043
OVERALL (#)	0.070	**0.049** *	0.084	0.083

(*) - Best performance measure score for a given variable/level

(#) - Overall, 48 questions and 192 responses

MARGIN OF ERROR FOR DIFFERENCE			
MLR (+)	MHDIS	MUSA	Ordinal
OVERALL (#) 0.141	**0.099** *	0.168	0.165

(+) - The Multiple Linear Regression has unfair advantages over all other methods as it produces a continuous predicted variable, where as MUSA, MHDIS and Ordinal Logit produces a discrete predicted variable

MUSA) with the value scores elicited from the learners in order to suggest which one provides the best prediction of value scores from the satisfaction scores. As mentioned before, weights of each of the four methods and the aggregated elicited value scores for each of the 47 value measures (43 e-learning system characteristics and four e-learning system dimensions) were transformed to a scale from 0 to 1. Subsequently, four performance measures were assessed: mean absolute difference (MAD), mean squared difference (MSD), standard error of difference (SED), and the margin of error for difference (MED). Results of the four performance measures are provided in Figure 8.

Results indicate that in spite of its unfair advantage of decimal predictions, multiple linear regression did not outperform the two MCDA techniques across all four performance measures. Moreover, ordinal logistic regression estimates of values were worse than those of the two MCDA methods across all four performance measures. Finally, the results indicate that MHDIS value estimates are reasonably accurate with an average 3.9% absolute difference from the actual values, standard error of difference about 4.9% and a margin of error 9.9%. The "margin of error" is a common summary of sampling error, which used in this analysis to provide a quantification of the error for the difference between weights resulted from a method and the actual values elicited from learners and is calculated as twice the standard error (95% confidence). Consequently, although both MCDA techniques (MHDIS and MUSA) outperform standard statistical methods

Figure 9. Results of perceived learning analysis: Pearson and Eta correlations

Pearson Correlation
(n=192, PercLearn No-Combined Categories)

	Overall Perc Learn	LEVIS_AC	VO_ACT	SO_ACT
LEVIS_AC	0.710 **	1.000		
VO_ACT	0.246	0.308	1.000	
SO_ACT	0.636 **	0.886 **	0.702 **	1.00

** Correlation is significant at the 0.01 level (2-tailed).

Eta Correlation (n=192)

	Overall Perc Learn
LEVIS_AC	0.768
VO_ACT	0.262
SO_ACT	0.736

(multiple linear regression and ordinal logistic regression), MHDIS provided the best overall prediction across all four performance measures. The results of these analyses are presented in Figure 8.

Perceived Learning Analysis and Result

As suggested in Chapter IV, it was fruitful also to investigate the relationship between overall perceived learning, a dependent variable measure in many pedagogical teaching effectiveness studies in technology mediated learning (TML) field, with the three main constructs measured in this study, namely overall satisfaction (S_o), overall value (V_o), and overall learners' perceived effectiveness (LeVIS). Results were done on the actual scores. Hence, S_{o_ACT} refers to the actual aggregated scores of overall satisfaction; V_{o_ACT} refers to the actual aggregated scores of overall value; and LeVIS $_{AC}$ refers to the actual aggregated scores of overall learners' perceived effectiveness. Additionally, as this analysis sought to investigate any relationship between these constructs, both linear (Pearson) and non-linear (Eta, η) correlations were measured.

Results show that perceived learning (noted as "PercLearn") is significantly correlated with LeVIS (Pearson Corr. = 0.71, $p < 0.01$, Eta Corr. = 0.77, n = 192) and is significantly correlated with Satisfaction (Pearson Corr. = 0.64, p

< 0.01, Eta Corr. = 0.74, n = 192) (see Figure 9). This is consistent with literature suggesting that satisfaction and perceived learning are correlated. However, perceived learning was found to have low correlation (Pearson Corr. = 0.246, Eta Corr. = 0.26, n = 192) with value suggesting no observed relationship between the two (see Figure 9). These results were not previously investigated in literature and provided added evidence for the validity for the use of value construct as a separate measure. Moreover, an ordinal logistic regression analysis was done using the three proposed predictors (S_o, V_o, and LeVIS) in order to predict perceived learning (PercLern). Results are presented in Figure 10 (left side). Although none of the predictors were found to be significant (at $p < 0.10$, overall satisfaction (S_o) was found to have $p = 0.136$), the overall model is reliable with:

$$-2 \text{ Log Likelihood} = 102.28, \chi^2(3) = 125.16, p < 0.001$$

(see Figure 10, left side). The estimates (or weights) show that perceived learning (PercLern) is LeVIS driven (largest weight), followed by the overall satisfaction (second largest weight), which is consistent with both Pearson and Eta correlations just noted. Moreover, the results show that overall value has the lowest weight among all three predictors (S_o, V_o, and LeVIS) in predicting perceived learning, which is also consistent with both Pearson and Eta correlations noted (see Figure 10, left side).

Since none of the three predictors (S_o, V_o, and LeVIS) was found to be significant at $p < 0.10$, however overall satisfaction was found to have $p = 0.136$, an attempt was made to group the few scores for low perceived learning in an effort to find significant predictors. This grouping was necessitated by the small number of cases with scores with low perceived learning. For PercLern = 1, there were a total of three cases out of 192 cases (~ 1.5%), whereas for PercLern = 2 there were a total of six out of 192 cases (~ 3%).

Consequently, grouping was proposed for the two low perceived learning scores (PercLern = 1 and 2). A second Ordinal Logistic Regression analysis was done using the same three proposed predictors with the newly grouped scores. Results are presented in Figure 10, noted as "PercLern Scores of 1 & 2 Grouped." None of the predictors was found to be significant (at $p < 0.10$), yet the overall model is reliable with:

$$-2 \text{ Log Likelihood} = 87.40, \chi^2(3) = 129.97, p < 0.001$$

Figure 10. Results of perceived learning analysis: Ordinal logistic regression

Perceived Learning Prediction from individual Sat, Val, and LeVIS
Ordinal Logistic Regression Analysis (n=192)
After Internal Contradictory Overall Scores Adjustment

PercLearn (No-Combined Categories)

PercLearning	Estimate	Std.Est%	Sig.
[PERCLEAR = 1]	3.2280		0.515
[PERCLEAR = 2]	5.3055		0.273
[PERCLEAR = 3]	6.4326		0.185
[PERCLEAR = 4]	7.5974		0.120
[PERCLEAR = 5]	11.5638		0.020 *
SO_ACT	1.6964	71.4%	0.136
VO_ACT	0.1020	3.4%	0.911
LEVIS_AC	2.9515	25.2%	0.694

PercLearn (Combined Categories 1&2)

PercLearning	Estimate	Std.Est%	Sig.
[PERCLEAR = 1]	1.3503		0.794
[PERCLEAR = 2]	2.3708		0.647
[PERCLEAR = 3]	3.4816		0.502
[PERCLEAR = 4]	7.5884		0.149
SO_ACT	0.8716	23.4%	0.468
VO_ACT	-0.9168	19.6%	0.366
LEVIS_AC	10.5012	57.1%	0.204

Model Fitting Information

Overall (PercLearning)		
Model	Intercept Only	Final
-2 Log Likelihood	227.44	102.28
Chi-Square		125.16
df		3
Sig.		0.000

Model Fitting Information

Overall (PercLearning)		
Model	Intercept Only	Final
-2 Log Likelihood	217.37	87.40
Chi-Square		129.97
df		3
Sig.		0.000

* p < 0.10

(see Figure 10, right side). The following equation provides the prediction probability for each category (1 and 2, 3, 4, or 5):

$$P(\text{Perceived Learning}) = \frac{1}{1 + \exp\left[-\left(b_o + .8716 \cdot S_{o\_Act} - .9168 \cdot V_{o\_Act} + 10.5012 \cdot \text{LeVIS}_{Ac}\right)\right]}$$

$$\text{where } b_o = \begin{cases} 1.3505 \text{ for category 1 and 2} \\ 2.3708 \text{ for category 3} \\ 3.4815 \text{ for category 4} \\ 7.5884 \text{ for category 5} \end{cases}$$

These results are consistent with the previous ordinal logistic regression analysis and with both Pearson and Eta correlations previously noted, showing that perceived learning (PercLern) is LeVIS driven (largest weight), followed by the overall satisfaction (second largest weight). Moreover, the results show that overall value has again the lowest weight among all three predictors (S_o, V_o, and LeVIS) in predicting perceived learning, and is also consistent with both Pearson and Eta correlations noted previously (see Figure 10, left side). Accordingly, results of these analyses addressed research question five (RQ5) by providing evidence on how the overall perceived learning measure related to the overall value, satisfaction and perceived effectiveness of e-learning systems.

The Value-Satisfaction and Effectiveness Grids of the E-Learning System Under Study

The Value-Satisfaction grids were developed in a similar manner to the SWOT proposed by marketing scholars (Andrews, 1987; Ansoff, 1965; Mintzberg et al., 1998; Porter, 1991). It was based on aggregated learner-elicited perceived satisfaction with e-learning system characteristics and dimensions as well as aggregated learner-elicited perceived value of e-learning system characteristics and dimensions. As suggested in Chapter V, aggregation using geometric mean provides appropriate results for cognitive measures over arithmetic mean. These aggregated measures result in two scores for each e-learning system characteristic (noted as *mean characteristic satisfaction* and *mean characteristic value*) and two scores for each e-learning system dimension (noted as *mean dimension satisfaction* and *mean dimension value*). The aggregated satisfaction score for each e-learning system characteristic is the *mean characteristic satisfaction* and noted as $\overline{S}_{a1}$,..., $\overline{S}_{a14}$, $\overline{S}_{b1}$,..., $\overline{S}_{b12}$, $\overline{S}_{c1}$,..., $\overline{S}_{c7}$, and $\overline{S}_{d1}$,..., $\overline{S}_{d15}$. It was calculated as:

$$\overline{S}_{a1} = \left(\prod_{i=1}^{n} \left(A_{1\_SAT} \right)_i \right)^{1/n},$$

where $\left(A_{1\_SAT} \right)_i$ is the *characteristics satisfaction* score rated by learner *i* for e-learning system characteristic A_1. And *n* is the number of cases in the data collected, which is 192 in this case study. In the same manner all other 47 *mean characteristic satisfaction* scores were calculated to provide the aggregated *characteristic satisfaction* score for all 48 e-learning system characteristics. Similarly, the aggregated value score for each e-learning system characteristic is the mean characteristic value and noted as $\overline{V}_{a1}, ..., \overline{V}_{a14}, \overline{V}_{b1}, ..., \overline{V}_{b12}, \overline{V}_{c1}, ..., \overline{V}_{c7}$, and $\overline{V}_{d1}, ..., \overline{V}_{d15}$. It will be calculated as:

$$\overline{V}_{a1} = \left(\prod_{i=1}^{n} \left(A_{1\_VAL}\right)_i \right)^{1/n},$$

where $\left(A_{1\_VAL}\right)_i$ is the *characteristics value* score rated by learner *i* for e-learning system characteristic A_1, and *n* is the number of cases in the data collected. In the same manner, all other 47 *mean characteristic value* scores are calculated to provide the aggregated *characteristic value* score for all 48 e-learning system characteristics.

The *mean dimension satisfaction* for each dimension is noted as $\overline{S}_a, \overline{S}_b, \overline{S}_c$, and $\overline{S}_d$. It will be calculated as:

$$\overline{S}_a = \left(\prod_{i=1}^{n} S_{ai} \right)^{1/n} \quad ; \quad \overline{S}_b = \left(\prod_{i=1}^{n} S_{bi} \right)^{1/n} \quad ; \quad \overline{S}_c = \left(\prod_{i=1}^{n} S_{ci} \right)^{1/n} \quad ; \quad \overline{S}_d = \left(\prod_{i=1}^{n} S_{di} \right)^{1/n},$$

where S_{ai}, S_{bi}, S_{ci}, and S_{di} are the *dimension satisfaction* score rated by learner *i* for dimensions A, B, C, and D respectively, and *n* is the number of cases in the data collected. Moreover, the *mean dimension value* for each dimension is noted as $\overline{V}_a, \overline{V}_b, \overline{V}_c$, and $\overline{V}_d$. It will be calculated as:

$$\overline{V}_a = \left(\prod_{i=1}^{n} V_{ai} \right)^{1/n} \quad ; \quad \overline{V}_b = \left(\prod_{i=1}^{n} V_{bi} \right)^{1/n} \quad ; \quad \overline{V}_c = \left(\prod_{i=1}^{n} V_{ci} \right)^{1/n} \quad ; \quad \overline{V}_d = \left(\prod_{i=1}^{n} V_{di} \right)^{1/n},$$

where V_{ai}, V_{bi}, V_{ci}, and V_{di} are the *dimension value* score rated by learner *i* for dimensions A, B, C, and D respectively, and *n* is the number of cases in the data collected.

The Value-Satisfaction grid for each dimension (noted as *dimension grid*) was constructed by positioning all the e-learning system characteristics of that dimension in the grid, where the *mean characteristics satisfaction* scores are positioned on the horizontal axis and the *mean characteristics value* score are positioned on the vertical axis as discussed in details in Chapter V. The *dimension grid* was developed for each of the four dimensions including the e-learning system characteristics as points in the grid. Furthermore, a Value-Satisfaction grid for the overall system (noted as *overall grid*) was constructed by positioning all the e-learning system dimensions as points in the grid, where the *mean dimension satisfaction* scores were positioned on the horizontal axis and the *mean dimension value* score were positioned on the vertical axis. The *overall grid* also included the four e-learning system dimensions as points in that grid.

Each aggregated score range was divided into two intervals representing *low* and *high*. Hence, the *mean satisfaction* score with e-learning systems was divided into *low satisfaction* measure and *high satisfaction* intervals respectively. Similarly, the *mean value* score of e-learning systems was divided into *low value* and *high value* intervals respectively. Additional information and interpretation of each quadrant in these Value-Satisfaction grids was provided in Chapter V.

There are several approaches proposed in literature in regards to the positioning of the cut-off-point between the low and high range of cognitive measures such as satisfaction and value. One approach suggests using the centroid of all points in the grid as the cut-off-point between low and high on both axes. One problem observed with this approach is the fact that this approach provides only a relative view, suggesting only the relative distance between the points in the grid, when a more accurate approach should look at the actual scale of the scores. Another approach suggests that in the case of no user scores in the low-low quadrant, it is more appropriate to rescale the cut-off-point between the low and high quadrants on both axes to 75% of the maximum scale (EBI, 2002). In this study as the measures scale ranges from 1 to 6, in the event that no scores will be below 3 in satisfaction and below 3 in value, resulting with 4.5 as the cut-off-point between low and high on both axes. The results of this analysis of the study addressed research question six (RQ6) by positioning the aggregated learners' perceptions of the overall value and overall satisfaction of the e-learning system under study in the Value-Satisfaction grid. This was done both for the overall system and separately for each of the four e-learning system dimensions as described in the preceeding paragraphs.

The Value-Satisfaction grids were developed for aggregated learners' measures of perceived satisfaction with e-learning system characteristics and dimensions, as well as aggregated learners perceived value of e-learning system characteristics and dimensions. As suggested previously, aggregation using geometric mean often provides adequate results when aggregating cognitive measures over arithmetic mean. Therefore, geometric mean was used in aggregating the two scores for each e-learning system characteristic (*mean characteristic satisfaction* and *mean characteristic value*) and two scores for each e-learning system dimension (*mean dimension satisfaction* and *mean dimension value*).

The Value-Satisfaction grids were constructed for the four dimensions (noted as *dimension grid*) and one for the overall system (noted as *overall grid*) using a cut-off-point between the low and high quadrants on both axes, set to 75% of the maximum scale, as suggested earlier. Additionally, effectiveness curves were also superimposed on the Value-Satisfaction grids for those LeVIS levels that correspond to the cut-off-point in order to divide the quadrants as noted in Chapter VI. The three LeVIS levels corresponding to the 0.75% of maximum scale cut-off-point are 0.375, 0.5625, and 0.75. Results are presented in Figures 11, 12, 13, 14, and 15 for Value-Satisfaction Dimension Grid for dimensions A, B, C, D, and Value-Satisfaction overall grid, respectively. Additionally, Figure 16 includes all 43 e-learning systems characteristics and four e-learning systems dimensions as well as the overall system and the effectiveness curves superimposed on the grid.

Results of the Value-Satisfaction Dimension Grid for dimension A (Figure 11) indicate that five e-learning system characteristics (A_1, A_2, A_3, A_4, and A_5) from the *technology and support* dimension are in the high-value-low-satisfaction quadrant (Q1). This implies that support via phone, support via e-mail, quality of support, system up-time, and reduced system errors are of high importance to students but have low satisfaction, suggesting first priority for improvement in such e-learning system characteristics of dimension A (technology and support). Results also indicate that seven e-learning system characteristics (A_6, $A_7, A_9, A_{10}, A_{11}, A_{12}$ and A_{13}) from the *technology and support* dimension are in the high-value-high-satisfaction quadrant (Q2), implying that system security, access to courses, learning at anytime, submit assignments from anywhere, different system tools, access of all courses from one area (portal), and taking quizzes remotely (off-campus) are high performance e-learning system characteristics that should be highlighted as part of the strengths of the e-learning system under study. One e-learning systems characteristic (A_{14}) from the *technology and support* dimension was resulted in the low-value-low-satisfaction quadrant (Q3) implying that course audios might not be needed as they are not important nor learners are satisfied from them when learning online. No e-learning system characteristics from the *technology and support* dimension were found to be in the low-value- high-satisfaction quadrant (Q4) implying that no wasted resources were found on any of the e-learning systems characteristics of dimension A (technology and support).

Results of the Value-Satisfaction Dimension Grid for dimension B (Figure 12) indicate that four e-learning system characteristics (B3, B4, B5, and B7) from the course dimension in the high-value-low-satisfaction quadrant (Q1). This implies that course content, interesting subject matter, difficulty of subject matter, and enjoyment from courses are of high importance to students but have low satisfaction suggesting first priority for improvement in such e-learning

Figure 11. Value-satisfaction dimension grid and effectiveness curves for dimension A

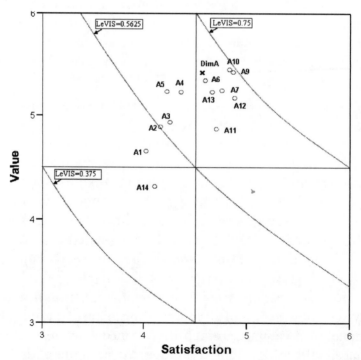

Dimension A: Technology and support; n = 192, after internal contradictory overall scores adjustment; low/high cut-off at 75% of scale maximum (6)

system characteristics of dimension B (course). Also, results of this grid indicate that six e-learning system characteristics ($B_1, B_2, B_8, B_9, B_{10}$, and B_{11}) from the *course* dimension are in the high-value-high-satisfaction quadrant (Q2), implying that availability of course content, quality content of courses, ease-of-use (with course content, navigation, interface, etc.), similarity of interface across all online courses, gathering information quickly, and organization of courses (content of courses, organization of assignments, etc. across all courses) are high performance e-learning system characteristics that should be highlighted as part of the strengths of the e-learning system under study. No e-learning system characteristic from the *Course* dimension were found in the low-value-low-satisfaction quadrant (Q3) and no e-learning system characteristics from the *course* dimension were found to be in the low-value-high-satisfaction quadrant (Q4) implying no e-learning system characteristics from

Figure 12. Value-satisfaction dimension grid and effectiveness curves for dimension B

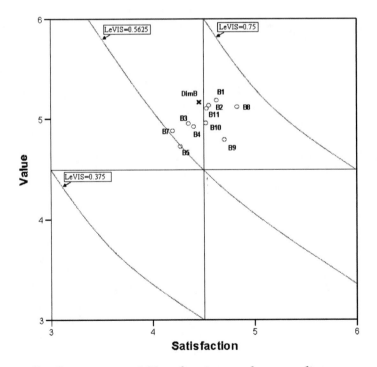

Dimension B: Course; n = 192, after internal contradictory overall scores adjustment; low/high cut-off at 75% of scale maximum (6)

the *course* dimension may need to discard or no wasted resources were found on any of the e-learning system characteristics of dimension B (course).

Results of the Value-Satisfaction Dimension Grid for dimension C (Figure 13) indicate that five e-learning system characteristics (C_1, C_2, C_4, C_6 and C_7) from the *professor* dimension are in the high-value-low-satisfaction quadrant (Q1). This implies that the mount of professor-to-student interactions, professor's attitude, quality of professor-to-student interactions, submission time window for assignments and quizzes, and online workload of courses are of high importance to students but have low satisfaction, suggesting first priority for improvement in such e-learning system characteristics of dimension C (professor). Results of this grid also indicate that one e-learning systems characteristic (C5) from the *professor* dimension is in the high-value-high-satisfaction quadrant (Q2), implying that freedom of learning (selective seeking and

Figure 13. Value-satisfaction dimension grid and effectiveness curves for dimension C

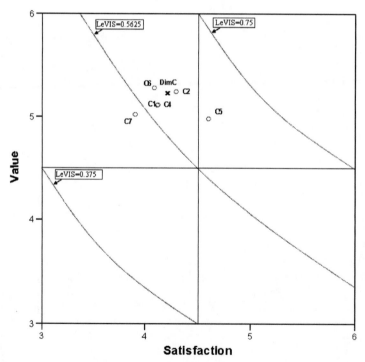

Dimension C: Professor; n = 192, after internal contradictory overall scores adjustment; low/high cut-off at 75% of scale maximum (6)

processing of information) should be highlighted as a strength of the e-learning system under study. No e-learning system characteristic from the *professor* dimension was found in the low-value-low-satisfaction quadrant (Q3) and no e-learning system characteristics from the *professor* dimension were found to be in the low-value-high-satisfaction quadrant (Q4) implying no e-learning system characteristics from the *professor* dimension may need to discard or no wasted resources were found on any of the e-learning system characteristics of dimension C (professor).

Results of the Value-Satisfaction Dimension Grid for dimension D (Figure 14) indicate that three e-learning system characteristics (D_1, D_9 and D_{10}) from the *learner* dimension are in the high-value-low-satisfaction quadrant (Q1). Due to the very low satisfaction (2.85) of D9 it was the only e-learning system characteristic not plotted in the grid. This implies that learning a lot in these

Figure 14. Value-satisfaction dimension grid and effectiveness curves for dimension D

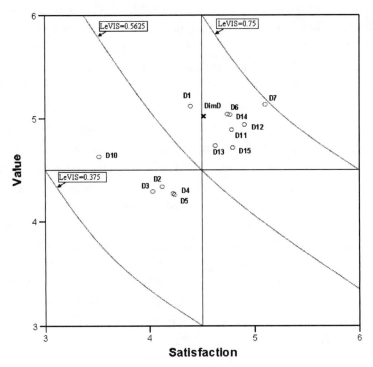

Dimension D: Learner; n = 192, after internal contradictory overall scores adjustment; low/high cut-off at 75% of scale maximum (6)

classes, cost of courses, and cost of ISP and Internet access have high importance for students but have low satisfaction, suggesting first priority for improvement in such e-learning system characteristics of dimension D (learner). Also, results of this grid indicate that seven e-learning system characteristics $(D_6, D_7, D_{11}, D_{12}, D_{13}, D_{14}$ and $D_{15})$ from the *learner* dimension are in the high-value-high-satisfaction quadrant (Q2), implying that learners' comfort with online learning and technology, learners' perceived Internet and computer skills, reduced travel cost/time (to and from campus), ability to travel while taking online courses (for business or other), employer support, attendance to family responsibilities, and family support are high performance e-learning system characteristics that should be highlighted as part of the strengths of the e-learning system under study. Four e-learning systems characteristics $(D_2, D_3, D_4,$ and $D_5)$ from the *learner* dimension were placed in the low-value-low-satisfaction quadrant (Q3), implying that the amount of interaction with classmates, quality of interaction with classmates, classmates' attitude, and being part of a "class" do not seem to be effective as they are not important nor learners are satisfied from it when learning online. Moreover, the LeVIS score for these four e-learning systems characteristics $(D_2, D_3, D_4,$ and $D_5)$ is low indicating further support. Additional information will be discussed in the LeVIS results to follow. These results suggest that for e-learning students may not find classmates an effective part of e-learning. No e-learning system characteristics from the *learner* dimension was found to be in the low-value-high-satisfaction quadrant (Q4) implying no wasted resources were found on any of the e-learning systems characteristics of dimension D (learner).

Finally, results of the Value-Satisfaction overall grid (Figure 15) indicate that e-learning system dimension B (courses) and C (professor) are in the high-value-low-satisfaction quadrant (Q1) implying that both the course and the professor dimensions are of high importance for students but of low satisfaction. This suggests that administrators of the e-learning system under study may need to focus their first attention for the improvement of these two e-learning systems dimensions (*courses* and *professor*). That may include enhancing courses with some games and adding some interactive features to the course content. Moreover, it may also suggest that seminars and workshops are needed to improve professors' performances (such as the amount of professor-to-student interaction, professor's attitude, quality of professor-to-student interaction, etc.). Results of this overall grid also indicate that in general, e-learning system dimensions A (technology and support) and D (learner) are in the high-value-high-satisfaction quadrant (Q2) implying that both the *tech-*

nology and support dimension as well as the *learner* dimension are effective and should be highlighted as part of the strengths of the e-learning system under study. No e-learning systems dimensions were found in the low-value-low-satisfaction quadrant (Q3) or the low-value-high-satisfaction quadrant (Q4).

Figure 16 integrates all the previous five grids together including all 43 e-learning system characteristics, four e-learning system dimensions, and the overall system. Results from this grid suggest some added interesting observations. For example, it is evident that in general, professor related e-learning system characteristics (Cs) appears to have high-value and low-satisfaction.

Figure 15. Value-satisfaction overall grid and effectiveness curves for overall system

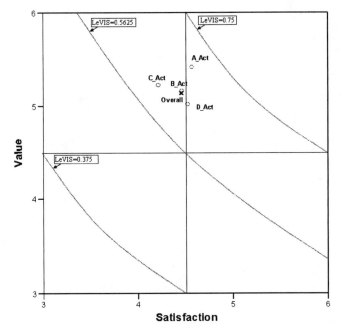

Overall e-learning system; n = 192, after internal contradictory overall scores adjustment; low/high cut-off at 75% of scale maximum (6)

Legend:

Dimension A: Technology and support

Dimension B: Course

Dimension C: Professor

Dimension D: Learner

Moreover, it is evident that classmates related e-learning system characteristics group together and appears to have low-value and low-satisfaction suggesting that online learning students may find classmates or classmates related e-learning system characteristics as ineffective (see Figure 16). The results of this analysis of the study addressed research question six (RQ6) by positioning the

Figure 16. Value-satisfaction dimension and overall grid including effectiveness curves for dimensions A, B, C, D, and overall

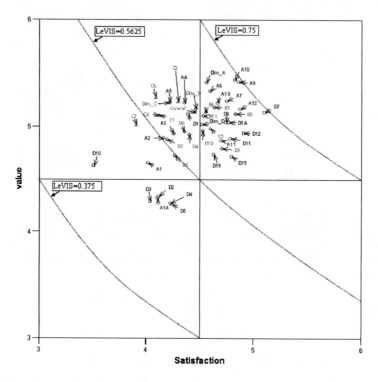

All 43 characteristics, four dimensions, and overall system; n = 192, after internal contradictory overall scores adjustment; low/high cut-off at 75% of scale maximum (6)

Legend:

Dimension A: Technology and support (O)

Dimension B: Course (◇)

Dimension C: Professor (△)

Dimension D: Learner (□)

Overall (x)

aggregated learners' perceptions of the overall value and overall satisfaction of the e-learning system under study in the Value-Satisfaction grid and superimpose it with the effectiveness curves. This was done both for the overall system and separately for each of the four e-learning system dimensions as described previously. Implications for future studies resulting from these Value-Satisfaction grids for the e-learning system under study is presented and discussed in the next chapter.

The LeVIS Index for the E-Learning System Under Study

LeVIS is proposed as a benchmarking tool combining the learners' perceived value and satisfaction in order to indicate learners' perceived e-learning systems effectiveness. Although the Value-Satisfaction grid proposed provides an indication for action and improvement priorities for e-learning system dimensions and e-learning systems characteristics, it is not providing a measure of the magnitude of e-learning systems effectiveness. The LeVIS index provides that measure as an overall index of learners' perceived effectiveness of e-learning systems by combining e-learning systems *value* measures and e-learning systems *satisfaction* measures. The Value-Satisfaction grid suggests that it is not sufficient that only value or only satisfaction measures are high, rather the combination of both value and satisfaction. Consequently, the LeVIS index was proposed as the multiplication of the *overall satisfaction* (S_o) by the *overall value* (V_o). LeVIS will provide a score of the overall magnitude of the effectiveness of e-learning system under study (see Figure 4 in Chapter III). The two items (S_o and V_o) are measured on a scale of 1 to 6. Bailey and Pearson (1983) suggested calibrating the overall score by dividing the actual score by the maximum possible score in the evaluating scale (p. 534). Therefore, the multiplication of the two measures was calibrated to provide the LeVIS index on a scale from 0 to 1 by dividing by 36. The LeVIS index was calculated as:

$$\text{LeVIS} = \left(\frac{1}{36}\right) \cdot V_o \cdot S_o \quad \Rightarrow \quad 0 \le \text{LeVIS} \le 1$$

The results provide assessment of the magnitude of learners' perceived effectiveness integrating all learners' *dimension value* measures and *dimensions satisfaction* measures with the e-learning system under study. The magnitude of LeVIS provides that measure by suggesting that when LeVIS is near 0, this indicates very low learners' perceived e-learning systems effectiveness. When LeVIS is near 1, this indicates very high learners' perceived e-learning systems effectiveness. This measure provides that if only one of the two measures (S_o or V_o) is high, the overall system measure (LeVIS) score is not high. One observed limitation of LeVIS is due to the equal importance given for value and satisfaction. For example, if $S_o = 5$ and $V_o = 6$, LeVIS produces the same measure as if $S_o = 6$ and $V_o = 5$. However, as indicated by the *effective* quadrant (Q2) of the Value-Satisfaction grid, it is the combination of both high-value and high-satisfaction that indicate high effectiveness of e-learning systems.

Similar effectiveness LeVIS indices were calculated for the four e-learning systems dimensions. These indices were noted as E_a, E_b, E_c, and E_d (See Figure 2 in Chapter VI) and were calculated as:

$$E_a = \left(\frac{1}{36}\right) \cdot V_a \cdot S_a; \; E_b = \left(\frac{1}{36}\right) \cdot V_b \cdot S_b; \; E_c = \left(\frac{1}{36}\right) \cdot V_c \cdot S_c; \; E_d = \left(\frac{1}{36}\right) \cdot V_d \cdot S_d$$

The results of each of the four indices provides assessment of the magnitude of learners' perceived effectiveness with the e-learning systems dimension by integrating all learners' *characteristic value* measures and *characteristic satisfaction* measures with the e-learning system under study. The magnitude of each index provides a measure of effectiveness suggesting that when an index (E_a, E_b, E_c, or E_d) is near 0, this indicates very low learners' perceived e-learning systems effectiveness for that dimension. When an index (E_a, E_b, E_c, or E_d) is near 1, this indicates very high learners' perceived e-learning systems effectiveness for that dimension. The results of this analysis of the study addresses research question seven (RQ7) by providing the learners' perceived effectiveness of e-learning systems as implied by LeVIS. This was done by integrating all learners' value measures and satisfaction measures for each of the e-learning systems dimension and overall system, as discussed previously.

The Value-Satisfaction grids provide an indication for e-learning systems effectiveness (low in Q3, high in Q2) and improvement priorities for e-learning systems dimensions as well as e-learning system characteristics. However, it is not providing a measure of the magnitude of e-learning systems effectiveness. Consequently, as proposed in Chapter VI, LeVIS provides a benchmarking tool combining the learners' perceived value and satisfaction in order to indicate learners' perceived e-learning systems effectiveness.

As suggested in Chapter VI, the LeVIS index is based on the multiplication of the *satisfaction* measures by the *value* measures. LeVIS provides a score of the overall magnitude of the e-learning system effectiveness under study (see Figure 2 in Chapter VI), whereas similar indices (E_a, E_b, E_c, and E_d) provide four scores of the magnitude of the effectiveness for the four e-learning systems dimensions (dimensions A, B, C, and D). Results are presented in Figures 17, 18, 19, 20, and 21 (in the current chapter) for the effectiveness of e-learning system characteristics in dimensions A, B, C, and D, and for the effectiveness of e-learning system dimensions as well as the overall LeVIS.

The magnitude of LeVIS provides assessment of the magnitude of learners' perceived effectiveness by suggesting that when LeVIS is near 0, this indicates very low learners' perceived e-learning systems effectiveness. When LeVIS is near 1, this indicates very high learners' perceived e-learning systems effectiveness. Similarly, the other indices for learners' perceived effectiveness of e-learning systems characteristics and of e-learning systems dimensions were calculated.

Results of the learners' perceived e-learning systems effectiveness of dimension A characteristics (technology and support) suggest relatively lower effectiveness for quick support via phone (A_1), quick support after-hours via e-mail (A_2), quality of support (A_3), and course audios (A_{14}) (see Figure 17). Furthermore, the results also suggest relatively high effectiveness for learning at anytime of the day (schedule flexibility) (A_9), the ability to submit assignments from anywhere (via the Internet) (A_{10}), and access to all courses from one area (portal) (A_{12}) (see Figure 17).

Results of the learners' perceived e-learning systems effectiveness of dimension B characteristics (course) suggest relatively lower effectiveness for difficulty of subject matter (B_5) and enjoyment from the courses/lessons (B_7) (see Figure 18). Moreover, the results also suggest relatively high effectiveness for availability of course content (B_1), quality content of courses (B_2), ease-of-use (with course content, navigation, interface, etc.) (B_8), and organization of courses (B_{11}) (see Figure 18).

Results of the learners' perceived e-learning systems effectiveness of dimension C characteristics (professor) suggest relatively lower effectiveness for quality of professor-to-student interaction (C_4) and online workload of courses (C_7) (see Figure 19). Additionally, the results also suggest relatively high effectiveness for freedom of learning (selective seeking and processing of information) (C_5) (see Figure 19).

Results of the learners' perceived e-learning systems effectiveness of dimension D characteristics (learner) suggest relatively lower effectiveness for e-learning system characteristics such as classmate related e-learning systems characteristics (D_2, D_3, D_4, and D_5), cost of courses (D_9), and cost of ISP and Internet access (D_{10}) (see Figure 20). Furthermore, the results also suggest relatively high effectiveness for learners' perceived comfort with online learning and technology (D_6), learners' perceived Internet and computer skills (D_7), reduced travel cost/time (to and from campus) (D_{11}), ability to travel while taking online courses (for business or other) (D_{12}), and attendance to family responsibilities (D_{14}) (see Figure 20).

The results of this analysis addressed research question seven (RQ7) by providing the learners' perceived effectiveness of e-learning systems as implied by LeVIS. Results of the LeVIS index (Figure 21) indicate that overall, the e-learning system under study is moderately effective (LeVIS = 0.637). Moreover, it evidently indicates relatively lower effectiveness for e-learning system dimension C (professor), and relatively higher effectiveness for e-learning system dimension A (technology and support). This is consistent to the results suggested from the Value-Satisfaction grids, indicating that, in general, more attention should be placed in e-learning systems characteristics from the *professor* dimension, while some e-learning systems characteristics from the *technology and support* dimension should be used in advertising and highlighted as the strength of the e-learning system under study.

Figure 17. LeVIS index of e-learning system characteristics in dimension A

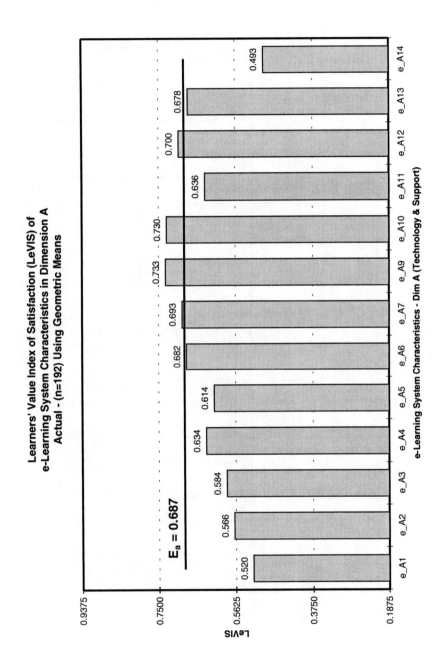

Figure 18. LeVIS index of e-learning system characteristics in dimension B

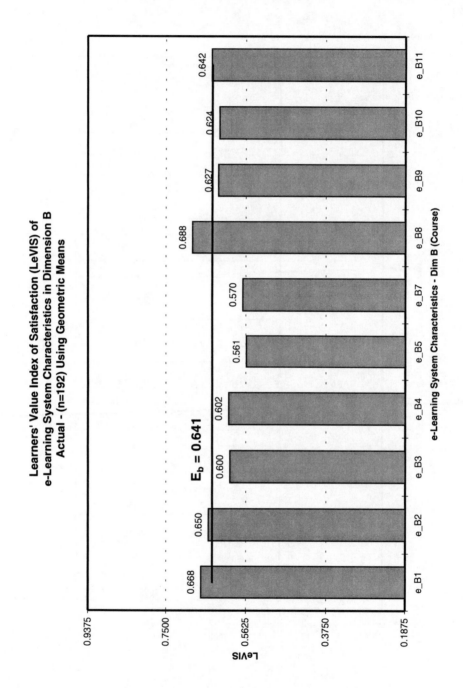

Figure 19. LeVIS index of e-learning system characteristics in dimension C

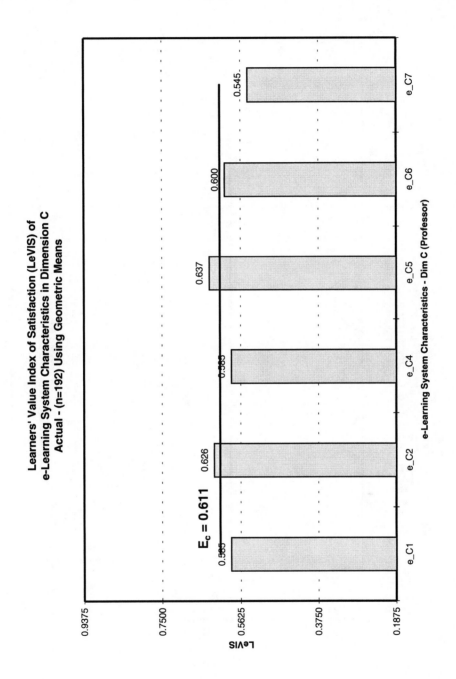

Figure 20. LeVIS index of e-learning system characteristics in dimension D

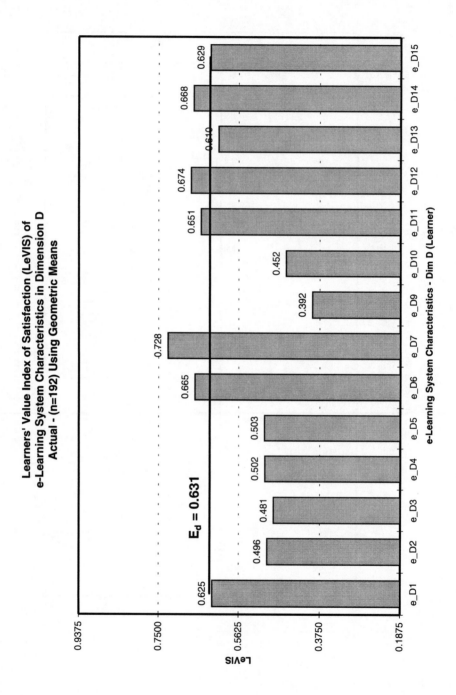

Figure 21. LeVIS index of e-learning system dimensions and overall system

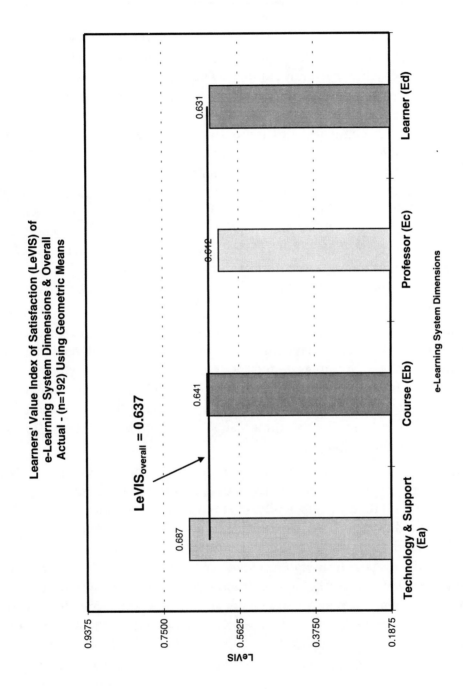

Chapter Summary

This chapter provides a detailed review of the results of all analyses performed and the results of all research questions proposed in Chapters IV, V, and VI in the context of the case study explored. The first phase of this study included qualitative techniques to gather e-learning system characteristics learners found important when learning online. Results of such approaches suggest 48 e-learning system characteristics as presented in Table 1. The second phase of this analysis included the development of a survey instrument and performed preliminary data collection on a pilot group (n = 141, or a 27% response rate) of undergraduate business students learning online via an e-learning system. The pilot data was subjected to an exploratory factor analysis using principal components analysis (PCA) done separately for the satisfaction measures and value measures. Results of such analyses helped improve the validity of the preliminary instrument by suggesting adjustments for items with low reliability as well as the constructions of the principal components. The revised instrument is available in the Appendix (see Appendix E).

The third phase of this study included the collection of data on a larger group (n = 207, or a 32% response rate) of undergraduate business students learning online via an e-learning system. The data was subjected to extensive pre-analyses data preparation in order to detect irregularities or problems with the collected data. As a result, seven cases were eliminated due to a response set and eight cases were eliminated due to multivariate outliers, leaving 192 cases available for final analyses.

Results of the factor analysis done in the process to validate the revised instrument suggested elimination of five e-learning system characteristics (A_8, B_6, C_3, D_8, and B_{12}). Consequently, the final analyses included only 43 out of the initial 48 e-learning system characteristics. Initially, it was the assumption that both satisfaction and value correspond to the same four e-learning system dimensions propose by literature. However, both Pearson and Eta correlations between value and satisfaction constructs were found to be low, indicating that they are two distinct uncorrelated constructs (see Table 3). These results provide further confirmation for the validity of analyzing the two constructs separately as done in this study and the argument that effectiveness can be indicated from the multiplication of the two. This is consistent with the literature. Moreover, results of the factor analyses done separately for value measures and satisfaction measures suggest that the two constructs have different factors (see Tables 4 and 5). This is consistent with Rokeach's (1969) argument that satisfaction and value constructs refers to two distinct constructs. Four *satisfaction factors* were resulted with a total cumulative variance explained of nearly 60% with three high and one moderate Cronbach's α (0.946, 0.940, 0.897, and 0.571 respectively). The four new *satisfaction factors* were named: course and professor; technology and support; learner and interface support; and cost. Similarly, four *value factors* were resulted with a total cumulative variance explained of nearly 61% with very high Cronbach's α (0.961, 0.857, 0.943, and 0.837 respectively). The four new *value factors* were named: course, professor and technology; learners' support environment; classmates; and technical support.

Results of the analysis of values suggest that although both MCDA techniques (MHDIS and MUSA) outperform standard statistical methods (multiple linear regression and ordinal logistic regression), MHDIS provided the best overall prediction across all four performance measures (see Figure 8). MHDIS value estimates are reasonably accurate with an average difference of 3.9% from actual values, standard error of 4.9% and margin of error of 9.9%. Consequently, these results provide indication that MHDIS is the best MCDA technique to be used for such imputation in the future.

Results of the perceived learning analysis indicate that perceived learning is significantly correlated with LeVIS (Pearson corr. $= 0.71$, $p < 0.01$, Eta corr. $= 0.77$) and with satisfaction (Pearson corr. $= 0.64$, $p < 0.01$, Eta corr. $= 0.74$) (see Figure 9). This is consistent with literature suggesting that satisfaction and perceived learning are correlated (Hiltz, 1998; Hiltz et al., 2000). However, perceived learning was found to have low correlation (Pearson corr. $= 0.246$ and Eta corr. $= 0.26$) with value suggesting no observed relationship between the two (see Figure 9). These results were not previously investigated in literature and provide added evidence for the validity for the use of value construct as a separate measure.

Results from the Value-Satisfaction grids indicate that e-learning system dimensions B (courses) and C (professor) are in the high-value-low-satisfaction quadrant (Q1) implying that both the course and the professor dimensions are perceived to have high importance but low satisfaction (See Figures 11 to 16). These results suggest that administrators of the e-learning system under study may need to focus much of their attention to improve these two e-learning system dimensions (*courses* and *professor*) by enhancing courses with some games and adding some interactive features to the course contents as well as by providing seminars and workshops for professors in order to improve their performance. Moreover, results also indicate that in general, e-learning system dimensions A (technology and support) and D (learner) are in the high-value-high-satisfaction quadrant (Q2) implying that both the *technology and support* dimension as well as the *learner* dimension are effective and should be highlighted as part of the strengths of the e-learning system under study. An interesting result from the *learner* dimension is the fact that online learning students did not find classmates or classmate related activities important nor were they satisfied with such characteristics indicating low effectiveness for classmate related e-learning system characteristics, at least for the e-learning system and population under this study. Furthermore, overall no e-learning system characteristics or e-learning system dimensions were found in the low-value-high-satisfaction quadrant (Q4). This is a good indication that no resources are being wasted in the e-learning system under this study.

Results of the LeVIS index (Figure 21) indicate that the overall e-learning system under study is relatively effective (LeVIS = 0.637). Results also indicated relatively high effectiveness for *technology and support* characteristics (see Figure 17). However, relatively low effectiveness was indicated for *professor*'s characteristics (see Figure 19), while e-learning system characteristics in the *course* and *learner* dimensions indicated average effectiveness (see Figures 18 and 20).

In summary, this chapter is built around the research design suggested in Figure 1. Moreover, it follows closely the structure of Chapters IV, V, and VI in providing a review of the specific results for each of the analyses performed for each of the research question proposed. Subsequently, Chapter VIII provides a review of the limitations of the current study. Moreover, Chapter VIII concludes by summarizing the significant results reviewed in this chapter and provides recommendations for practitioners on ways to improve implementations of e-learning systems as well as recommendations for researchers on future studies needed to continue this stream of research.

Chapter VIII

Discussion and Conclusion

Introduction

This chapter provides a discussion of findings and a summary of the results of the case study conducted. The discussion also includes a section on the limitations of the case study followed by two sections highlighting the contributions of the theoretical model, the effectiveness benchmarking tools proposed, and the results of the case study. The first study contributions section includes implications for business and practice, while the second contributions section includes implications for research, scholars, and recommendations for future studies. The chapter concludes with a summary.

Summary of the Results

IS literature has been given major attention in the past two decades to IS user satisfaction. However, no attention has been given to the rationale, definition, or measurement of users' perceived value of IS. Moreover, IS literature includes many definitions of IS effectiveness, with very little consensus. The main purpose of this study was to enlighten IS literature about the importance of the value construct especially as a construct contributing to users' effectiveness of IS. Consequently, this study addressed the central research question: Is there a relationship between learners' perceived satisfaction with e-learning systems and learners' perceived value for effectiveness of e-learning systems? Moreover, seven more specific research questions were addressed in order to guide the exploratory and theory building approach taken in this study. This section provides a brief summary of the results and drawing some conclusions from each of the specific research questions addressed in this study.

The first research question asked what characteristics of e-learning systems are important for learners. Results of the qualitative phase of this study provided an initial list of 48 e-learning system characteristics that online learners find important; however, later analyses via the use of principal components analysis (PCA) with varimax rotation loadings, Cronbach α when item deleted, and *similar vector analysis* reduced the list to 43 reliable e-learning system characteristics (see Table 1 in Chapter VII). Accordingly, future research may rely on the final list of 43 e-learning system characteristics when conducting assessments of satisfaction and/or value of such systems.

The second and third research questions asked about the significant factors for learners' perceived value of e-learning systems and perceived satisfaction of e-learning systems. This study used the four main dimensions (factors) proposed by Webster and Hackley (1997), namely: *technology and support*, *course*, *professor*, and *learner*, and examined if these four factors still hold. Moreover, literature suggests that value and satisfaction constructs are different (Feather, 1975; Rokeach, 1969, 1973, 1979). Consequently, it was suspected that the two constructs may have different factors and therefore need separate analysis. Thus, prior to conducting the factor analyses, an analysis was done to check the level of association between value measures and satisfaction measures using linear association tests (Pearson correlations) and non-linear association tests (Eta, η, correlation). Results suggest that there are no observed correlations (linear or non-linear) between value and satisfaction measures (See Table 3 in Chapter VII). These results are quite profound as they suggest that value and satisfaction are two distinct uncorrelated constructs. Moreover, these results add to the validity of conducting separate analyses for each one (value and satisfaction measures separately) and add for the validity of the whole model proposed in this book. The factor analyses results also confirm that the two constructs (value and satisfaction) have different factors, and most of these factors are consistent with prior literature. Learners' perceived satisfaction measures resulted in four factors: *course and professor*, *technology and support*, *learner and interface support*, and *cost* (see Figure 4 in Chapter VII). Learners' perceived value measures resulted in four different factors: *course, professor and technology*; *learners' support environment*; *classmates*; and *technical support* (see Figure 5 in Chapter VII). These are interesting results since learners' satisfaction of e-learning system characteristics of *course and professor* were grouped together for one component, whereas for the value analyses such e-learning system characteristics were grouped together with ones related to technology.

These results suggest that learners find e-learning system characteristics related to technology also related to characteristics on course and professor when learning online. Moreover, technology related e-learning system characteristics were consistent with literature in grouping with support related e-learning system characteristics in the factor analysis done for the satisfaction measures. However, interestingly enough, technology related e-learning system characteristics were not grouped with support related e-learning system characteristics in the factor analysis done for the value measures, rather they were grouped with the course's and professor's e-learning system characteristics. Since value analysis of such e-learning system characteristics were never done prior to this study, no comparison for consistency with literature is available. Nevertheless, a plausible explanation for such a difference may be that learners find the satisfaction levels from technology related e-learning system characteristics similar to support characteristics, whereas their perceived importance for technology related e-learning system characteristics in online learning environments may more resemble that of course's and professor's e-learning system characteristics. Thus, it is evident that due to the nature of learning online, learners find course, professor, and technology related e-learning system characteristics similarly in nature in regards to their perceived importance. Another interesting result from these analyses is the fact that *cost* came as a separate factor in regards to satisfaction measures, whereas no such factor resulted from the value measure. This suggests that online learners may not be satisfied with and may be sensitive to the costs associated with learning online. However, when considering the importance of such costs, they do not find the cost as a factor by itself. This may suggest that they found other more crucial issues such as course related characteristics than costs when learning online.

Additional results from these analyses are the fact that classmates resulted as a separate factor for value related measures. A plausible explanation for such a result may lie in the fact that online learners may not find classmate related characteristics as important. It may be that their whole notion of taking part in online education is to reduce interaction with classmates. The fact that classmate related characteristics grouped together in respect to value may be an interesting area to further investigate in the future. Additional information is provided in the *Recommendations for Future Research* section to follow.

Finally, the results suggest that e-learning system characteristics related to technical support appear to form a separate factor from e-learning system characteristics related to technology when learners consider the importance of such characteristics. A plausible explanation for this result is due to the learners' level of Internet and computer skills (D_6) as well as learners' comfort with online learning (D_7). As suggested from Figures 16 and 20 in Chapter VII, learners' comfort with online learning (D_7) was noted by all 192 learners as the highest satisfactory measure, indicating that the learners feel very comfortable with online learning. Moreover, learners' Internet and computer skills (D_6), were also high across all 192 respondents, indicating that their technical skills are satisfactory. Consequently, these students who feel highly comfortable with online learning as well as their Internet and computer skills may not need as much technical support. It will be interesting to investigate if such phenomenon also occurs in a case were large number of students, maybe at another college or institution, have significantly lower level of perceived Internet and computer skills as well as significantly lower level of perceived comfort with online learning.

The fourth research question asked how well the actual value measures elicited from learners fit the imputed value measures derived via the conventional statistical techniques such as multiple linear regression and ordinal logistic regression as well as from the data mining techniques such as MUSA and MHDIS. Additionally, the question asked which MCDA technique provides the best fit and how it compared with statistical estimation procedures such as multiple linear regression and ordinal logistic regression. Weights of each of the four methods and the aggregated elicited value scores for each of the 47 value measures (43 e-learning system characteristics and four e-learning system dimensions) were transformed to a scale from 0 to 1. As suggested in Chapter VII, four performance measures were assessed. Results indicate that in spite of its unfair advantage of decimal predictions, multiple linear regression did not outperform the two MCDA techniques across all four performance measures (see Figure 8 in Chapter VII). Moreover, ordinal logistic regression estimates of values were worse than those of the two MCDA techniques across all four performance measures. Finally, the results indicate that MHDIS value estimates are reasonably accurate with an overall average absolute difference 3.9%, standard error of difference 4.9%, and margin of error for difference of 9.9%. Consequently, although both MCDA techniques (MHDIS and MUSA) outperform standard statistical methods (multiple linear regression and ordinal logistic regression), MHDIS provided the best overall prediction across all four performance measures.

The fifth research question asked how the overall perceived learning measure is related to the overall value, overall satisfaction and overall perceived effectiveness of e-learning systems. Results show that perceived learning was found significantly correlated with LeVIS and is significantly correlated with satisfaction (see Figure 9 in Chapter VII). This is consistent with literature suggesting that satisfaction and perceived learning are correlated. However, perceived learning was found to have low correlation with value suggesting no observed relationship between the two (see Figure 9 in Chapter VII). These results were not previously investigated in literature and provide added evidence for the validity for the use of value construct as a separate measure. Moreover, ordinal logistic regression analysis was done to further validate these conclusions. Results of the ordinal logistic regression analysis show that perceived learning is LeVIS driven (largest weight), followed by the overall satisfaction (second largest weight). Whereas overall value has the lowest weight among all three predictors (S_o, V_o, and LeVIS) in predicting perceived learning, and is also consistent with both Pearson and Eta correlations noted previously (see Figure 10 in Chapter VII, left side). Overall these results are consistent with literature suggesting that measurement of learners' perceived satisfaction do provide an indicator for learners' perceived learning.

The sixth research question asked how the aggregated learners' perceptions of the overall value and overall satisfaction of the e-learning system under study are positioned in the Value-Satisfaction grid (overall and separately for each of the four e-learning system dimensions). Although new factors were found for value and satisfaction measures, further analyses of this study was done using the initial four factors proposed in the literature. Additional information related to this issue is provided in the *Study Limitation* and *Recommendation for Future Research* sections. Nevertheless, results of the analyses using the four e-learning system dimensions suggested by literature still provide fruitful information in indicating the effectiveness of e-learning systems. Consequently, five Value-Satisfaction grids were developed and constructed as suggested in Chapter V, one for the overall e-learning system under study and one for each of the four e-learning system dimensions. Results of the Value-Satisfaction overall grid (Figure 16 in Chapter VII) indicate that e-learning system dimensions A (technology and support) and D (learner) are in the high-value-high-satisfaction quadrant (Q2) implying that both the *technology and support* dimension as well as the *learner* dimension are effective and should be highlighted as strengths of the e-learning system under study. However, results also indicate that e-learning system dimensions B (courses) and C (professor) are in the high-value-low-satisfaction quadrant (Q1) implying that both the course and the professor dimensions are in high importance for students; however, they are found to have lower satisfaction. This suggests that attention should be given to course and professor related e-learning system characteristics in order to improve their overall effectiveness as perceived by learners. This may include enhancing the course with games and adding interactive features to the course content. Moreover, it may also suggest that seminars and workshops are needed to improve professors' performances (such as professor-to-student interaction, professor's attitude, quality of professor-to-student interaction, etc.). No dimensions were found in the low-value-low-satisfaction quadrant (Q3) or the low-value-high-satisfaction quadrant (Q4) within the e-learning system under study.

Finally, the seventh research question asked what is the learners' perceived effectiveness of e-learning systems (as implied by LeVIS) for each of the e-learning system dimension (technology and support, course, professor, and learners' dimension) and overall. As suggested previously, the Value-Satisfaction grid provides a tool in spotting the e-learning system characteristics and e-learning system dimensions that are effective, as well as suggesting some improvement. However, the grid does not provide a measurable index for the magnitude of e-learning systems effectiveness. Consequently, as proposed in chapter VI, LeVIS was developed to provide a benchmarking tool combining learners' perceived value and satisfaction in order to indicate learners' perceived e-learning systems effectiveness. Results of the LeVIS index (Figure 21 in Chapter VII) indicate that overall, the e-learning systems under study is moderately effective (LeVIS = 0.637). Relatively higher effectiveness than the whole system was found for e-learning system dimension A (technology and support, with $E_a = 0.687$), whereas relatively lower effectiveness than the whole system was found for e-learning system dimension C (professor, $E_c = 0.612$). Both e-learning system dimensions B (course) and D (learner) were found to have about the same effectiveness as the whole system with $E_b = 0.641$ and $E_d = 0.631$ respectively. These results again are consistent with the results suggested from the Value-Satisfaction grids, indicating that in general more attention should be placed in e-learning system characteristics from the *professor* dimension. Furthermore, some e-learning system characteristics from the *technology and support* dimension can be used in advertising and highlighted as the strength of the e-learning system under study.

Contributions of the Study

This research study provides four main contributions. IS literature include numerous studies assessing IS effectiveness by the measurement of primarily user satisfaction for decision support systems. Value theory (Rokeach, 1969, 1973, 1979) suggests that *value* is a core construct across all of the social sciences. However, the *value* construct in IS effectiveness is lacking. Furthermore, several scholars such as Brown (1976), criticized management and organizational behavior scholars for neglecting value construct in their theories (p. 16). Therefore, the first contribution of this study to the IS knowledge domain is by identifying, defining, and articulating the relationship between *value* and *satisfaction* constructs in order to indicate users' perceived IS effectiveness. The review done in Chapters II and III provides the outcome of such contributions.

Literature of distance learning suggests a list of characteristics and dimensions of e-learning systems. However, advances in technology have yet to be accounted for. Consequently, qualitative approaches were used to gather data from the learners' point of view on all e-learning system characteristics they find important when learning online. Subsequently, a survey instrument was constructed to empirically assess the findings of the qualitative study and generate a list of factors that contribute to learners' overall value and learners' overall satisfaction of e-learning systems. These methods and approaches provide the second contribution of this research by providing guidelines to researchers on the process of gathering e-learning system characteristics learners' value and find important when learning online. This contribution is significant, as other researchers who might wish to pursue investigation of different types of systems than e-learning systems can follow the procedure done in their development of list of IS characteristics users' value and find important when using the system(s) under study. Additional information is provided in the *Recommendation for Future Research* section to follow.

Brown (1976) contends that measuring satisfaction as well as value is a major burden on the respondents and poses a burden for researchers in the data collection process (p. 20). Consequently, a burden on the respondents along with respondents fatigue from long questionnaires makes it difficult for researchers to gather both learners' value and satisfaction measures of e-learning systems. With the use of statistical methods such as multiple linear regression and ordinal logistics regression, this study reliably provided evidence for imputing value scores from satisfaction scores. The survey instrument used included both learners' value measures and learners' satisfaction measures on the four dimensions of e-learning systems. However, following this study, new assessment of the e-learning system under this study will not require asking users to answer their perceived values, rather it will be sufficient to measure the satisfaction level for each of the e-learning system characteristics and e-learning system dimensions. This reduces the survey length while maintaining reliable results on future assessment of the same e-learning system. Clearly, new types of systems will require going through the same path proposed in this study by developing and validating a new instrument as well as validating again the imputations of values. Additional information is provided in the *Recommendation for Future Research* section.

IS literature provides little agreement on the methods of assessing IS effectiveness. Kim (1989) claimed that "measuring MIS effectiveness is a complex task because of the difficulties of tracing and measuring the effects of MIS through a web of intermediate factors" (p. 1). Yuthas and Eining (1995) claimed that "despite the importance of IS effectiveness ... research in the field has not been successful in its attempts to identify the factors that influence IS effectiveness" (p. 69). However, Grover, Jeong, and Segars (1996) proposed a very promising general approach for measurement of IS effectiveness. Extending their innovative approach, this study provided a contribution on the development and validation of a set of tools to indicate learners' perceived effectiveness of e-learning systems. Finally, the fourth contribution of this research is in the development and validation of the Value-Satisfaction grids, the effectiveness curves, and LeVIS as benchmarking tools indicating learners' perceived effectiveness of e-learning systems. Moreover, the set of tools developed and validated in this study helps researchers as system benchmarking tools without ignoring the multi-dimensionality of such systems. Therefore, this study helps researchers by identifying key e-learning system characteristics and e-learning system dimensions that warrant attention for future studies of e-learning systems. Additional information about such implications on future research is provided in the *Recommendations for Future Research* section. Moreover, the results of this study also helps practitioners by providing guidelines on channeling funds to effective e-learning system characteristics and e-learning system dimensions and redesign or eliminate non-effective ones. Additional information about the contributions of this study for practitioners is provided in the *Implications for Practice* section.

Implications for Practice

The first implication of this research study to practitioners is by providing research-based support for the use of value construct in order to indicate learners' perceived effectiveness of e-learning systems. This study provides practitioners with the mindset that although measurement of satisfaction is beneficial, one can "totally miss the boat" if value, or level of importance, is not accounted for. Consequently, as demonstrated by this study, if online learners' perceived value was not measured, no accurate assessment of the learners' effectiveness could have resulted. For example, Gale (1994) noted that "AT&T was reporting satisfaction levels of 90% or more yet was still losing customers" (pp. 77-78). Clearly, if AT&T were to assess their customers' perceived value as well as their customers' perceived satisfaction a different picture might have emerged.

A second implication of this research study to practitioners is by the development of a reliable survey instrument to assess satisfaction and value in order to indicate learners' perceived effectiveness of e-learning systems in the context of such systems. With the use of the qualitative approaches, the quantitative factor analysis, and reliability measures, (e.g., Cronbach's α) the final instrument can be used by any institution or corporate training center that utilizes e-learning systems in order to measure learners' perceived satisfaction and value in order to indicate learners' perceived effectiveness of their e-learning systems (see Appendix Q).

A third implication of this research study to practitioners is by the development of the benchmarking tools to indicate learners' perceived effectiveness of e-learning systems. Value-Satisfaction grids, the effectiveness curves, and the LeVIS index validated in this study are useful tools for administrators of online learning programs, both in academic institutions as well as corporate training centers. Administrators of such programs who wish to improve their programs can collect data from their users with the final survey and develop their Value-Satisfaction grids, effectiveness curves, and calculate the LeVIS index as suggested in this study to learn more about the effectiveness of their e-learning system characteristics. Knowledge about e-learning system characteristics that are not effective can help practitioners by providing guidelines on channeling funds and redesigning those characteristics that are important for learners, but have low satisfaction or eliminate non-effective characteristics that are not as important. Moreover, if administrators of such programs wish to start an advertising campaign or attract new students, knowledge of effective e-learning system characteristics can help them promote the strengths of their online learning programs successfully. Moreover, knowledge about the satisfaction, value and learners' perceived effectiveness of their e-learning system characteristics is essential in order to increase student retention, reduce students' frustration with e-learning systems, and extend the longevity of such programs.

Measuring and Implementing Value in Your E-Learning Program

One major benefit this book can bring to administrators, directors, and managers of e-learning programs is the ability to implement the tools that were validated here in their own programs. In order to measure value in a given e-learning program, administrators are encouraged to utilize the final instrument available in Appendix Q. Doing so will save them time by eliminating the phases conducted in this study. The three phase approach (qualitative focus groups, pilot data collection, and main data collection) were done in order to validate the proposed theory. Thus, practitioners may follow the steps provided in subsequent paragraphs in order to collect data in their own institution regarding their e-learning program. Minor changes to the text of each question (like switching WebCT™ with Blackboard™ or any other e-learning platform) is acceptable in order to customize the survey for any given e-learning program. However, major changes such as: eliminations of questions (items), substitution of questions (items) with others, and major modification for question (item) text are not appropriate as it may change the overall validity and reliability of the results.

The following steps are recommended for administrators, directors, and managers of e-learning programs in collecting data in their e-learning programs. Additionally, these steps will provide a process of data analysis, construction of Value-Satisfaction grids, and development of the LeVIS index for each e-learning dimension as well as the overall e-learning program. Additionally, guidelines for feedback loop are provided based on the results within a specific e-learning program.

Collecting Data About Your E-Learning Program

1. Develop a Web-based system to collect data based on the revised instrument (Appendix Q: Final Survey Instrument). It is highly recommended to collect data via a Web-based system. As noted in chapter seven there are many benefits from doing it via the Web. However if this is not feasible, administrators can either collect data via a paper survey or contact the author of this book for help in enabling a Web-based survey mechanism. With the great advances of tools available nowadays, administrators can utilize their technical group to use the survey presented in Appendix Q and convert it to a Web-based system. This can be done either by a shelf product, survey Web site enablers, or by a package like MS®FrontPage®. The Web-based survey system should collect responses via the Internet and Web browser, where learners submit a Web form to a server that collects the data and submits it to a centralized database. Additionally, during the submission process, each selection by the user should translate automatically to a numeric score for ease of analysis. For *satisfaction* measures, the database entries should be set to submit 1 for *extremely unsatisfied* to 6 for *extremely satisfied*. For *value* measures, the database entries should be set to submit 1 for *not important* to 6 for *extremely important*. Once the Web-based survey is constructed, a full testing session should be made to ensure an error-free process.

2. Request approval from the Institutional Review Board (IRB) for data collection as the study falls under the category of research that includes "human subjects." However, since no specific student's identifiable information should be collected, thus there is no link between a given respondent that submitted the survey and the response itself (essentially no one knows which student submitted which submission), the study should be qualified for "exempt from further IRB review." Contact the IRB representative and/or the IRB office before conducting the data

collection. Once the study is approved by IRB and is exempt from further review, the IRB representative or IRB office will supply specific guidelines of sections of text to use in the letter of consent. If the data collection will be done online (highly recommended), this text should be included in the first welcoming page of the survey. However, if the data collection will be done via paper survey (not recommended) the text should be included in the consent form provided to respondents.

3.   Develop a solicitation strategy. The process of encouraging students to take the survey is crucial for the success of the study and also for increasing the validity of the results based on a high response rate. Additionally, try to look for a higher administrator's (e.g., dean, provost, chancellor, and president) support for the study and get their "blessings" for it. Asking them to suggest the importance of the study for students, faculty, and other administrators will help increase the response rate as well. As proposed in this study, a three-phase approach should be taken to solicit students to participate in the study, which should help capture a high response rate. All three phases should be made to all students taking online courses, asking them to submit the survey. The following three phases are listed in the chronological order of execution.

a.   The first phase in soliciting survey participants should be done via e-mail to all students attending online courses in the program. It is assumed that administrators of the program have access to all e-mail addresses of their students. Thus, developing an e-mail list should be trivial. A solicitation e-mail should be short, to the point, and should include a direct link to the welcome page of the survey. The solicitation e-mail should be sent during the last week of the term asking students to submit the survey. It is recommended that the message will be sent from either the technical support group or the director of the program to ensure students will pay attention to the message. It is not recommended to ask faculty to send the solicitation e-mail to students. Additionally, a revised message should also be sent out a second time, about a week after courses are over, in order to help future increase response rates. The revised message may include a statement thanking those who already submitted the survey, and asking those who have not yet done it to go ahead and submit their survey.

b.   The second phase in soliciting survey participants should be done by individual faculty members or the technical support group. This should include posting a request message during the last week of the term in the homepages of all online courses asking students to assist in improving the program by submitting their survey. As in the case of the e-mail, this message should also be short, to the point, and should include a direct link to the welcome page of the survey. The message should be posted until two weeks after the end of the term or until students' access to the online course has terminated.

c.   The third phase in soliciting survey participants should be done by creating a pop-up window that will be implemented in the last week of the term on the e-learning system or portal access page (see Figure 3 in Chapter VII). The message will pop-up to all students taking online courses as they access the site. However, it should be noted that if the students' browser includes a pop-up blocker, this message may not be displayed. One solution for that can be posting the solicitation message also on the portal access page itself rather than as a pop-up. The message should be in place until two weeks after the end of the term or shortly before a new term is started.

Preparing and Analyzing Your Data

Once data is collected, it should be organized in a spreadsheet file where students' responses are the rows and each of the survey items is a column. Prior to analysis, a pre-analysis data preparation should be done to clear any irregularities or problems with the collected data. For simplicity, data preparation may only include investigation of data accuracy, outliers, and response-sets (assuming no missing data is evident). See the *Pre-Analysis Data Preparation* section in Chapter VII for additional information related to preparing the data collected for analysis.

After performing the basic pre-analysis data preparations noted earlier, the raw data should be ready for analysis. It is recommended to assemble the final data received from the survey in a spreadsheet where each row in the table represents individual submission for all sections of the survey and each column of the table is a given survey item. For simplicity of instructions, this spreadsheet will be noted as Spreadsheet A. In this case, there should be two measures (satisfaction and value) for each characteristics (e.g., A1_sat and A1_val), for each overall dimension (e.g., A_sat and A_val), and overall system wide (e.g., O_sat and O_val). Subsequently, averages for each survey item (column in the

Table 1. Structuring your data for analysis (Spreadsheet A)

CASE_NO	A1_SAT	A1_VAL	A2_SAT	A2_VAL	A3_SAT	A3_VAL	A4_SAT	A4_VAL	...
1	4	3	5	5	6	6	6	6	...
2	4	2	5	5	6	6	5	6	...
3	6	6	6	6	6	6	6	6	...
4	4	6	4	6	5	6	5	6	...
5	5	6	4	5	4	4	5	5	...
6	4	4	4	4	4	4	4	4	...
7	4	6	4	6	5	6	4	6	...
8	6	6	6	6	5	5	6	6	...
9	4	4	3	5	3	5	1	6	...
10	4	6	4	6	4	6	5	6	...
...	...	...	...	...	...	...	...	...	...
Averages >	3.91	4.66	4.03	4.89	4.14	4.93	4.28	5.21	...

spreadsheet) can be computed (See Table 1). These averages are used for the constructions of the Value-Satisfaction grids to follow and will be transformed to a newer spreadsheet for ease of analysis. These averages will represent each survey item in an aggregated format across all respondents to the survey.

Constructing Your Value-Satisfaction Grids

In order to construct the Value-Satisfaction grids, it will be more productive to work with the aggregated data produced in Spreadsheet A instead of the raw data. The following are instructions on the steps to construct the Value-Satisfaction grids:

1. Place the aggregated averages from Spreadsheet A into a new spreadsheet file (noted as Spreadsheet B) where the names of the measure (characteristics, dimensions, and overall) are noted in the first column, followed by the aggregated average satisfaction score, followed by the value score for each measure (See Table 2). Spreadsheet B can either be used directly in order to construct the Value-Satisfaction grids (the dimensions and the overall grids) or as a source data file for statistical package such as SPSS™. The grids produces in this study were done via SPSS™ for better accuracy and presentation; however, similar results can be produced by using spreadsheet software.

2. In order to produce the Value-Satisfaction grid for a specific dimension using spreadsheet software, select only the characteristics and the overall

Table 2. Structuring your data for value-satisfaction grids (Spreadsheet B)

Char/Dim/O	SAT	VAL
A1	3.912	4.660
A2	4.034	4.891
A3	4.136	4.934
A4	4.280	5.214
...	...	...
A	4.566	5.417
B1	4.637	5.185
B2	4.557	5.135
B3	4.357	4.955
B4	4.403	4.926
...	...	...
B	4.466	5.168
C1	4.124	5.111
C2	4.300	5.240
C4	4.120	5.110
C5	4.602	4.984
...	...	...
C	4.213	5.228
D1	4.393	5.121
D2	4.122	4.335
D3	4.037	4.293
D4	4.231	4.269
...	...	...
D	4.523	5.021
Overall	4.460	5.141

of that dimension (e.g., A1, A2,... and A for dimension A in Spreadsheet B, see Table 2). In order to produce the Value-Satisfaction grid for the whole system, select all the characteristics, all dimensions measures, and the overall measure (e.g., A1, A2,..., B1, B2,..., C1, C2,..., D1, D2,..., A, B, C, D and O in Spreadsheet B, see Table 2). Once the data source is selected, produce an XY scatter plot using the spreadsheet software. Make sure to assign the satisfaction scores as the data for the X axis and to assign the value scores as the data for the Y axis. Once the graph is produced, change the scale on each axis from "auto" to: Minimum = 3, Maximum = 6, Major unit = 1.5, Minor unit = 1 and Value (y) axis crosses at = 3. Additionally, set the gridlines under "chart options" for major gridlines for both X and Y axes. The resulting 2×2 grid should look like Figure 1 (Also see Figures 9 to 12 in Chapter VII). Same process should be repeated for each of the other dimensions. Additionally, another grid can be produced to include only the dimensions measures and the overall measure (see Figure 13 in Chapter VII). Furthermore, another grid can be produced to include all the characteristics, the dimensions measures and the overall measure (see Figure 14 in Chapter VII). Details on interpreting

Figure 1. Sample value-satisfaction grid

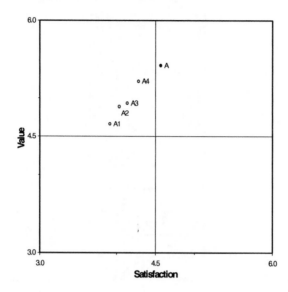

the Value-Satisfaction grids are presented in the *Understanding Your Value-Satisfaction Grids and LeVIS Index for Improvement* section.

Calculating Your LeVIS Index

The Value-Satisfaction grid provides a key tool to indicate action and improvement priorities for e-learning systems as well as an overall map to indicate the learners' perceived effectiveness of e-learning systems. However, the Value-Satisfaction grid does not provide a specific score of the effectiveness. Consequently, the LeVIS index is constructed in order to provide a measure of the magnitude of the learners' perceived effectiveness of e-learning systems utilizing the aggregated value and satisfaction scores available in Spreadsheet B. Similar indices can be calculated for each characteristic and each dimension.

The calculation of the precise effectiveness index of each characteristic and dimension as well as the overall system-wide (LeVIS) measure can be done directly in Spreadsheet B. In order to produce these effectiveness indices, multiply the satisfaction score and the value score for that given characteristic (can be noted as e_i, where it notes the effectiveness of characteristic i, see Figure 2 in Chapter VI), dimension (can be noted as E_a, E_b, E_c, and E_d, where

Table 3. Sample spreadsheet of calculating effectiveness indices (Spreadsheet B)

Char/Dim/O	SAT	VAL	E
A1	3.912	4.660	0.520
A2	4.034	4.891	0.566
A3	4.136	4.934	0.584
A4	4.280	5.214	0.634
...	...	...	...
A	4.566	5.417	0.687
B1	4.637	5.185	0.668
B2	4.557	5.135	0.650
B3	4.357	4.955	0.600
B4	4.403	4.926	0.602
...	...	...	...
B	4.466	5.168	0.641
C1	4.124	5.111	0.585
C2	4.300	5.240	0.626
C4	4.120	5.110	0.585
C5			0.637
...	...	...	...
C	4.213	5.228	0.612
D1	4.393	5.121	0.625
D2	4.122	4.335	0.496
D3	4.037	4.293	0.481
D4	4.231	4.269	0.502
...	...	...	...
D	4.523	5.021	0.631
Overall	4.460	5.141	0.637

it notes the effectiveness of dimensions *a*, *b*, *c*, and *d*) and the overall system measures (LeVIS). The four effectiveness indices for each of the four dimensions are calculated as the multiplication of the dimension satisfaction (S_a, S_b, S_c, and S_d) by the corresponding dimension value (V_a, V_b, V_c, and V_d). The overall LeVIS is computed by multiplying the *overall satisfaction* (S_o) by the *overall value* (V_o). The resulted column will include all of the calibrated indices (See Table 3). All indices need to be calibrated by dividing the multiplication score by 36 to provide an index score on a scale from 0 to 1 (see Figure 2 in Chapter VI). Details on interpreting these indices and the LeVIS index are presented in the *Understanding Your Value-Satisfaction Grids and LeVIS Index for Improvement* section.

Understanding Your Value-Satisfaction Grids and LeVIS Index for Improvements

The main goal of the value approach proposed in this book is to combine the value measure with the traditional satisfaction measure in order to help

Figure 2. Understanding your LeVIS index

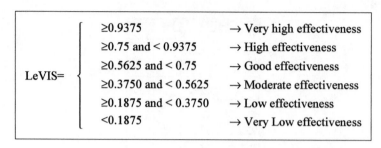

LeVIS=

≥0.9375	→ Very high effectiveness
≥0.75 and < 0.9375	→ High effectiveness
≥0.5625 and < 0.75	→ Good effectiveness
≥0.3750 and < 0.5625	→ Moderate effectiveness
≥0.1875 and < 0.3750	→ Low effectiveness
<0.1875	→ Very Low effectiveness

practitioners improve their e-learning programs by having benchmarking tools that provide a valid measure of e-learning systems effectiveness. Improvement or a feedback loop is required by many accreditations bodies, such as AACSB, for the survival of the program. Thus, understanding the Value-Satisfaction grids and the LeVIS index is crucial as these tools can indicate the areas that need more attention for improvements or continued attention for sustaining competitive edge.

One overall "dashboard" indicator for the effectiveness of an e-learning program is the LeVIS index proposed in Chapter VI. Additionally, the effectiveness of each dimension can be measured by the dimensions' indices (i.e., E_a, E_b, E_c, and E_d, see Figure 2 in Chapter VI). Administrators are encouraged to look at the LeVIS index for the e-learning program as it provides a benchmarking tool to suggest precise magnitude of effectiveness of e-learning systems as perceived by learners. Although there is no clear cut for the LeVIS index scale, Figure 2 presents scale intervals of the index and its interpretation to indicate effectiveness.

Although the LeVIS index can provide a specific effectiveness score for the overall system, and similar indices can provide the specific effectiveness score for each key system dimension as well as for each system characteristic, additional information is needed to clarify the score calculated. Thus, the second key "dashboard" indicator for the effectiveness of specific characteristics of the e-learning program is the Value-Satisfaction grid proposed in Chapter V. Value-Satisfaction grids can be done for the overall system or each key dimension separately as noted previously.

After the Value-Satisfaction grids are constructed for all four dimensions and the overall program, administrators should spend time understanding the

Figure 3. Understanding your value-satisfaction grids

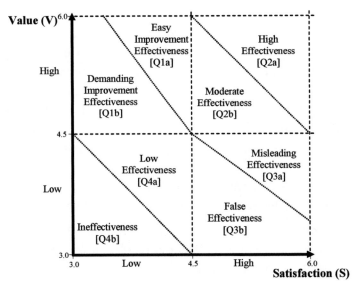

results. It is recommended to look separately at the Value-Satisfaction grid that was produced for each dimension. Then look over the overall program Value-Satisfaction grid. Additionally, in order to simplify the process for administrators, linear curves can be drawn directly on the Value-Satisfaction grids to serve as a piece-wise linear approximation for the effectiveness curves. Although these linear approximation curves are not fully precise effectiveness curves (as those proposed in Chapter VI), they can provide a very well estimation of the characteristics positions within the grids. The corners (x_1, y_1) and (x_2, y_2) of the linear approximation curves are (see Figure 3):

- For the Q1 curve, the corners are (3.375, 6.0) and (4.5, 4.5)
- For the Q2 curve, the corners are (4.5, 6.0) and (6.0, 4.5)
- For the Q3 curve, the corners are (4.5, 4.5) and (6.0, 3.375)
- For the Q4 curve, the corners are (3.0, 4.5) and (4.5, 3.0)

Constructing these linear approximation curves for each grid will provide administrators an immediate report on the effectiveness level of given characteristics in their e-learning program. Characteristics falling under Q1a should be first in the improvement priority followed by characteristics falling under Q1b.

Improvement in such characteristics could occur by providing more resources to increase learners' satisfaction with the characteristics that are valued highly, hence help avoid learners' attrition. For example, if characteristics such as C1 (amount of professor-to-student interaction), C2 (professor's attitude), and C4 (quality of professor-to-student interaction) appears in the Q1a or Q1b sections, administrators may require faculty who teaches e-learning courses to attend special training sessions on issues related to interaction with students. Clearly, repeated measures in subsequent terms may tell administrators if those special training sessions were successful by looking at the position of the same characteristics over time. Ultimately, if those training sessions were successful, C1, C2, and C4 characteristics should move into the Q2 quadrant or at least move toward that quadrant.

Administrators will be happy to look for characteristics that fall in the Q2a and Q2b sections since they are the effective characteristics suggesting the strength of their e-learning program or areas that they are doing exceptionally well. Although noted as effective characteristics, administrators should continue to provide resources for these characteristics to ensure maintaining their level of effectiveness. For example, if characteristics related to technical support (i.e., A1, A2, and A3) appear to fall under Q2a or Q2b, funding and resources provided to the technical support group clearly should remain the same to ensure maintaining, or improving, the effectiveness of the service.

Characteristics falling under Q3a and Q3b are noted as "misleading effectiveness" and "false effectiveness" due to the fact that the satisfaction level is reported high, however the value is relatively low. This is the area where past measures that relay on satisfaction only may have been misleading or providing false indication of effectiveness. Using the Value-Satisfaction model proposed here, clearly these characteristics are not as effective as ones falling in the Q2 quadrant and are simply not as important to the learners. Resources invested in maintaining these e-learning system characteristics may be more appropriately utilized if transferred to other characteristics located in the Q1 quadrant. For example, if B12 (taking practice test prior to graded test) ended up in the Q3 quadrant, whereas B9 (similar interface across all online courses) was measured in the Q1 quadrant, it would have been more beneficial to direct the resources places in creating the practice tests to the resources given for ensuring similar interface across all online courses. So, if faculty are developing their own courses, based on the results it may well be beneficial to provide them tools on developing similar interfaces across all online courses in the e-learning program and suggest to them that devoting time on developing practice tests is not needed as students don't see high value in it. If the development is done by a development group, administrators can direct them to spend less time on developing practice tests for new developed courses and devote more time to ensure similar interfaces across all online courses.

Administrators should also spend time investigating the characteristics that fall in the Q4 quadrant. Characteristics that fall under Q4a may require closer investigation to look for the particular reasons why they fall in this section. For example, if characteristics related to classmates D2 (amount of interactions with classmates), D3 (quality of interaction with classmates), D4 (classmates' attitude), and D5 (being part of the class) fall in the Q4a section, this may indicate low effectiveness for classmates activities. However, with a closer investigation, administrators may find out that most of the courses in their program do not require students to produce any group work. This information may be important for e-learning programs that are under accreditation bodies that may require students to have some exposure for group work. Consequently, administrators may ask faculty to incorporate group work as part of their course activities. Clearly, repeated assessment of this study on their e-learning program may provide additional information on the success, or lack thereof, of the policies implemented as a result of these findings.

Characteristics that fall under Q4b may not be needed or even discarded. For example, if A14 (review of course audios) was found to fall close to the origin of the grid (0.50, 0.50), administrators may propose faculty to stop spend their efforts on recording their lectures and providing it via online audios, as it is appeared to be ineffective for students. Clearly, if the examples provided in this section were found, it would be more appropriate to divert the efforts and resources spent on audio recording to professors' training, technical support, or ensuring similar interfaces across all online courses.

Recommendations for Future Research

The research study addressed in this book provides the ground work for two new streams of research in the IS field. The first research stream that can result from this study may continue the investigation of learners' perceived effectiveness in the area of e-learning systems. More work is needed in the validation of the new e-learning system dimensions for satisfaction and value respectively. This study followed the four e-learning system dimensions found in literature in analyses of the results. However, results of research question two (RQ2) and research question three (RQ3) suggest slightly different e-learning system dimensions for satisfaction and value. Consequently, a more appropriate approach should be taken by collecting and analyzing new data based on the four new e-learning system dimensions proposed in this study. This included the development of the Value-Satisfaction grids, effectiveness curves, and the LeVIS index based on the new e-learning system dimensions rather than the ones done in this study.

As noted in Chapter III, Grover et al. (1996) proposed three methods to evaluate IS effectiveness from the individual's unit of analysis: a comparative, a normative, and an improvement measurement (p. 180). The focus of the study detailed in this book was on the normative measurement of IS effectiveness. However, the two other methods to evaluate IS effectiveness (comparative and improvement) were not part of this study but can be derived from the normative approach. The improvement measurement determines IS effectiveness by comparing the effectiveness of a particular system over time. Consequently, another future study can be done by looking at the changes of satisfaction, value and learners' perceived effectiveness of the same e-learning system over an extended period of time. Additionally, the comparative measurement determines IS effectiveness by comparing the effectiveness of a particular system with "peer systems" in other organizations. Consequently, another future study can be done to compare the effectiveness of the e-learning system used in this study with "peer systems" in other universities. This may include comparison of several higher educational institutions using the same type of e-learning systems or a comparison with another program that uses different types of e-learning systems. For example, a comparison study can be done on a group of students attending a program that uses an asynchronous e-learning system (e.g., WebCT™ or Blackboard™ with another group of students attending a program that uses synchronous e-learning system (e.g., Centra™ or PlaceWare™. Such approach may lead us to better understanding of what types of e-learning systems are more effective for any given group of students.

Another study in this research stream of e-learning systems can be done by investigating the satisfaction, value and learners' perceived effectiveness of e-learning systems used in corporate employee training centers. Although one can hypothesize that results from corporate employee training centers that utilizes e-learning systems will resemble results of this study of e-learning systems used in higher educational institutions, no such studies exist in prior literature to confirm or deny it.

Additional study in this research stream of e-learning systems can be done in order to fully investigate the issue of classmates and classmates related e-learning system characteristics. Results of this study suggest that classmate related e-learning system characteristics group together and appear to have low-value and low-satisfaction. This suggest that online learning students may find classmates or classmate related e-learning system characteristics ineffective. One approach for future study of classmates related e-learning system characteristics can look at the effect of demographic characteristics (e.g., age, hours of employment per week, marital status, etc.) on the level of satisfaction, value, and learners' perceived effectiveness. These approaches have never been taken in prior literature. Results of such a study will help us better assist online learning students by increasing student retention and reducing their frustration with e-learning systems.

The second research stream that can result from this study may utilize the methodology proposed here to develop similar surveys for other types of information systems. For example, a new study can be conducted for the exploration of system characteristics and dimensions for Web-based airline reservation systems. This study can follow the qualitative approaches proposed in the first phase of this study to seek a list of airline reservation system characteristics. Following these approaches, a preliminary survey can be done to assess both satisfaction and value of such systems. Prior to data collection, the new proposed survey can be provided to two focus groups. One focus group can consist of frequent users of such systems, whereas the other focus group can consist of employees, managers, and supervisors of such systems. This will provide added validity for the list of characteristics as well as to the preliminary survey instrument. Pilot data can be collected using the preliminary survey on a small group of users who utilizes Web-based airline reservation systems. The pilot data can be analyzed to propose revisions to the preliminary survey in order to provide a reliable and valid final instrument. These revisions may include the elimination of characteristics that do not add to the overall reliability of each factor as done in the study detailed in this book. The analyses of the data can also help extract the system dimensions with the use of factor analysis. Subsequently, the revised instrument can be used to collect new data on a larger group of users who frequently utilizes web-based airline reservation systems. That data can be used to develop the Value-Satisfaction grids and effectiveness curves for each of the systems' dimension found in the previous phase. Results of such grids can help managers and supervisors of web-based airline reservation systems to improve characteristics with low effectiveness by channeling funding to such characteristics and eliminate characteristics that have low value and low satisfaction. Moreover, that data can be used to develop an index similar to LeVIS (e.g., users' value index of satisfaction or UsVIS), in order to suggest the users' effectiveness of such systems. Such index can provide measures for the magnitude of users' effectiveness of such system characteristics, dimensions and the overall systems.

Chapter Summary

In conclusion, the study detailed in this book provided the argument for the use of value construct along with satisfaction construct in order to explore users' perceived IS effectiveness in the context of e-learning systems. The central research question of this study asked if there is a relationship between learners' perceived satisfaction with e-learning systems and learners' perceived value for effectiveness of e-learning systems. Results of this study suggest that value and satisfaction constructs are two distinct uncorrelated constructs. This is consistent with the literature. Moreover, results of this study show that there is a solid validity for the use of the two distinct constructs together in order to indicate the learners' perceived effectiveness of e-learning systems. Additionally, such combination of the two constructs (value and satisfaction) yields powerful results by mapping the characteristics and dimensions on the Value-Satisfaction grids along with the effectiveness curves and the precise assessment of such effectiveness done by the LeVIS index.

The results of this study provided four satisfaction factors and four value factors with high reliability (Cronbach's α). Three benchmarking tools (Value-Satisfaction grids, effectiveness curves, and the LeVIS index) were proposed and validated to indicate learners' perceived effectiveness of e-learning system characteristics, e-learning system dimensions and the overall system. Results suggest relatively high effectiveness for technology and support characteristics. However, relatively low effectiveness was indicated for professor's characteristics, while course and learner characteristics indicated average effectiveness. Results also indicate that MHDIS provide the most accurate prediction of values and that both MCDA techniques (MHDIS and MUSA) outperform standard statistical methods (multiple linear regression and ordinal logistic regression) in predicting the values across all four performance measures. Results also show that perceived learning is LeVIS driven, followed by the overall satisfaction. Furthermore, the results show that overall value was uncorrelated (both via linear correlation, Pearson, and via non-linear correlation, Eta, η) and is not significant in predicting perceived learning, however, value is a key in understanding IS effectiveness. These results further strengthen the construct validity of value, suggesting that measuring it can provide fruitful information in the analyses of information systems.

This chapter also provides a "cookbook" approach for administrations who wish to implement the validated the Value-Satisfaction model in their e-learning programs. The chapter provides guidelines on proper steps to collect data from your e-learning program, steps on preparing and analyzing the data, steps on how to develop your Value-Satisfaction grids, steps on how to calculate your LeVIS index, and elaborated section on how to understand your Value-Satisfaction grids and LeVIS index in order to improve your e-learning program.

References

Aczel, J., & Saaty, T.L. (1983). Procedures for synthesizing ratio judgments. *Journal of Mathematical Psychology, 27*(1), 93-102.

Ahituv, N. (1980). A systematic approach toward assessing the value of an information system. *MIS Quarterly, 4*(4), 61-75.

Alavi, M. (1994). Computer-mediated collaborative learning: An empirical evaluation. *MIS Quarterly, 18*(2), 159-179.

Alavi, M., & Leidner, D. (2001a). Research commentary: Technology mediated learning-a call for greater depth and breadth of research. *Information Systems Research, 12*(1), 1-10.

Alavi, M., & Leidner, D. (2001b). *Virtual learning systems*. Unpublished manuscript.

Alavi, M., Wheeler, B., & Valacich, J. (1995). Using IT to reengineer business education: An exploratory investigation of collaborative telelearning. *MIS Quarterly, 19*(3), 293-311.

Alavi, M., Yoo, Y., & Vogel, D. (1997). Using information technology to add value to management education. *Academy of Management Journal, 40*(6), 1310-1333.

Allport, G.W. (1935). Attitudes. In C. Murchison (Ed.), *A handbook of social psychology*. Worcester, MA: Clark University Press.

Allport, G.W. (1961). *Pattern and growth in personality*. New York: Holt, Rinehart, Winston.

Allport, G.W., Vernon, P., & Lindzey, G. (Eds.). (1951). *Study of values* (revised edition). *Manual of directions*. Boston: Houghton Mifflin.

Andrews, K.R. (1987). *The concept of corporate strategy*. Homewood, IL: Irwin.

Ansoff, H.I. (1965). *Corporate strategy*. New York: McGraw-Hill.

Arnold, V. (1995). Discussion of an experimental evaluation of measurements of information system effectiveness. *Journal of Information Systems, 9*(2), 85-91.

Bailey, J.E., & Pearson, S.W. (1983). Development of a tool for measuring and analyzing computer user satisfaction. *Management Science, 29*(5), 530-546.

Baroudi, J.J., & Orlikowski, W.J. (1988). A short-form measure of user information satisfaction: A psychometric evaluation and notes on use. *Journal of Management Information Systems, 4*(4), 44-60.

Beatty, S.E., Kahle, L.R., Homer, P.M., & Misra, S. (1985). Alternative measurement approaches to consumer values: The list of values and the Rokeach value survey. *Psychology and Marketing, 2*(3), 181-200.

Brown, M. (1976). Value—A necessary but neglected ingredient of motivation on the job. *Academy of Management Review, 1*(4), 15-24.

Bures, E., Abrami, P., & Amundsen, C. (2000). Student motivation to learn via computer conferencing. *Research in Higher Education, 41*(5), 593-621.

Carswell, L., Thomas, P., Petre, M., Price, B., & Richards, M. (1999). Understanding the "electronic" student: Analysis of functional requirements for distributed education. *Journal of Asynchronous Learning Networks, 3*(1), 7-18. Retrieved on January 24, 2005, from *http://www.aln.org/publications/jaln/v3n1/pdf/v3n1_carswell.pdf*

Cook, T.D., & Campbell, D.T. (1979). *Quasi-experimentation: Design and analysis issues for field settings*. Boston: Houghton Mifflin.

Chapman, D.W., Blackburn, R.W., & Austin, A.E. (1983). Expanding analytic possibilities of Rokeach values data. *Educational and Psychological Measurement, 43*(3), 419-421.

Connor, P.E., & Becker, B.W. (1979). Values and the organization: Suggestions for research. In M. Rokeach (Ed.), *Understanding human values*. New York: The Free Press.

Coyne, B.J. (1988). The predictive validity of the Rokeach value survey for college academic achievement. *Educational and Psychological Measurement, 48*(2), 165-173.

Davis, G.B., & Olson, M.H. (1985). *Management information systems: Conceptual foundations, structure and development.* New York: McGraw-Hill.

DeLone, W.H., & McLean, E.R. (1992). Information system success: The quest for the dependent variable. *Information Systems Research, 3*(1), 60-95.

DeLone, W.H., & McLean, E.R. (2002). Information systems success revisited. In *Proceedings of the 35th Hawaii International Conference on System Sciences*, Big Island, Hawaii, (pp. 238-250).

Doll, W., & Torkzadeh, G. (1988). The measurement of end-user computing satisfaction. *MIS Quarterly, 12*(2), 259-274.

Doll, W., & Torkzadeh, G. (1991). The measurement of end-user computing satisfaction: Theoretical and methodological issues. *MIS Quarterly, 15*(1), 5-9.

Doll, W., Xia, W., & Torkzadeh, G. (1994). A confirmatory factor analysis of the end-user computing satisfaction instrument. *MIS Quarterly, 18*(4), 453-461.

Doumpos, M., Zanakis, S.H., & Zopoundidis, C. (2001). Multicriteria preference disaggregation for classification problems with an application to global investing risk. *Decision Sciences, 32*(2), 333-385.

Durgee, J.F., O'Connor, G.C., & Veryzer, R.W. (1996). Observations: Translating values into product wants. *Journal of Advertising Research, 36*(6), 90-100.

England, G.W. (1967). Personal value systems of American managers. *Academy of Management Review, 10*(1), 56-68.

Etezadi-Amoli, J., & Farhoomand, A.F. (1991). On end-user computing satisfaction. *MIS Quarterly, 15*(1), 1-5.

Feather, N.T. (1967). An expectancy-value model of information-seeking behavior. *Psychological Review, 74*(5), 242-360.

Feather, N.T. (1975). *Values in education and society.* New York: The Free Press.

Flowler, F.J. (1995). *Improving survey questions, design and evaluation.* Thousand Oaks, CA: Sage Publication.

Fowler, F.J. (1993). *Survey research methods*. Newbury Park, CA: Sage Publication.

Gale, B.T. (1994). *Managing customer value*. New York: The Free Press.

Galletta, D.F., & Lederer, A.L. (1989). Some cautions on the measurement of user information satisfaction. *Decision Sciences, 20*(3), 419-439.

Grover, V., Jeong, S.R., & Segars, A.H. (1996). Information systems effectiveness: The construct space and patterns of application. *Information & Management, 31*(4), 177-191.

Hendrickson, A.R., Glorfeld, K., & Cronan, T.P. (1994). On the repeated test-retest reliability of the end-user computing satisfaction instrument: A comment. *Decision Sciences, 25*(4), 655-668.

Hiltz, R.S. (1993). *The virtual classroom: Learning without limits via computer networks*. Norwood, NJ: Ablex Publishing Corporation.

Hiltz, R.S. (1998). Collaborative learning in asynchronous learning networks: Building learning communities. In *Proceedings for WebNet 98 World Conference of the WWW, Internet, and Intranet*.

Hiltz, R.S., Coppola, N., Rotter, N., & Turoff, M. (2000). Measuring the importance of collaborative learning for the effectiveness of ALN: A multi-measure, multi-method approach. *Journal of Asynchronous Learning Networks, 4*(2). Retrieved on January 24, 2005, from *http://www.sloan-c.org/publications/jaln/v4n2/pdf/v4n2_hiltz.pdf*

Hiltz, R.S., & Johnson, K. (1990). User satisfaction with computer-mediated communication systems. *Management Science, 36*(6), 739-765.

Hiltz, R.S., & Wellman, B. (1997). Asynchronous learning networks as a virtual classroom. *Communications of the ACM, 40*(9), 44-49.

Ives, B., & Jarvenpaa, S. (1996). Will the Internet revolutionize business education and research? *Sloan Management Review, 37*(3), 33-41.

Ives, B., Olson, M.H., & Baroudi, J.J. (1983). The measure of user information satisfaction. *Communications of the ACM, 26*(10), 785-794.

Jacquet-Lagreze, E., & Siskos, J. (1982). Assessing a set of additive utility functions for multicriteria decision-making, the UTA method. *European Journal of Operationale Research, 10*(2), 151-165.

Johonson, A.H. (1978). *Modes of value*. New York: Philosophical Library, Inc.

Kahle, L.R. (1983). *Social values and social change: Adaptation to life in America*. New York: Praeger.

Kahle, L.R., & Chiagouris, L. (1997). *Values, lifestyles, and psychographics*. Mahwah, NJ: L. Erlbaum Associates.

Kahle, L.R., Beatty, S.E., & Homer, P. (1986). Alternative measurement approaches to consumer values: The list of values (LOV) and value and life style (VALS). *Journal of Consumer Research, 13*(3), 405-409.

Kahle, L.R., & Kennedy, P. (1988). Using the list of values (LOV) to understand consumers. *The Journal of Services Marketing, 2*(4), 49-56.

Keeney, R.L. (1992). *Values focus thinking*. Cambridge, MA: Harvard University Press.

Keeney, R.L. (1994). Using values in operations research. *Operations Research, 42*(5), 793-813.

Keeney, R.L. (1999). The value of Internet commerce to the customer. *Management Science, 45*(4), 533-542.

Keeney, R.L., & McDaniels, D. (1999). Identifying and structuring values to guide integrated resource planning at BC gas. *Operations Research, 47*(5), 651-662.

Keeney, R.L., & Raiffa, H. (1993). *Decisions with multiple objectives: Preferences and value tradeoffs*. Cambridge, MA: Harvard University Press. (First published in 1976 by Wiley, New York).

Kerlinger, F.N., & Lee, H.B. (2000). *Foundations of behavioral research* (4th ed.). Toronto: Wadsworth Thomson Learning.

Kettinger, W.J., & Lee, C.C. (1994). Perceived service quality and user satisfaction with the information service function. *Decision Sciences, 25*(5/6), 737-767.

Kim, K.K. (1989). User satisfaction: A synthesis of three different perspectives. *Journal of Information Systems, 4*(1), 1-12.

King, W., & Epstein, B. (1983). Assessing information system value: An empirical study. *Decision Sciences, 14*(1), 34-45.

Kluckhohn, C. (1951). Values and value-orientations in the theory of action. In T. Parsons & E. Shils (Eds.), *Towards a general theory of action*. Cambridge, MA: Harvard University Press.

Lee, S.M., Kim, Y.R., & Lee, J. (1995). An empirical study of the relationships among end-user information systems acceptance, training, and effectiveness. *Journal of Management Information Systems, 12*(2), 189-203.

Leidner, D., & Jarvenpaa, S. (1993). The Information age confronts education: case studies on electronic classrooms. *Information Systems Research, 4*(1), 24-54.

Leidner, D., & Jarvenpaa, S. (1995). The use of information technology to enhance management school education: A theoretical view. *MIS Quarterly, 19*(3), 265-291.

Levy, Y., & Murphy, K. (2002). Toward a value framework for online learning systems. In *Proceedings for the Hawaii International Conference on System Sciences (HICSS-35)*, Hawaii, (pp. 1-9).

Marks, B. (2000). Determinants of student evaluations of global measures of instructor and course value. *Journal of Marketing Education, 22*(2), 108-119.

McHanry, R., & Cronan, T.P. (1998). Computer simulation success: on the use of the end-user computing satisfaction instrument: A comment. *Decision Sciences, 29*(2), 525-537.

McHanry, R., Hightower, R., & Pearson, J. (2002). A validation of the end-user computing satisfaction instrument in Taiwan. *Information & Management, 39*(6), 503-512.

Mertler, C.A., & Vannatta, R.A. (2001). Advanced and multivariate statistical methods. Los Angeles, CA: Pyrczak Publishing.

Mintzberg, H., Ahlstrand, B., & Lampel, J. (1998). *Strategy safari: A guide through the wilds of strategic management.* New York: The Free Press.

Moore, M., & Kearsley, G. (1996). *Study guide for distance education: A systems view.* Belmont, CA: Wadsworth Publishing Company.

Newcomb, T.M., Turner, R.H., & Converse, P.E. (1965). *Social psychology.* New York: Holt, Rinehart, & Winston.

Ng, S.H. (1982). Choosing between the ranking and rating procedure for the comparison of values across culture. *European Journal of Social Psychology, 12*(2), 169-172.

Palvia, P.C. (1996). A model and instrument for measuring small business user satisfaction with information technology. *Information & Management, 31*(3), 151-163.

Payne, S.L. (1988). Values and ethics-related measures for management education. *Journal of Business Ethics, 7*(4), 273- 278.

Piccoli, G., Ahmad, R., & Ives, B. (2001). Web-based virtual learning environments: A research framework and a preliminary assessment of effectiveness in basic IT skills training. *MIS Quarterly, 25*(4), 401-426.

Pitt, L.F., Watson, R.T., & Kavan, C.B. (1995). Service quality: A measure of information systems effectiveness. *MIS Quarterly, 19*(2), 173-187.

Porter, M.E. (1991). Toward a dynamic theory of strategy. *Strategic Management Journal, 12*(1), 95-117.

Posner, B.Z., & Munson J.M. (1979). The importance of values in understanding organizational research. *Human Resource Management, 18*(3), 14-22.

Prescott, S., & Hopkins, G. (1984). The value and attitude structure of special educators. *College Student Journal, 18*(2), 56-59.

Reynolds, T.J., & Jolly, J.P. (1980). Measuring personal values: An evaluation of alternative methods. *Journal of Marketing Research, 17*(4), 531-536.

Rokeach, M. (1969). *Beliefs, attitudes, and values.* San Francisco: Jossey-Bass, Inc., Publishers.

Rokeach, M. (1973). *The nature of human values.* New York: The Free Press.

Rokeach, M. (1979). *Understanding human values.* New York: The Free Press.

Salmon, G. (2000). Computer mediated conferencing for management learning at the open university. *Management Learning, 31*(4), 491-502.

Sampson, S. E. (1999). Axiomatic justification for a geometric quality aggregation function. *Decision Sciences, 30*(2), 415-441.

Seddon, P., & Yip, S.K. (1992). An empirical evaluation of user information satisfaction (UIS) measures for use with general ledger accounting software. *Journal of Information Systems, 6*(1), 75-93.

Sethi, V., & King, R.C. (1999). Nonlinear and noncompensatory models in user information satisfaction measurement. *Information Systems Research, 10*(1), 87-96.

Sethi, V., Hwang, K.T., & Pegles, C. (1993). Information technology and organizational performance: A critical evaluation of computer world's index of information systems effectiveness. *Information and Management, 25*(4), 193-205.

Srinivasan, A. (1985). Alternatives measures of system effectiveness: Associations and implications. *MIS Quarterly, 9*(3), 243-253.

Stone, D.N. (1990). Assumptions and values in the practice of information system evaluation. *Journal of Information Systems, 5*(1), 1-17.

Straub, D. (1989). Validating instruments in MIS research. *MIS Quarterly, 13*(2), 147-170.

Sun, S. (2001). Base closure: An application of the analytic hierarchy process. *Infor, 39*(1), 17-32.

Swan, K. (2002). Building learning communities in online courses: The importance of interaction. *Education, Communication and Information, 2*(1), 23-49.

Swan, K., Shea, P., Frederickson, E., Pickett, A., Pelz, W., & Maher, G. (2000). Building knowledge building communities: Consistency, contact, and communication in the virtual classroom. *Journal of Educational Computing Research, 23*(4), 389-413.

Thompson, B., Levitov, J.E., & Miederhoff, P.A. (1982). Validity of the Rokeach value survey. *Educational and Psychological Measurement, 42*, 899-914.

Torkzadeh, G., & Doll, W. (1991). Test-retest reliability of the end-user computing satisfaction instrument. *Decision Sciences, 22*(1), 26-38.

Valentin, E.K. (2001). SWOT analysis from a resource-based view. *Journal of Marketing Theory and Practice, 9*(2), 54-70.

Watson, G. (1966). *Social psychology: Issues and insights*. Philadelphia: Lippincott.

Webster, J., & Hackley, P. (1997). Teaching effectiveness in technology-mediated distance learning. *Academy of Management Journal, 40*(6), 1282-1309.

Williams, R.M. (1979). Change and stability in values and value system: A sociological perspective. In M. Rokeach (Ed.), *Understanding human values*. New York: The Free Press.

Woodruff, A.D. (1942). Personal values and the direction of behavior. *School Review, 50*, 32-42.

Yuthas, K., & Eining, M.M. (1995). An experimental evaluation of measurements of information system effectiveness. *Journal of Information Systems, 9*(2), 69-84.

Zopoundidis, C., Doumpos, M., & Zanakis, S.H. (1999). Stock evaluation using a preference disaggregation methodology. *Decision Sciences, 30*(2), 313-334.

Terms and Definitions

E-learning system (ELS): The entire technological, organizational, and management system that facilitates and enables students learning via the Internet.

End-user computing: A person who combines the two roles of developing the reports as well as utilizing the system output (the reports) to aid in the decision-making process.

Learners' perceived effectiveness of e-learning systems: An e-learning system is considered effective when learners perceive its characteristics as highly important and are highly satisfied by those same characteristics.

1. **Comparative system effectiveness:** A comparison of an e-learning system with peer e-learning system.

2. **Improvement system effectiveness**: A comparison of an e-learning system over time.

3. **Normative system effectiveness**: A comparison of an e-learning system with a theoretically ideal e-learning system.

Learners' satisfaction items (satisfaction items): The measures of the perceived performance level learners find at a post-experience point of time with each e-learning system characteristic.

Learners' value items (value items): The measures of the importance of enduring core beliefs concerning each characteristic of e-learning systems when learning online.

Learners' dimension satisfaction measure: The aggregation of all perceived learners' satisfaction items with each dimension.

Learners' dimension value measure: The aggregation of all perceived learners' value items with each dimension.

Learners' overall satisfaction (overall satisfaction): The aggregation of all four learners' dimension satisfaction measures.

Learners' overall value (overall value): The aggregation of all four learners' dimension value measures.

Proposed e-learning system characteristics: The attributes (or features) associated with e-learning systems (e.g., quality of technical support, interaction with professor, quality of course content, learner's comfort with technology, etc.).

Proposed e-learning system dimensions: (1) Technology and support; (2) Course; (3) Professor; (4) Learner. These are extended categories of e-learning system characteristics from literature.

Survey items: Questions that seek to measure users' perceptions on characteristics.

Satisfaction: The perceived performance level users find at a post-experience point of time with e-learning systems.

Value (overall, for the whole e-learning system): An enduring core belief about the level of importance learners attribute to e-learning system as a whole.

Values (importance, preferences, desirables, and weights in the context of e-learning systems): Enduring principles learners use to evaluate the importance of e-learning system characteristics.

Appendices

Appendix A: List of Acronyms

CAI   Computer-Assisted Instruction
DA   Discriminant Analysis
EUCS   End-User Computer Satisfaction
IS   Information Systems
GDSS   Group Decision Support System
LeVIS   Learners' Value Index of Satisfaction
LOV   List Of Values
MIS   Management Information Systems
OR   Operations Research
PCA   Principal Component Analysis
RVS   Rokeach's Value Survey
TML   Technology Mediated Learning
UIS   User Information Satisfaction
VLE   Virtual Learning Environment (Another name for e-learning system)

Appendix B: Open-Ended Questionnaire (Phase I)

Section 1:

Please identify five things that are important for you when learning online:

1. _____
2. _____
3. _____
4. _____
5. _____

Section 2:

A. System, Technology, Network and Support

Now, please think about issues related to *System, Technology, Network and Support* and try to identify five more things that are important for you when learning online:

1. _____
2. _____
3. _____
4. _____
5. _____

B. Content of Course

Now, please think about issues related to *Content of Courses* and try to identify five more things that are important for you when learning online:

1. _____
2. _____
3. _____
4. _____
5. _____

C. Instructors

Now, please think about issues related to *Instructors* and try to identify five more things that are important for you when learning online:

1. _____
2. _____
3. _____
4. _____
5. _____

D. Student or Learner

Now, please think about issues related to *Student or Learner* and try to identify five more things that are important for you when learning online:

1. _____
2. _____
3. _____
4. _____
5. _____

Appendix C: PCA Results for Satisfaction — Pilot Data

PCA Varimax Rotated Component Matrix (Satisfaction) + Recoded Variables
Pilot Study (n=141)

	1	2	3	4	5	6	7	8	9
B11_SAT	0.823	0.196	0.114	0.079	0.057	0.231	0.115	0.107	-0.004
B2_SAT	0.739	0.269	0.183	0.125	0.176	0.145	0.071	-0.089	0.151
B3_SAT	0.738	0.225	0.178	0.081	0.270	0.112	0.038	-0.042	-0.010
B10_SAT	0.705	0.127	0.158	0.218	0.207	0.077	0.137	-0.065	0.113
B5_SAT	0.690	0.187	0.156	0.164	0.243	0.059	0.085	-0.247	0.116
D1_SAT	0.689	0.225	0.154	-0.001	0.279	0.348	-0.031	0.000	0.159
C6_SAT	0.682	-0.082	0.127	0.277	0.161	0.291	0.071	0.098	-0.035
B7_SAT	0.677	0.172	0.159	0.090	0.237	0.359	0.138	-0.049	0.038
B4_SAT	0.658	0.243	0.209	0.072	0.121	0.200	0.121	-0.149	0.151
B1_SAT	0.631	0.205	0.297	0.287	0.126	0.158	0.030	-0.196	0.081
B8_SAT	0.614	0.243	0.282	0.229	0.145	0.097	0.133	0.034	-0.034
C5_SAT	0.571	0.093	0.269	0.176	0.157	0.447	0.104	0.022	0.065
C7_SAT	0.536	-0.007	0.154	0.166	0.339	0.360	0.086	-0.302	-0.010
B9_SAT	0.506	0.338	0.394	0.174	0.157	0.054	0.139	0.100	-0.013
A2_SAT	0.085	0.823	0.037	0.091	0.163	0.032	0.103	-0.095	0.109
A3_SAT	0.233	0.809	0.123	0.086	0.132	0.003	0.054	-0.083	0.062
A1_SAT	0.140	0.762	0.162	0.134	0.164	-0.017	0.052	-0.125	0.026
A8_SAT_R	-0.159	-0.759	-0.047	-0.135	-0.044	-0.055	-0.150	0.182	0.045
A5_SAT	0.230	0.731	0.039	0.212	-0.030	0.194	0.027	0.133	0.063
A4_SAT	0.104	0.660	0.208	0.326	0.071	0.076	-0.105	0.062	-0.029
A6_SAT	0.184	0.638	0.114	0.354	0.048	0.178	0.085	0.135	0.028
A7_SAT	0.175	0.606	0.194	0.518	0.145	0.026	-0.035	0.082	-0.097
A14_SAT	0.421	0.451	0.055	0.417	0.125	-0.010	0.079	-0.243	0.112
D15_SAT	0.078	0.060	0.812	0.244	0.196	0.116	0.096	-0.092	0.181
D14_SAT	0.240	0.053	0.803	0.234	0.150	0.079	0.030	-0.150	0.157
D11_SAT	0.388	0.231	0.715	-0.033	-0.013	0.156	0.046	0.077	-0.117
D13_SAT	0.207	0.147	0.712	0.266	0.093	0.118	0.140	-0.191	0.153
D12_SAT	0.413	0.207	0.671	0.089	0.073	0.103	-0.049	0.025	-0.171
D6_SAT	0.433	0.307	0.438	-0.055	0.293	0.230	0.030	0.338	-0.076
D7_SAT	0.127	0.124	0.434	0.173	0.201	0.043	-0.106	0.182	0.017
A10_SAT	0.111	0.473	0.264	0.699	0.088	0.051	0.032	-0.030	-0.072
A11_SAT	0.373	0.325	0.104	0.693	0.068	0.095	-0.012	-0.151	0.034
A13_SAT	0.296	0.414	0.264	0.670	0.010	0.003	-0.028	0.011	0.037
A12_SAT	0.207	0.482	0.295	0.643	0.101	0.008	0.020	0.020	0.036
A9_SAT	0.104	0.472	0.329	0.556	0.090	0.132	-0.054	0.028	-0.047
D3_SAT	0.378	0.144	0.142	0.051	0.800	0.154	0.203	0.021	0.073
D2_SAT	0.384	0.193	0.107	0.098	0.760	0.172	0.136	0.056	0.093
D4_SAT	0.262	0.066	0.142	0.149	0.740	0.221	0.171	-0.009	0.143
D5_SAT	0.455	0.169	0.343	0.082	0.607	0.216	0.039	-0.041	-0.030
D8_SAT_R	-0.127	-0.293	-0.197	0.014	-0.481	-0.055	-0.048	0.270	0.241
C2_SAT	0.381	0.011	0.122	0.068	0.230	0.811	0.101	-0.010	0.059
C4_SAT	0.460	0.121	0.204	0.037	0.203	0.778	0.102	0.011	0.058
C1_SAT	0.497	0.135	0.216	0.106	0.208	0.655	0.106	-0.001	0.044
C3_SAT_R	-0.409	-0.429	-0.031	0.075	-0.131	-0.565	-0.048	0.430	-0.029
D10_SAT	0.275	0.187	0.144	0.024	0.122	0.080	0.828	-0.016	-0.020
D9_SAT	0.180	0.048	-0.050	-0.056	0.296	0.159	0.824	-0.088	0.147
B6_SAT_R	-0.480	-0.265	-0.112	-0.093	-0.040	-0.076	-0.154	0.542	0.103
B12_SAT	0.358	0.148	0.214	-0.030	0.138	0.149	0.136	0.047	0.804
Cronbach	0.9537	0.79 (.91)	0.8914	0.9201	0.68 (.93)	0.17 (.94)	0.7834	-	-
% of Var	42.29	10.34	5.43	4.39	2.97	2.95	2.63	2.49	2.12
Cumul %	42.29	52.63	58.07	62.46	65.43	68.37	71.00	73.49	75.61

Appendix D: PCA Results
for Value — Pilot Data

PCA Varimax Rotated Component Matrix (Value) + Recoded Variables
Pilot Study (n=141)

	1	2	3	4	5	6	7	8	9	10
C4_VAL	0.748	0.257	0.095	0.171	0.127	0.110	0.032	0.024	0.220	0.091
C2_VAL	0.728	0.135	0.131	0.044	0.173	0.212	0.119	-0.020	0.145	-0.068
C5_VAL	0.677	0.334	0.103	0.198	0.102	0.135	0.049	0.089	0.129	-0.056
C1_VAL	0.673	0.070	0.195	0.150	0.155	0.183	0.084	0.126	0.163	0.105
C7_VAL	0.629	0.246	0.205	0.233	0.020	-0.038	0.167	-0.053	0.009	0.073
C6_VAL	0.617	0.268	0.217	-0.020	0.113	0.202	0.125	0.106	0.080	0.121
D6_VAL	0.528	0.227	0.099	0.163	0.236	0.272	0.459	0.067	-0.052	-0.141
B1_VAL	0.519	0.408	0.181	-0.001	0.160	0.009	-0.138	0.445	-0.053	-0.119
D7_VAL	0.474	0.096	0.006	0.273	0.293	0.277	0.325	0.053	-0.117	0.080
B12_VAL	0.443	0.229	0.072	0.329	0.041	0.343	0.028	0.051	-0.050	0.253
D8_VAL_R	-0.400	-0.178	-0.201	-0.250	-0.154	-0.280	-0.283	-0.054	-0.088	0.065
D1_VAL	0.388	0.289	0.066	0.219	0.164	0.163	0.340	0.005	0.204	-0.145
B4_VAL	0.320	0.695	0.008	0.212	0.176	0.051	0.155	0.196	0.006	-0.109
B5_VAL	0.041	0.694	0.011	0.148	0.090	-0.065	0.227	0.148	0.064	0.118
B11_VAL	0.363	0.597	0.135	-0.006	0.195	0.276	0.105	-0.031	0.081	0.251
B3_VAL	0.317	0.588	0.081	0.284	0.194	0.176	-0.107	0.016	0.280	0.039
B10_VAL	0.282	0.588	0.069	0.140	0.253	0.305	0.051	-0.132	0.159	0.115
B9_VAL	0.281	0.585	0.210	0.003	0.073	0.064	0.013	-0.041	-0.182	0.290
B8_VAL	0.228	0.543	0.277	0.098	0.244	0.223	0.287	-0.061	0.095	-0.219
B7_VAL	0.249	0.539	0.139	0.287	0.142	0.197	0.146	0.030	0.151	-0.092
B2_VAL	0.430	0.507	0.168	0.046	0.212	-0.048	-0.017	0.331	0.072	-0.137
A2_VAL	0.130	0.118	0.885	0.024	0.098	0.152	0.014	0.007	-0.118	0.032
A1_VAL	0.092	0.100	0.854	0.008	0.103	0.158	0.219	0.012	-0.019	-0.032
A3_VAL	0.217	0.132	0.727	0.015	0.329	0.037	0.110	0.045	0.122	0.010
A5_VAL	0.254	0.083	0.684	0.017	0.416	0.003	0.134	0.142	0.015	-0.035
A4_VAL	0.160	0.050	0.657	-0.059	0.468	-0.039	0.109	0.085	0.001	0.089
A6_VAL	0.319	0.046	0.518	0.021	0.407	-0.086	-0.089	0.007	0.166	0.258
D2_VAL	0.118	0.122	-0.001	0.908	0.025	0.129	0.020	-0.086	0.062	0.095
D3_VAL	0.125	0.173	0.016	0.905	0.003	0.167	0.096	-0.041	0.071	0.055
D4_VAL	0.189	0.065	-0.047	0.898	0.017	0.034	0.080	0.088	0.024	0.016
D5_VAL	0.149	0.163	0.043	0.855	0.063	0.109	0.163	0.130	0.002	0.070
A10_VAL	0.123	0.139	0.337	-0.061	0.731	0.148	0.098	0.179	0.039	-0.013
A11_VAL	0.131	0.196	-0.020	0.204	0.705	0.018	-0.074	-0.043	0.097	0.147
A13_VAL	0.186	0.199	0.257	-0.074	0.654	0.163	0.180	0.118	-0.033	-0.009
A9_VAL	0.184	0.148	0.346	-0.013	0.652	0.194	-0.031	0.115	0.033	0.033
A7_VAL	0.086	0.050	0.389	0.022	0.597	0.122	0.159	0.094	-0.047	0.154
A12_VAL	0.082	0.366	0.356	0.144	0.593	0.039	-0.021	-0.066	0.094	0.000
D14_VAL	0.263	0.137	0.150	0.158	0.104	0.816	0.088	0.063	-0.009	-0.029
D15_VAL	0.225	0.133	0.067	0.230	0.109	0.815	0.022	0.028	0.068	0.104
D13_VAL	0.169	0.091	0.097	0.125	0.233	0.659	0.427	0.244	0.070	0.016
D9_VAL	0.094	0.201	0.148	0.089	0.013	0.080	0.748	0.010	-0.023	-0.043
D10_VAL	0.102	0.034	0.235	0.334	-0.091	-0.006	0.715	-0.016	0.071	0.285
D11_VAL	0.325	0.031	0.023	-0.121	0.269	0.333	0.528	0.266	-0.056	-0.078
A8_VAL_R	0.080	-0.088	-0.509	-0.146	-0.146	-0.076	0.039	-0.657	-0.132	-0.237
D12_VAL	0.278	0.138	-0.037	0.014	0.172	0.307	0.312	0.653	0.060	0.057
C3_VAL_R	-0.308	-0.086	0.018	-0.098	-0.052	-0.038	-0.030	0.019	-0.851	-0.022
B6_VAL_R	-0.178	-0.480	-0.036	-0.034	-0.070	-0.053	0.021	-0.261	-0.596	-0.026
A14_VAL	0.055	0.118	0.099	0.240	0.251	0.081	0.044	0.107	0.040	0.847
Cronbach	0.84 (.91)	0.8918	0.9093	0.9484	0.8696	0.8604	0.6412	-1.221	0.6628	.
% of Var	32.04	11.64	6.38	5.30	3.87	3.22	2.85	2.73	2.57	2.24
Cumul %	32.04	43.68	50.05	55.36	59.23	62.45	65.30	68.02	70.60	72.84

Appendix E: Revised Survey Instrument

Online Learning Experience

The following is a list of items related to the **technology and support** of online learning (across all online courses).
Please read each item and rate your level of **satisfaction** AND the level of **importance** you attribute to each item when learning online.
Please rate the level of **satisfaction** for each item from: 'Extremely Unsatisfied' to 'Extremely Satisfied'. And at the same time...please rate the level of **importance** for each item from: 'Not Important' to 'Extremely Important'.

A. The following items related to technology and support:

Items	Level of Satisfaction						Level of Importance					
	Extremely unsatisfied	Very unsatisfied	Unsatisfied	Satisfied	Very satisfied	Extremely satisfied	Not Important	Not so Important	Slightly Important	Important	Very Important	Extremely Important
A1. Quick answer from technical support via phone	☐	☐	☐	☐	☐	☐	☐	☐	☐	☐	☐	☐
A2. Quick answer from technical support after-hours via e-mail	☐	☐	☐	☐	☐	☐	☐	☐	☐	☐	☐	☐
A3. Quality of technical support	☐	☐	☐	☐	☐	☐	☐	☐	☐	☐	☐	☐
A4. System operation time (up-time)	☐	☐	☐	☐	☐	☐	☐	☐	☐	☐	☐	☐
A5. Reduced system errors	☐	☐	☐	☐	☐	☐	☐	☐	☐	☐	☐	☐
A6. System security (discourage hacking, secure access, etc.)	☐	☐	☐	☐	☐	☐	☐	☐	☐	☐	☐	☐
A7. Access to courses from anywhere in the world (via the Internet)	☐	☐	☐	☐	☐	☐	☐	☐	☐	☐	☐	☐
A8. Low network availability & High network congestion	☐	☐	☐	☐	☐	☐	☐	☐	☐	☐	☐	☐
A9. Learning at anytime of the day (schedule flexibility)	☐	☐	☐	☐	☐	☐	☐	☐	☐	☐	☐	☐
A10. Submit assignments from anywhere (via the Internet)	☐	☐	☐	☐	☐	☐	☐	☐	☐	☐	☐	☐
A11. Different system tools (chat, bulletin board or discussion forums, etc.)	☐	☐	☐	☐	☐	☐	☐	☐	☐	☐	☐	☐
A12. Access of all courses from one area (My WebCT)	☐	☐	☐	☐	☐	☐	☐	☐	☐	☐	☐	☐
A13. Taking quizzes remotely (off-campus)	☐	☐	☐	☐	☐	☐	☐	☐	☐	☐	☐	☐
A14. Review course audios	☐	☐	☐	☐	☐	☐	☐	☐	☐	☐	☐	☐
A15. Overall, how would you rate your level of **satisfaction** with the **technology and support**?	☐	☐	☐	☐	☐	☐						
A16. Overall, how **important** are **technology and support** to you when learning online?	→		→		→		☐	☐	☐	☐	☐	☐

Appendix E:
Revised Survey Instrument (cont.)

Online Learning Experience

The following is a list of items related to **online course content** (across all online courses) of online learning.

Please read each item and rate your level of **satisfaction** AND the level of **importance** you attribute to each item when learning online.

Please rate the level of **satisfaction** for each item from: 'Extremely Unsatisfied' to 'Extremely Satisfied'. And at the same time...please rate the level of **importance** for each item from: 'Not Important' to 'Extremely Important'.

B. The following items related to the online content of courses:

Items	Level of Satisfaction						Level of Importance					
	Extremely unsatisfied	Very unsatisfied	Unsatisfied	Satisfied	Very satisfied	Extremely satisfied	Not Important	Not so Important	Slightly Important	Important	Very Important	Extremely Important
B1. Availability of course content	☐	☐	☐	☐	☐	☐	☐	☐	☐	☐	☐	☐
B2. Quality content of courses	☐	☐	☐	☐	☐	☐	☐	☐	☐	☐	☐	☐
B3. Amount of material in courses	☐	☐	☐	☐	☐	☐	☐	☐	☐	☐	☐	☐
B4. Interesting subject matter	☐	☐	☐	☐	☐	☐	☐	☐	☐	☐	☐	☐
B5. Difficulty of subject matter	☐	☐	☐	☐	☐	☐	☐	☐	☐	☐	☐	☐
B6. Lack of availability of other Content (syllabus, objectives, assignments, schedule)	☐	☐	☐	☐	☐	☐	☐	☐	☐	☐	☐	☐
B7. Enjoyment from the courses/lessons	☐	☐	☐	☐	☐	☐	☐	☐	☐	☐	☐	☐
B8. Ease-of-use (with content of courses, navigation, interface, etc.)	☐	☐	☐	☐	☐	☐	☐	☐	☐	☐	☐	☐
B9. Similar of interface across all online courses	☐	☐	☐	☐	☐	☐	☐	☐	☐	☐	☐	☐
B10. Gathering information quickly	☐	☐	☐	☐	☐	☐	☐	☐	☐	☐	☐	☐
B11. Organization of courses (content of courses, organization of assignments, etc. across all courses)	☐	☐	☐	☐	☐	☐	☐	☐	☐	☐	☐	☐
B12. Taking practice tests prior to graded test	☐	☐	☐	☐	☐	☐	☐	☐	☐	☐	☐	☐
B13. Overall, how would you rate your level of **satisfaction** with **online content of courses**?	☐	☐	☐	☐	☐	☐						
B14. Overall, how **important** is **online content of courses** to you when learning online?	→		→		→		☐	☐	☐	☐	☐	☐

Appendix E:
Revised Survey Instrument (cont.)

Online Learning Experience

The following is a list of items related to **the professors** when learning online (across all online professors).

Please read each item and rate your level of **satisfaction** AND the level of **importance** you attribute to each item when learning online.

Please rate the level of **satisfaction** for each item from: 'Extremely Unsatisfied' to 'Extremely Satisfied'. And at the same time...please rate the level of **importance** for each item from: 'Not Important' to 'Extremely Important'.

C. The following items related to the professors:

Items	Level of Satisfaction						Level of Importance					
	Extremely unsatisfied	Very unsatisfied	Unsatisfied	Satisfied	Very satisfied	Extremely satisfied	Not Important	Not so Important	Slightly Important	Important	Very Important	Extremely Important
C1. Amount of professor-to-student online interaction	☐	☐	☐	☐	☐	☐	☐	☐	☐	☐	☐	☐
C2. Professors' attitude (across all professors)	☐	☐	☐	☐	☐	☐	☐	☐	☐	☐	☐	☐
C3. Not learning a lot from the Professors (across all courses)	☐	☐	☐	☐	☐	☐	☐	☐	☐	☐	☐	☐
C4. Quality of professor-to-student online interaction	☐	☐	☐	☐	☐	☐	☐	☐	☐	☐	☐	☐
C5. Freedom of learning (selective Seeking and processing of information)	☐	☐	☐	☐	☐	☐	☐	☐	☐	☐	☐	☐
C6. Submission time window for assignments and quizzes	☐	☐	☐	☐	☐	☐	☐	☐	☐	☐	☐	☐
C7. Online workload of courses	☐	☐	☐	☐	☐	☐	☐	☐	☐	☐	☐	☐
C8. Overall, how would you rate your level of **satisfaction** with the **professors**?	☐	☐	☐	☐	☐	☐						
C9. Overall, how **important** are **professors** to you when learning online?	→		→		→		☐	☐	☐	☐	☐	☐

Appendix E:
Revised Survey Instrument (cont.)

Online Learning Experience

The following is a list of items related to **learner self assessment** when learning online (across all online courses).
Please read each item and rate your level of **satisfaction** AND the level of **importance** you attribute to each item when learning online.
Please rate the level of **satisfaction** for each item from: 'Extremely Unsatisfied' to 'Extremely Satisfied'. And at the same time...please rate the level of **importance** for each item from: 'Not Important' to 'Extremely Important'.

D. The following items related to learner self-assessment:

Items		Level of Satisfaction						Level of Importance					
		Extremely unsatisfied	Very unsatisfied	Unsatisfied	Satisfied	Very satisfied	Extremely satisfied	Not Important	Not so Important	Slightly Important	Important	Very Important	Extremely Important
D1.	Learning a lot in these classes	☐	☐	☐	☐	☐	☐	☐	☐	☐	☐	☐	☐
D2.	Amount of interaction with classmates	☐	☐	☐	☐	☐	☐	☐	☐	☐	☐	☐	☐
D3.	Quality of interaction with classmates	☐	☐	☐	☐	☐	☐	☐	☐	☐	☐	☐	☐
D4.	Classmates' attitude (across all courses)	☐	☐	☐	☐	☐	☐	☐	☐	☐	☐	☐	☐
D5.	Being part of a 'class' although it was online	☐	☐	☐	☐	☐	☐	☐	☐	☐	☐	☐	☐
D6.	Your comfort with online learning and technology	☐	☐	☐	☐	☐	☐	☐	☐	☐	☐	☐	☐
D7.	Your Internet and computer skills	☐	☐	☐	☐	☐	☐	☐	☐	☐	☐	☐	☐
D8.	Lack of self-discipline and time management	☐	☐	☐	☐	☐	☐	☐	☐	☐	☐	☐	☐
D9.	Cost of courses	☐	☐	☐	☐	☐	☐	☐	☐	☐	☐	☐	☐
D10.	Cost of ISP and Internet access	☐	☐	☐	☐	☐	☐	☐	☐	☐	☐	☐	☐
D11.	Reduced travel cost/time (to and from campus)	☐	☐	☐	☐	☐	☐	☐	☐	☐	☐	☐	☐
D12.	Ability to travel while taking online courses (for business or other)	☐	☐	☐	☐	☐	☐	☐	☐	☐	☐	☐	☐
D13.	Employer support and your ability to work while learning	☐	☐	☐	☐	☐	☐	☐	☐	☐	☐	☐	☐
D14.	Attendance to family responsibilities	☐	☐	☐	☐	☐	☐	☐	☐	☐	☐	☐	☐
D15.	Family support	☐	☐	☐	☐	☐	☐	☐	☐	☐	☐	☐	☐
D16.	Overall, how would you rate your level of **satisfaction** with the **above items** when learning online?	☐	☐	☐	☐	☐	☐						
D17.	Overall, how **important** are the **above items** to you when learning online?	→		→		→		☐	☐	☐	☐	☐	☐

Appendix E:
Revised Survey Instrument (cont.)

Global Questions:												
G1.	Taking into account all your previous answers about **satisfaction** (including this section and the previous three sections), what is your overall **SATISFACTION** level from the online learning?	☐ Extremely unsatisfied	☐ Very unsatisfied	☐ Unsatisfied	☐ Satisfied	☐ Very satisfied	☐ Extremely satisfied						
G2.	Taking into account all your previous answers about the **important** level (including this section and the previous three sections), overall how **IMPORTANT** all the items to you when learning online?	→		→		→		☐ Not Important	☐ Not so Important	☐ Slightly Important	☐ Important	☐ Very Important	☐ Extremely Important
G3.	Taking into account all your previous answers on both **satisfaction** and **importance** level (including all items in this section and the previous three sections), how would you rate your **overall educational LEARNING** outcomes?				→		☐ Extremely Poor	☐ Poor	☐ Slightly Poor	☐ Slightly Good	☐ Good	☐ Extremely Good

Appendix F: Cases Cleaning and Reflection Priority

Cases Cleaning and Reflection Priority (n=207)

Case No	SAT 1&2	SAT 3&4	Maha (SAT)	SAT44 1	2	3	4	5	6	SAT4 1	2	3	4	5	6	KS SAT	Refl SAT	VAL 1&2	VAL 3&4	Maha (VAL)	VAL44 1	2	3	4	5	6	VAL4 1	2	3	4	5	6	KS VAL	Refl VAL
1				0	1	2	5	12	24	0	0	0	2	0	2	0.318					1	0	1	3	7	32	0	0	0	1	0	3	0.136	4
3				2	0	0	4	1	37	0	0	0	0	0	4	0.159		99			3	1	2	1	0	37	0	0	0	0	0	4	0.159	
4				0	2	1	18	15	8	0	0	0	4	0	0	0.523		95			0	4	0	3	1	36	0	0	0	0	2	2	0.318	
7				0	1	1	8	1	33	0	0	0	1	1	2	0.250					0	0	0	0	1	43	0	0	0	0	0	4	0.023	2
8				0	0	1	7	11	25	0	0	0	1	0	3	0.182					0	0	0	7	7	30	0	0	1	0	0	3	0.091	3
9		Q+A		14	6	4	14	6	0	2	0	0	1	1	0	0.182				Q	0	2	2	8	13	19	0	0	1	0	0	3	0.318	
10				0	1	1	5	15	22	0	0	0	0	1	3	0.250					0	0	0	1	2	41	0	0	0	0	0	4	0.068	3
12				0	0	0	0	0	44	0	0	0	0	0	4	0.000	Delete				0	0	0	0	0	44	0	0	0	0	0	4	0.000	Delete
13				0	0	1	10	16	17	0	0	0	1	3	0	0.386					0	0	3	1	11	29	0	0	0	0	1	3	0.091	3
15				0	1	3	10	6	24	0	0	1	1	1	1	0.295					1	0	0	1	5	37	0	0	0	0	1	3	0.091	3
16			Q	3	4	2	12	9	14	1	0	0	1	1	1	0.182					0	0	0	4	4	36	0	0	0	0	0	4	0.182	
17				0	2	4	15	10	13	0	0	0	2	1	1	0.136	4	99		Q+A	4	5	4	12	12	7	0	0	0	0	3	1	0.568	
18		95		7	9	2	14	9	3	0	1	0	2	1	0	0.159					0	1	3	8	7	25	0	0	0	1	0	3	0.182	
19				0	0	2	20	15	7	0	0	0	2	2	0	0.159					0	3	5	12	16	8	0	0	0	1	2	1	0.205	
20				1	2	4	17	14	6	0	0	1	3	0	0	0.455				Q	0	0	7	6	12	19	0	0	1	1	2	0	0.432	
21				0	0	0	2	11	31	0	0	0	0	1	3	0.045	2				0	0	0	0	9	35	0	0	0	0	0	4	0.205	
22				0	0	8	6	0	30	0	0	1	0	0	3	0.068	3				0	0	0	0	0	44	0	0	0	0	0	4	0.000	1
23				0	0	3	22	18	1	0	0	0	3	1	0	0.182					0	0	0	0	0	44	0	0	0	0	0	4	0.000	1
24				0	0	1	1	8	34	0	0	0	1	1	2	0.273					0	0	0	1	1	42	0	0	0	0	0	4	0.045	2
25	99		Q+A	19	7	4	10	3	1	2	1	0	1	0	0	0.159					0	0	4	5	6	29	0	0	0	1	1	2	0.159	
26				0	0	2	16	17	9	0	0	0	2	1	1	0.091	3				0	0	0	1	25	18	0	0	0	0	2	2	0.091	3
27				0	0	4	34	6	0	0	0	0	4	0	0	0.136	4				0	0	0	5	15	24	0	0	0	1	0	3	0.205	
28	99			12	10	9	13	0	0	1	1	2	0	0	0	0.205		99		Q+A	11	7	6	9	5	6	1	1	0	0	0	2	0.250	
29			Q+A	4	8	15	5	12	0	0	1	1	0	2	0	0.227					0	0	1	12	13	18	0	0	0	1	0	3	0.341	
30				0	0	6	17	18	3	0	0	1	0	2	1	0.273				Q+A	3	5	0	7	18	11	0	0	0	2	1	1	0.182	
32				0	0	1	27	14	2	0	0	1	2	1	0	0.227		99			0	0	4	23	9	8	0	0	0	1	3	0	0.364	
33	99			1	1	2	18	8	14	0	0	1	2	1	0	0.318			95		0	4	0	5	14	21	0	0	0	0	0	4	0.523	
35	99			5	18	1	20	0	0	1	1	0	2	0	0	0.136	4				0	0	0	43	1	0	0	0	0	4	0	0	0.023	2
36				0	0	0	44	0	0	0	0	0	4	0	0	0.000	Delete				0	0	0	44	0	0	0	0	0	4	0	0	0.000	Delete
37				0	1	5	17	4	17	0	0	0	2	1	1	0.136	4				0	0	2	12	5	25	0	0	0	0	1	3	0.318	
38				0	2	0	6	13	23	0	0	0	1	1	2	0.068	3				0	0	0	1	1	43	0	0	0	0	1	3	0.227	
39				1	0	0	3	11	29	4	0	0	0	0	0	0.977					0	0	0	0	2	42	0	0	0	0	0	4	0.045	2
40			Q+A	3	4	5	13	5	14	2	0	0	1	1	0	0.432					0	1	0	5	32	6	0	0	0	0	3	1	0.136	4
42				0	0	1	15	14	14	0	0	2	2	0	0	0.318					0	0	0	0	11	33	0	0	0	0	1	3	0.000	
43				0	0	2	9	24	9	0	0	0	1	2	1	0.045	2				0	1	3	10	13	17	0	0	0	2	1	1	0.182	
44				0	0	0	31	5	8	0	0	0	4	0	0	0.295				Q	1	3	11	18	4	7	0	0	1	3	0	0	0.250	
47				3	4	8	15	8	6	0	1	0	1	1	1	0.182			95		1	3	2	4	9	25	0	0	0	1	1	2	0.136	4
48				0	0	2	13	12	17	0	0	0	1	1	2	0.114	4				0	0	0	0	0	44	0	0	0	0	0	4	0.000	1
51				0	2	3	30	9	0	0	0	1	3	0	0	0.205					0	0	6	21	15	2	0	0	1	2	1	0	0.136	4
52				1	7	3	28	0	5	0	1	0	3	0	0	0.114	4				0	0	0	1	0	43	0	0	0	0	0	4	0.023	2
53				0	2	3	5	19	15	0	0	0	1	0	3	0.409					0	0	0	4	13	27	0	0	0	0	1	3	0.136	4
55				1	0	1	14	19	9	0	0	0	2	1	1	0.136	4				0	0	0	7	4	33	0	0	0	0	0	4	0.250	
56		95	Q+A	0	5	5	11	16	7	0	1	2	1	0	0	0.523		99			1	2	2	5	12	22	0	0	4	0	0	0	0.886	
57		95		8	3	3	5	3	22	2	0	0	0	0	2	0.318					0	0	0	1	4	39	0	0	0	0	0	4	0.114	4
59			Q+A	6	1	4	15	7	11	0	0	0	2	0	2	0.250					0	1	2	14	9	18	0	0	0	1	0	3	0.341	
60				0	0	6	19	8	11	0	0	1	1	1	1	0.114	4	99			2	13	26	1	1	1	0	1	3	0	0	0	0.091	3
62				1	1	4	6	1	31	0	0	1	0	0	3	0.136					0	0	2	3	0	39	0	0	0	1	0	3	0.136	4
65				0	3	13	28	0	0	0	0	1	3	0	0	0.114	4				0	0	4	36	4	0	0	0	1	3	0	0	0.159	
67				0	0	0	3	15	26	0	0	0	0	1	3	0.091					0	0	0	4	16	24	0	0	0	0	2	2	0.091	3
68				1	1	8	31	2	1	0	0	2	1	1	0	0.273					0	0	0	11	31	2	0	0	0	1	3	0	0.045	2
69				0	0	4	36	4	0	0	0	0	4	0	0	0.091	3				0	0	2	9	24	9	0	0	0	0	3	1	0.250	
71				0	0	0	3	39	2	0	0	0	0	4	0	0.068	3				0	0	0	1	41	2	0	0	0	0	4	0	0.045	2
75				0	0	3	11	27	3	0	0	0	1	3	0	0.068	3				0	0	0	10	23	11	0	0	0	0	4	0	0.250	
77				0	0	0	0	0	44	0	0	0	0	0	4	0.000	Delete				0	0	0	0	0	44	0	0	0	0	0	4	0.000	Delete
81				0	0	0	44	0	0	0	0	0	4	0	0	0.000	1				0	0	0	44	0	0	0	0	0	0	4	0	0.000	1
82				0	1	1	11	10	21	0	0	0	3	0	1	0.455				Q	1	0	4	8	6	25	0	1	0	1	0	2	0.227	
83				0	0	2	19	21	2	0	0	2	2	0	0	0.045	2	99		Q	3	1	3	11	21	5	0	0	0	0	4	0	0.409	
84				0	0	6	38	0	0	0	0	1	3	0	0	0.114	4				0	0	0	38	6	0	0	0	0	3	1	0	0.114	4
85				0	0	0	36	8	0	0	0	0	3	1	0	0.068	3				0	0	0	0	44	0	0	0	0	0	4	0	0.000	1
86				2	13	13	15	1	0	0	1	1	2	0	0	0.136	4				0	0	0	1	43	0	0	0	0	0	4	0	0.023	2
87			Q+A	1	6	1	20	12	4	0	2	0	1	0	1	0.341			95	Q+A	0	6	1	2	10	25	0	0	0	0	1	3	0.205	
88	95			2	3	1	29	2	7	0	0	0	2	2	0	0.295					0	0	1	17	1	25	0	0	0	1	0	3	0.409	
89				1	3	10	25	3	2	0	0	1	3	0	0	0.114	4				0	0	0	0	0	44	0	0	0	0	0	4	0.000	1
91				0	0	4	16	19	5	0	0	1	1	2	0	0.159					0	0	1	4	19	20	0	0	0	0	2	2	0.114	4
93				1	0	0	3	6	34	0	0	0	0	1	3	0.091	3				1	1	0	3	5	34	0	0	0	1	1	2	0.273	

Appendix F: Cases Cleaning and Reflection Priority (cont.)

Cases Cleaning and Reflection Priority (n=207)

Case No	SAT FS 1&2	SAT FS 3&4	SAT Maha	S44-1	S44-2	S44-3	S44-4	S44-5	S44-6	S4-1	S4-2	S4-3	S4-4	S4-5	S4-6	KS SAT	Refl SAT	VAL FS 1&2	VAL FS 3&4	VAL Maha	V44-1	V44-2	V44-3	V44-4	V44-5	V44-6	V4-1	V4-2	V4-3	V4-4	V4-5	V4-6	KS VAL	Refl VAL
97				0	0	12	21	11	0	0	0	1	2	1	0	0.023	2				0	0	0	37	7	0	0	0	0	0	4	0	0.159	
98				0	0	6	9	21	8	0	0	0	2	2	0	0.182					0	1	0	5	23	15	0	0	0	1	2	1	0.114	4
99				1	1	3	20	14	5	0	0	0	2	2	0	0.114	4				0	3	3	7	21	10	0	0	0	0	4	0	0.295	
103				0	0	4	40	0	0	0	0	0	4	0	0	0.091	3	99			0	6	4	34	0	0	0	0	0	4	0	0	0.227	
104				0	1	2	5	29	7	0	0	0	1	2	1	0.091	3				0	0	0	4	11	29	0	0	0	0	1	3	0.091	3
106				0	0	0	0	0	44	0	0	0	0	0	4	0.000	Delete				0	0	0	0	0	44	0	0	0	0	0	4	0.000	Delete
110				0	0	7	37	0	0	0	0	0	4	0	0	0.159					0	0	0	41	3	0	0	0	0	4	0	0	0.068	3
114				0	0	0	44	0	0	0	0	0	4	0	0	0.000	1				0	0	0	0	0	44	0	0	0	0	0	4	0.000	1
115				0	0	1	6	12	25	0	0	0	1	0	3	0.182					0	0	0	6	38	0	0	0	0	0	4	0	0.136	4
116				0	0	0	1	23	20	0	0	0	0	2	2	0.045	2				0	0	1	22	21	0	0	0	0	2	2	0	0.023	2
120				4	2	6	17	7	8	0	0	3	1	0	0	0.477		95		Q+A	3	0	0	3	21	17	0	0	0	2	1	1	0.364	
121		99	Q	3	2	6	15	13	5	0	0	1	3	0	0	0.409					0	4	1	9	21	9	0	0	0	2	2	0	0.205	
122		95		2	1	5	22	14	0	0	0	0	2	2	0	0.182					0	0	0	7	32	5	0	0	1	3	0	0	0.114	4
123				0	0	1	11	19	13	0	0	0	1	2	1	0.045	2				0	0	0	10	21	13	0	0	0	1	2	1	0.045	2
124				0	1	1	10	6	26	0	0	0	1	0	3	0.159					0	0	2	0	0	42	0	0	0	0	0	4	0.045	2
125		95	Q+A	14	8	5	14	1	2	1	0	2	1	0	0	0.250		95		Q+A	3	3	3	5	8	22	0	0	1	1	1	1	0.250	
127				0	0	3	17	9	15	0	0	0	2	0	2	0.159			99		0	7	3	8	9	17	0	0	0	1	2	1	0.227	
129				1	0	0	4	14	25	2	0	0	1	1	0	0.636					0	0	0	6	6	32	0	0	0	1	0	3	0.114	4
128				0	1	10	23	9	1	0	0	0	2	2	0	0.273		95			0	1	11	15	13	4	0	0	0	4	0	0	0.386	
133				1	3	8	28	4	0	1	1	1	0	0	1	0.477			99	Q+A	4	2	0	9	8	21	0	0	0	0	1	3	0.341	
136			Q	1	0	4	20	4	15	0	0	0	2	0	2	0.159					0	0	0	6	38	0	0	0	0	0	0	4	0.136	4
137				0	2	1	13	17	11	0	0	0	4	0	0	0.636					0	0	2	9	16	17	0	0	0	1	2	1	0.136	4
140				0	0	1	10	0	33	0	0	0	0	0	4	0.250					0	0	0	0	0	44	0	0	0	0	0	4	0.000	1
141				0	0	0	2	26	16	0	0	0	0	3	1	0.114	4				0	0	0	0	9	35	0	0	0	1	3	0	0.795	
144				0	2	0	26	16	0	0	0	0	1	2	1	0.205					0	3	9	15	17	0	0	0	1	2	1	0	0.136	4
145				0	0	0	20	22	2	0	0	0	0	4	0	0.455					0	0	4	20	18	2	0	0	0	2	2	0	0.091	3
149				0	0	2	5	20	17	0	0	0	1	2	1	0.136	4				0	0	0	1	13	30	0	0	0	0	1	3	0.068	3
150	95			1	5	2	30	5	1	0	0	0	3	0	1	0.227					0	0	0	5	29	10	0	0	0	0	3	1	0.114	4
151				0	0	0	10	30	4	0	0	0	2	2	0	0.273					0	0	0	1	38	5	0	0	0	0	4	0	0.114	4
154				1	0	0	13	18	12	0	0	0	1	1	2	0.227					0	0	0	13	23	8	0	0	0	1	2	1	0.068	
155	99	99		12	3	1	4	8	19	1	0	0	1	0	2	0.091	3				0	0	0	0	0	44	0	0	0	0	0	4	0.000	1
158				2	0	0	0	0	42	0	0	0	0	0	4	0.045	Delete				0	0	0	0	0	44	0	0	0	0	0	4	0.000	Delete
160				0	0	4	6	15	19	0	0	1	1	1	1	0.273					0	0	0	2	14	28	0	0	0	0	2	2	0.136	4
161			Q+A	5	5	19	12	3	0	0	2	1	1	0	0	0.273					0	7	12	20	4	1	0	0	2	2	0	0	0.159	
163	95	95		3	0	8	15	7	11	0	0	1	1	0	2	0.250			95		2	3	2	3	9	25	0	0	0	0	1	3	0.227	
164	99		Q	7	0	0	31	0	6	0	0	0	4	0	0	0.159					0	0	0	31	0	13	0	0	0	4	0	0	0.295	
166				0	0	0	0	34	10	0	0	0	0	3	1	0.023	2				0	0	0	0	34	10	0	0	0	0	3	1	0.023	2
167				0	0	0	2	0	42	0	0	0	0	0	4	0.045	2				0	0	1	0	0	43	0	0	0	0	0	4	0.023	2
168			Q+A	4	5	4	9	8	14	1	0	0	0	1	2	0.250			99	Q	7	0	0	1	3	33	0	0	0	0	0	4	0.250	
169				1	0	5	13	9	16	0	0	0	1	2	1	0.182					1	0	0	3	5	35	0	0	0	0	1	3	0.091	3
170				0	0	3	23	14	4	0	0	1	1	2	0	0.182					0	1	1	16	20	6	0	0	0	2	2	0	0.136	4
172				0	0	2	10	26	6	0	0	0	3	1	0	0.477					0	0	0	24	18	2	0	0	0	2	2	0	0.045	2
173				0	0	0	3	27	14	0	0	0	0	2	2	0.182					0	0	0	3	24	17	0	0	0	0	2	2	0.114	4
175				2	2	3	16	11	10	0	0	1	2	1	0	0.227					0	0	0	13	14	17	0	0	0	1	2	1	0.136	4
176				2	2	4	19	8	9	0	0	0	2	2	0	0.205		95		Q+A	0	6	10	9	8	11	0	0	0	2	2	0	0.364	
177				1	1	2	12	5	23	0	0	1	0	1	2	0.227					0	0	0	4	0	40	0	0	0	0	0	4	0.091	3
178				0	0	0	8	15	21	0	0	0	1	1	2	0.068	3				0	0	2	9	5	28	0	0	1	0	0	3	0.205	
179	99			4	9	0	11	18	2	0	0	1	1	2	0	0.295		99			4	9	0	7	23	1	0	1	0	0	2	1	0.227	
180				2	2	3	34	2	1	0	0	0	3	0	1	0.227					0	0	2	3	39	0	0	0	0	0	4	0	0.114	4
181	99			8	3	3	12	16	2	1	0	0	1	2	0	0.091	3				0	0	2	14	17	11	0	0	0	1	2	1	0.114	4
183				2	1	2	22	16	1	0	0	0	3	0	1	0.227					0	0	0	1	43	0	0	0	0	0	4	0	0.023	2
184	95	99		0	44	0	0	0	0	0	0	0	0	4	0	0.000	1	99			0	0	13	0	31	0	0	0	1	0	3	0	0.045	2
185	.	99		1	1	3	9	10	20	0	0	0	1	0	3	0.455					0	0	0	8	8	28	0	0	0	0	1	3	0.182	
186				0	0	1	0	36	7	0	0	0	0	4	0	0.159					0	0	0	0	0	44	0	0	0	0	0	4	0.045	2
187				2	1	9	19	8	5	0	0	1	1	1	1	0.205					0	0	6	25	5	8	0	0	3	0	0	1	0.136	
189				0	0	3	1	36	4	0	0	0	0	4	0	0.091	3				0	0	0	4	29	11	0	0	0	0	4	0	0.250	
190				1	3	3	11	22	4	0	1	0	2	1	0	0.341		95	99	Q+A	4	9	8	11	10	2	0	1	1	2	0	0	0.273	
191				0	0	0	44	0	0	0	0	0	4	0	0	0.000	1				0	2	0	1	15	26	0	0	0	1	1	2	0.182	
193	95			0	2	0	3	11	28	4	0	0	0	0	0	1.000					0	0	1	0	2	41	0	0	0	0	0	4	0.068	3

Appendix F: Cases Cleaning
and Reflection Priority (cont.)

Cases Cleaning and Reflection Priority (n=207)

Case No	Satisfaction																		Value																
	SAT Factor Scores BiPlots		Mahalanobis Outliers	Count (SAT) (44)						Count (SAT) (4)						KS Test	Reflecting Priority	VAL Factor Scores BiPlots		Mahalanobis Outliers	Count (VAL) (44)						Count (VAL) (4)						KS Test	Reflecting Priority
	1&2	3&4		1	2	3	4	5	6	1	2	3	4	5	6	SAT	SAT	1&2	3&4		1	2	3	4	5	6	1	2	3	4	5	6	VAL	VAL
194	99	99		12	1	0	0	0	31	1	0	0	0	0	3	0.045	2				0	0	0	0	5	39	0	0	0	0	0	4	0.114	4
195				0	0	0	44	0	0	0	0	0	4	0	0	0.000	Delete				0	0	0	44	0	0	0	0	0	4	0	0	0.000	Delete
196				0	0	0	0	0	44	0	0	0	0	0	4	0.000	Delete				0	0	0	0	0	44	0	0	0	0	0	4	0.000	Delete
197				0	0	3	26	10	5	0	0	0	2	2	0	0.159					0	3	1	15	20	5	0	0	0	2	2	0	0.114	4
198				0	0	1	9	34	0	0	0	0	1	3	0	0.023	2				0	1	3	14	25	1	0	0	0	3	1	0	0.341	
200				0	3	2	37	2	0	0	1	0	3	0	0	0.182	2		95	Q+A	0	10	1	4	22	7	0	1	0	0	2	1	0.091	3
203	99	99	Q,D,A	12	11	7	9	1	4	1	0	0	3	0	0	0.432					0	1	4	6	9	24	0	0	0	2	1	1	0.295	
205				0	0	2	21	15	6	0	0	0	2	2	0	0.136	4				0	0	4	10	20	10	0	0	0	1	3	0	0.227	
206				0	0	1	40	3	0	0	0	0	4	0	0	0.068	3				1	1	0	37	5	0	1	0	0	3	0	0	0.227	
207				0	0	0	1	43	0	0	0	0	0	4	0	0.023	2				0	0	0	0	41	3	0	0	0	0	4	0	0.068	

Cases Key:

Deleted Case	7
Close to a full set (retain)	3
Cases Eliminated from Final Analysis	8
Same score for all negative questions	
Same score for all questions	

Factor Scores BiPlots key:
99 - Factor Score Outlier of 99% Ellipses
95 - Factor Score Outlier of 95% Ellipses

Mahalanobis key:
Q - Mahalanobis Outlier on Questions only
D - Mahalanobis Outlier on Overall & Dimensions only
A - Mahalanobis Outlier on All

KS Test Key:
Diff = 0
Diff between 0 and .05
Diff between 0.05 and .10
Diff between 0.10 and .15

Count:

	SAT
4	1 - First SAT to reflect (diff=0)
11	2 - Second SAT to reflect (0<diff<.05)
15	3 - Third SAT to reflect (.05<diff<.10)
16	4 - Forth SAT to reflect (.10<diff<.15)

	VAL
10	1 - First VAL to reflect (diff=0)
17	2 - Second VAL to reflect (0<diff<.05)
16	3 - Third VAL to reflect (.05<diff<.10)
27	4 - Forth VAL to reflect (.10<diff<.15)

Reflect:
1 --> 6
2 --> 5
3 --> 4
4 --> 3
5 --> 2
6 --> 1

Appendix G: PCA Factor
Score Bi-Plots Ellipsoids

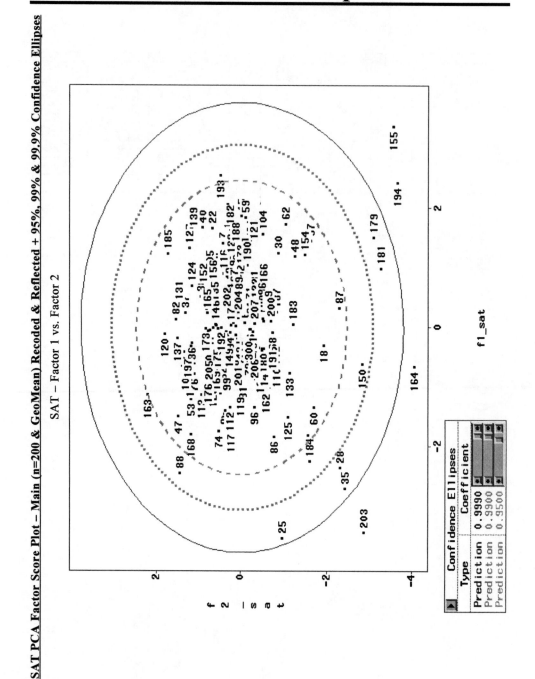

SAT PCA Factor Score Plot – Main (n=200 & GeoMean) Recoded & Reflected + 95%, 99% & 99.9% Confidence Ellipses

SAT – Factor 1 vs. Factor 2

f1_sat

Confidence Ellipses	
Type	Coefficient
Prediction	0.9990
Prediction	0.9900
Prediction	0.9500

Appendix G: PCA Factor
Score Bi-Plots Ellipsoids (cont.)

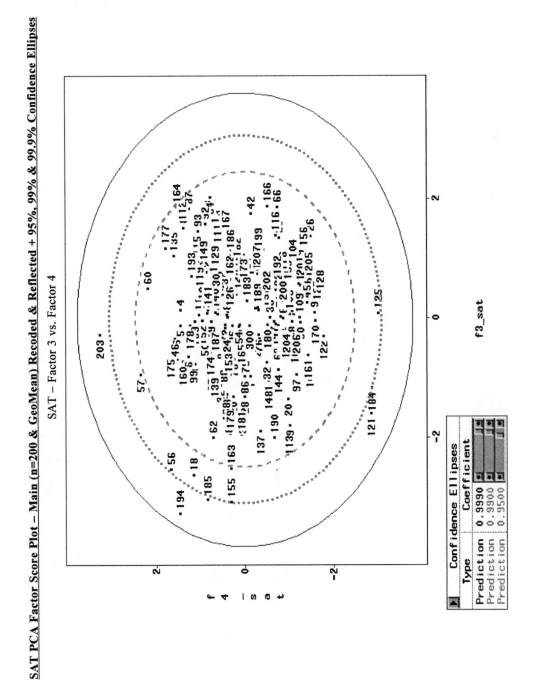

Appendix G: PCA Factor Score Bi-Plots Ellipsoids (cont.)

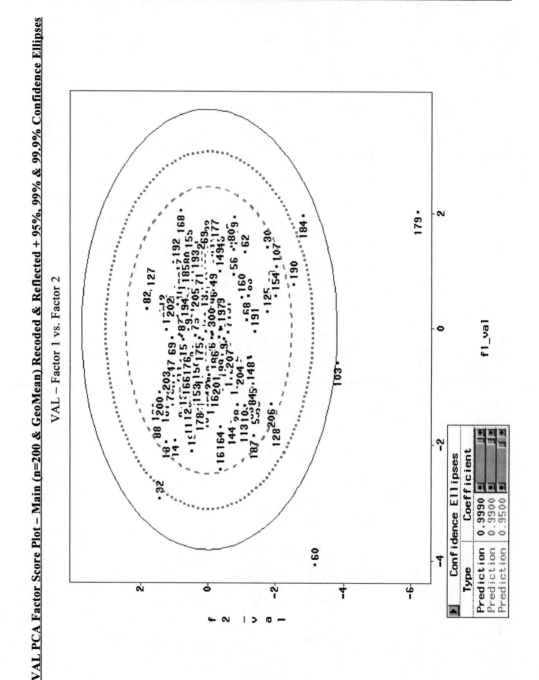

VAL PCA Factor Score Plot – Main (n=200 & GeoMean) Recoded & Reflected + 95%, 99% & 99.9% Confidence Ellipses

VAL – Factor 1 vs. Factor 2

Appendix G: PCA Factor
Score Bi-Plots Ellipsoids (cont.)

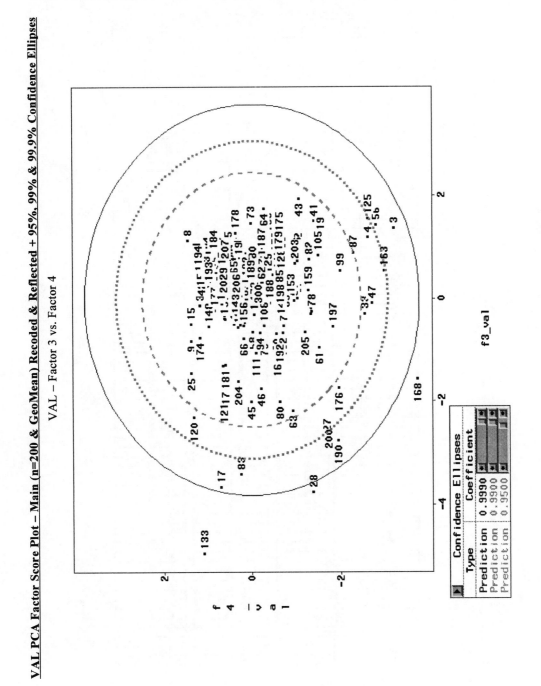

Appendix H: Internal Contradictory Overall Scores Check

Overall SAT (So_Act) - Internal Contradictory Overall Scores Check (n=192)

Case_No	Sa_ACT	Sb_ACT	Sc_ACT	Sd_ACT	So_Act	Change to:	Min	Max	Flag range
203	1	1	4	5	1		1	5	0
28	1	2	1	2	2		1	2	0
60	1	4	5	6	6		1	6	0
181	1	5	5	5	5		1	5	0
155	1	6	6	5	5		1	6	0
194	1	6	6	6	6		1	6	0
184	2	2	2	2	2		2	2	0
35	2	2	4	4	4		2	4	0
18	2	4	4	5	5		2	5	0
179	2	5	5	5	5		2	5	0
9	3	1	1	1	1		1	3	0
86	3	2	2	4	3		2	4	0
161	3	3	3	4	3		3	4	0
113	3	3	3	4	4		3	4	0
163	3	3	3	5	4		3	5	0
168	3	5	2	4	3		2	5	0
97	3	5	4	4	4		3	5	0
121	3	5	5	4	4		3	5	0
185	3	6	5	5	5		3	6	0
160	3	6	6	6	6		3	6	0
25	4	1	1	2	1		1	4	0
88	4	2	4	4	4		2	4	0
125	4	3	1	1	3		1	4	0
133	4	3	1	4	4		1	4	0
74	4	3	3	4	2	3	3	4	1
96	4	3	4	4	3		3	4	0
200	4	4	2	3	2		2	4	0
47	4	4	2	4	3		2	4	0
180	4	4	2	4	3		2	4	0
78	4	4	2	4	4		2	4	0
29	4	4	3	3	4		3	4	0
65	4	4	3	4	3		3	4	0
84	4	4	3	4	4		3	4	0
89	4	4	3	4	4		3	4	0
94	4	4	3	4	4		3	4	0
103	4	4	3	4	4		3	4	0
90	4	4	3	5	5		3	5	0
98	4	4	3	5	5		3	5	0
68	4	4	4	3	4		3	4	0
27	4	4	4	4	4		4	4	0
32	4	4	4	4	4		4	4	0
46	4	4	4	4	4		4	4	0
51	4	4	4	4	4		4	4	0
52	4	4	4	4	4		4	4	0
99	4	4	4	4	4		4	4	0
109	4	4	4	4	4		4	4	0
110	4	4	4	4	4		4	4	0
120	4	4	4	4	4		4	4	0
122	4	4	4	4	4		4	4	0
132	4	4	4	4	4		4	4	0
134	4	4	4	4	4		4	4	0
144	4	4	4	4	4		4	4	0
191	4	4	4	4	4		4	4	0
79	4	4	4	5	4		4	5	0
162	4	4	4	5	4		4	5	0
102	4	4	4	5	5		4	5	0
150	4	4	4	5	5		4	5	0
85	4	4	5	4	4		4	5	0
206	4	4	5	4	4		4	5	0
53	4	4	5	5	5		4	5	0
137	4	4	5	5	5		4	5	0
40	4	5	2	3	3		2	5	0
44	4	5	4	4	4		4	5	0
63	4	5	4	4	4		4	5	0
6	4	5	4	4	5		4	5	0
164	4	5	4	6	6		4	6	0
20	4	5	5	4	4		4	5	0

Appendix H: Internal Contradictory Overall Scores Check (cont.)

Overall SAT (So_Act) - Internal Contradictory Overall Scores Check (n=192)

Case_No	Sa_ACT	Sb_ACT	Sc_ACT	Sd_ACT	So_Act	Change to:	Min	Max	Flag range
23	4	5	5	4	4		4	5	0
30	4	5	5	4	4		4	5	0
56	4	5	5	5	4		4	5	0
73	4	5	5	5	5		4	5	0
138	4	5	5	5	5		4	5	0
107	4	5	6	5	5		4	6	0
154	4	5	6	6	5		4	6	0
183	4	6	4	5	5		4	6	0
7	4	6	6	6	5		4	6	0
62	4	6	6	6	6		4	6	0
87	5	3	2	5	4		2	5	0
117	5	3	3	5	4		3	5	0
204	5	4	1	4	4		1	5	0
16	5	4	1	5	3		1	5	0
175	5	4	2	4	5		2	5	0
61	5	4	3	3	3		3	5	0
17	5	4	3	4	4		3	5	0
54	5	4	3	4	4		3	5	0
148	5	4	3	4	4		3	5	0
119	5	4	3	5	5		3	5	0
57	5	4	4	4	3	4	4	5	1
55	5	4	4	4	4		4	5	0
58	5	4	4	4	4		4	5	0
80	5	4	4	4	4		4	5	0
91	5	4	4	4	4		4	5	0
176	5	4	4	4	4		4	5	0
187	5	4	4	4	4		4	5	0
192	5	4	4	4	4		4	5	0
197	5	4	4	4	4		4	5	0
201	5	4	4	4	4		4	5	0
128	5	4	4	4	5		4	5	0
4	5	4	4	5	5		4	5	0
142	5	4	4	5	5		4	5	0
157	5	4	5	4	4		4	5	0
76	5	4	5	4	5		4	5	0
153	5	4	5	4	5		4	5	0
59	5	4	6	3	4		3	6	0
135	5	5	3	5	4		3	5	0
169	5	5	3	5	5		3	5	0
69	5	5	4	4	4		4	5	0
174	5	5	4	4	4		4	5	0
171	5	5	4	4	5		4	5	0
190	5	5	4	4	6		4	6	0
49	5	5	4	5	5		4	5	0
50	5	5	4	5	5		4	5	0
105	5	5	4	5	5		4	5	0
177	5	5	4	5	5		4	5	0
136	5	5	4	6	5		4	6	0
41	5	5	5	4	4		4	5	0
75	5	5	5	4	4		4	5	0
114	5	5	5	4	5		4	5	0
131	5	5	5	4	5		4	5	0
189	5	5	5	4	5		4	5	0
205	5	5	5	4	5		4	5	0
70	5	5	5	5	4	5	5	5	1
172	5	5	5	5	4	5	5	5	1
2	5	5	5	5	5		5	5	0
19	5	5	5	5	5		5	5	0
71	5	5	5	5	5		5	5	0
81	5	5	5	5	5		5	5	0
83	5	5	5	5	5		5	5	0
100	5	5	5	5	5		5	5	0
141	5	5	5	5	5		5	5	0
145	5	5	5	5	5		5	5	0
147	5	5	5	5	5		5	5	0
149	5	5	5	5	5		5	5	0
165	5	5	5	5	5		5	5	0
166	5	5	5	5	5		5	5	0
186	5	5	5	5	5		5	5	0
188	5	5	5	5	5		5	5	0
198	5	5	5	5	5		5	5	0
199	5	5	5	5	5		5	5	0
202	5	5	5	5	5		5	5	0
43	5	5	5	6	5		5	6	0

Appendix H: Internal Contradictory Overall Scores Check (cont.)

Overall SAT (So_Act) - Internal Contradictory Overall Scores Check (n=192)

Case_No	Sa_ACT	Sb_ACT	Sc_ACT	Sd_ACT	So_Act	Change to:	Min	Max	Flag range
123	5	5	5	6	5		5	6	0
146	5	5	5	6	6		5	6	0
38	5	5	6	4	5		4	6	0
170	5	5	6	5	4	5	5	6	1
5	5	5	6	5	5		5	6	0
45	5	5	6	5	5		5	6	0
72	5	5	6	5	5		5	6	0
95	5	5	6	5	5		5	6	0
151	5	5	6	5	5		5	6	0
15	5	6	2	5	4		2	6	0
22	5	6	4	4	4		4	6	0
126	5	6	4	4	5		4	6	0
104	5	6	5	4	5		4	6	0
11	5	6	5	5	5		5	6	0
48	5	6	5	5	5		5	6	0
140	5	6	5	5	5		5	6	0
207	5	6	5	5	6		5	6	0
10	5	6	6	4	5		4	6	0
34	5	6	6	5	6		5	6	0
152	5	6	6	6	5		5	6	0
178	5	6	6	6	5		5	6	0
39	5	6	6	6	6		5	6	0
139	5	6	6	6	6		5	6	0
26	6	4	4	4	4		4	6	0
31	6	4	4	4	4		4	6	0
42	6	4	4	4	4		4	6	0
101	6	4	4	4	5		4	6	0
13	6	4	5	5	5		4	6	0
8	6	4	5	6	5		4	6	0
33	6	5	4	4	4		4	6	0
127	6	5	4	4	4		4	6	0
156	6	5	4	4	4		4	6	0
37	6	5	4	4	5		4	6	0
14	6	5	4	5	5		4	6	0
124	6	5	4	5	5		4	6	0
111	6	5	5	5	5		5	6	0
143	6	5	5	5	5		5	6	0
159	6	5	5	5	5		5	6	0
173	6	5	5	6	5		5	6	0
130	6	5	5	6	6		5	6	0
108	6	5	6	4	4		4	6	0
115	6	5	6	5	5		5	6	0
112	6	5	6	6	5		5	6	0
129	6	5	6	6	6		5	6	0
66	6	6	4	5	5		4	6	0
116	6	6	5	5	5		5	6	0
118	6	6	5	5	5		5	6	0
82	6	6	6	4	5		4	6	0
1	6	6	6	5	6		5	6	0
182	6	6	6	5	6		5	6	0
21	6	6	6	6	5	6	6	6	1
92	6	6	6	6	5	6	6	6	1
3	6	6	6	6	6		6	6	0
24	6	6	6	6	6		6	6	0
64	6	6	6	6	6		6	6	0
67	6	6	6	6	6		6	6	0
93	6	6	6	6	6		6	6	0
167	6	6	6	6	6		6	6	0
193	6	6	6	6	6		6	6	0

Total out:	7

PCA Varimax Rotated Component Matrix (Satisfaction) + Recoded Variables
Main Study (n=200)

	1	2	3	4	5	6	7	8	9	Pilot Loading
B3_SAT	0.784	0.087	0.096	0.089	0.148	0.212	0.072	0.006	-0.002	1
B4_SAT	0.742	0.159	0.078	0.127	0.172	0.263	0.004	-0.184	-0.200	1
B2_SAT	0.741	0.237	0.159	0.125	0.210	0.291	0.009	0.012	-0.050	1
B7_SAT	0.712	0.073	0.137	0.068	0.343	0.316	0.098	-0.102	-0.137	1
B11_SAT	0.697	0.216	0.168	0.248	0.289	0.115	0.117	0.103	0.060	1
B5_SAT	0.693	0.106	0.119	0.149	0.179	0.103	0.054	0.138	-0.066	1
B10_SAT	0.647	0.235	0.191	0.316	0.143	0.151	0.113	0.264	0.024	1
B1_SAT	0.610	0.278	0.173	0.265	0.087	0.169	-0.024	0.142	0.055	1
B8_SAT	0.608	0.355	0.069	0.254	0.078	0.174	-0.039	0.316	0.114	1
D1_SAT	0.605	0.101	0.078	0.147	0.344	0.362	-0.011	-0.086	-0.202	1
B12_SAT	0.584	0.002	0.137	0.324	0.149	-0.115	0.187	0.109	-0.247	9
B9_SAT	0.563	0.203	0.121	0.271	-0.092	0.147	-0.067	0.352	-0.011	1
C7_SAT	0.535	0.026	0.157	0.181	0.270	0.094	0.427	0.186	0.031	1
A10_SAT	0.114	0.847	0.285	0.186	0.067	0.046	0.043	0.028	-0.069	4
A12_SAT	0.159	0.795	0.348	0.128	0.067	-0.005	-0.026	0.040	0.027	4
A9_SAT	0.237	0.764	0.302	0.126	0.080	0.044	-0.071	-0.019	-0.010	4
A11_SAT	0.098	0.757	0.298	0.058	0.218	0.071	0.143	0.028	0.045	4
A13_SAT	0.257	0.735	0.283	0.157	0.127	0.064	0.092	0.128	0.008	4
A7_SAT	0.122	0.730	0.405	0.180	-0.119	-0.001	0.016	0.042	-0.046	2
A3_SAT	0.169	0.248	0.797	0.079	0.101	0.127	-0.054	-0.094	-0.083	2
A2_SAT	0.135	0.243	0.792	0.115	0.079	0.088	0.020	-0.015	0.000	2
A1_SAT	0.099	0.240	0.768	0.054	0.081	0.105	-0.089	-0.013	-0.030	2
A5_SAT	0.173	0.334	0.733	0.023	0.081	0.084	-0.004	0.035	-0.012	2
A4_SAT	0.157	0.471	0.658	0.054	0.052	0.082	-0.022	0.077	0.127	2
A6_SAT	0.144	0.517	0.584	0.174	-0.085	0.089	0.055	0.168	0.046	2
A14_SAT	0.124	0.433	0.547	0.107	0.010	-0.026	0.225	0.149	-0.090	2
a8_sat_rc	-0.029	-0.381	-0.517	-0.031	-0.039	-0.132	-0.113	-0.514	0.085	2
D12_SAT	0.174	0.198	0.077	0.800	0.074	0.120	0.005	0.085	-0.066	3
D13_SAT	0.204	0.123	0.043	0.793	0.091	0.054	0.104	0.044	-0.131	3
D14_SAT	0.232	0.167	0.095	0.738	0.126	0.248	0.199	0.070	0.046	3
D11_SAT	0.123	0.123	0.101	0.726	0.173	0.165	0.043	0.072	0.069	3
D15_SAT	0.357	0.053	0.150	0.687	0.110	0.173	0.037	-0.019	-0.087	3
D7_SAT	0.280	0.369	-0.012	0.442	-0.096	0.149	-0.203	0.118	0.031	3
C4_SAT	0.288	0.029	0.074	0.137	0.831	0.251	0.126	0.063	-0.058	6
C1_SAT	0.309	0.106	0.066	0.111	0.797	0.180	0.051	0.150	0.083	6
C2_SAT	0.404	0.109	0.091	0.125	0.750	0.123	0.011	-0.119	-0.135	6
C5_SAT	0.498	0.157	0.059	0.416	0.511	0.162	0.080	0.024	-0.034	1
C6_SAT	0.405	0.068	0.247	0.251	0.427	-0.024	0.376	0.155	-0.048	1
D2_SAT	0.261	0.075	0.095	0.159	0.249	0.773	0.127	0.071	0.003	5
D3_SAT	0.294	0.018	0.149	0.122	0.218	0.762	0.157	0.082	0.014	5
D5_SAT	0.289	0.082	0.132	0.235	0.311	0.661	0.181	0.010	-0.114	5
D4_SAT	0.342	-0.030	0.164	0.251	0.033	0.562	0.043	0.059	-0.039	5
D6_SAT	0.352	0.269	0.034	0.375	-0.010	0.493	-0.062	0.040	-0.156	3
D9_SAT	0.175	0.015	-0.052	-0.026	0.041	0.201	0.835	-0.213	-0.265	7
D10_SAT	0.014	0.100	-0.058	0.198	0.097	0.152	0.651	0.178	0.225	7
b6_sat_rc	-0.262	-0.099	0.024	-0.173	-0.143	-0.108	-0.007	-0.730	0.205	8
c3_sat_rc	-0.328	0.000	-0.038	-0.066	-0.467	-0.103	-0.019	-0.237	0.682	6
d8_sat_rc	-0.102	0.020	-0.079	-0.253	0.191	-0.499	-0.024	-0.318	0.576	5
Cronbach	0.9421	0.937	0.78 (.91)	0.881	0.8934	0.8716	0.5737	-	0.5794	
% of Var	36.53	12.82	5.04	4.10	3.76	3.07	2.96	2.63	2.19	
Cumul %	36.53	49.35	54.39	58.49	62.25	65.33	68.29	70.92	73.11	

Appendix I: PCA Results for Satisfaction — Main Data

Appendix J: PCA Results for Value — Main Data

PCA Varimax Rotated Component Matrix (Value) + Recoded Variables
Main Study (n=200)

	1	2	3	4	5	6	7	8	9	Pilot Loading
B10_VAL	0.762	0.186	0.125	0.199	0.172	-0.018	0.171	0.034	-0.092	2
B4_VAL	0.727	0.232	0.209	0.209	0.017	0.221	-0.051	0.030	0.000	2
B11_VAL	0.702	0.215	0.182	0.092	0.195	0.003	0.150	0.080	0.094	2
B2_VAL	0.678	0.335	0.220	0.079	0.149	0.164	0.092	0.093	0.075	2
B7_VAL	0.670	0.183	0.185	0.257	0.192	0.111	-0.001	-0.061	0.102	2
B3_VAL	0.668	0.235	0.152	0.223	-0.042	0.259	0.110	0.111	-0.036	2
B9_VAL	0.662	0.167	0.158	0.242	0.098	0.066	0.229	0.018	-0.074	2
B8_VAL	0.649	0.328	0.256	-0.015	0.218	0.036	-0.023	-0.029	0.083	2
B1_VAL	0.583	0.324	0.222	0.026	0.126	0.214	0.189	0.124	0.050	1
C2_VAL	0.572	0.217	0.169	0.174	0.186	0.253	-0.174	0.071	0.230	1
D1_VAL	0.559	0.181	0.207	0.151	0.154	0.206	-0.115	0.177	0.088	1
B5_VAL	0.556	0.092	0.118	0.256	0.033	0.446	0.127	0.101	0.004	2
C1_VAL	0.527	0.303	0.022	0.271	0.057	0.218	0.091	-0.065	0.304	1
C4_VAL	0.490	0.292	0.110	0.214	0.154	0.241	-0.064	-0.065	0.453	1
C6_VAL	0.488	0.322	0.336	0.110	0.093	0.257	0.038	0.110	0.017	1
D6_VAL	0.455	0.283	0.447	0.221	0.078	0.166	0.118	0.172	0.072	1
C7_VAL	0.383	0.195	0.053	0.149	0.268	0.033		0.125	0.366	1
A9_VAL	0.234	0.765	0.151	0.015	0.076	0.113	-0.020	0.022	0.073	5
A10_VAL	0.248	0.764	0.165	-0.032	0.008	0.105	-0.079	0.083	-0.001	5
A12_VAL	0.255	0.720	0.194	0.094	0.103	0.040	0.080	0.038	0.125	5
A5_VAL	0.335	0.670	0.023	-0.013	0.298	0.149	-0.059	0.139	0.090	3
A11_VAL	0.296	0.663	0.142	0.156	0.055	-0.071	0.252	-0.246	0.272	5
A13_VAL	0.054	0.660	0.254	0.083	0.199	0.149	0.032	0.163	0.154	5
A7_VAL	0.227	0.652	0.152	0.137	0.031	0.102	0.098	0.049	-0.397	5
A6_VAL	0.301	0.616	0.038	0.141	0.222	0.146	0.068	0.137	0.076	3
A4_VAL	0.251	0.582	0.114	-0.025	0.327	0.121	-0.193	0.125	0.034	3
a8_val_rc	-0.149	-0.562	-0.119	-0.107	-0.129	-0.284	-0.363	0.063	0.257	8
A14_VAL	0.239	0.442	0.194	0.200	0.311	-0.149	0.329	-0.043	-0.094	10
D15_VAL	0.301	0.108	0.806	0.195	0.100	0.007	-0.132	0.015	-0.044	6
D13_VAL	0.146	0.173	0.802	0.239	0.038	-0.002	0.092	0.056	0.037	6
D12_VAL	0.161	0.228	0.744	0.083	0.116	0.176	0.160	0.049	0.069	8
D14_VAL	0.411	0.147	0.698	0.116	0.098	0.144	-0.203	0.027	-0.121	6
D11_VAL	0.172	0.170	0.661	0.027	0.013	0.113	0.186	0.292	0.281	7
D7_VAL	0.449	0.146	0.455	0.136	0.028	0.136	0.071	0.162	0.014	1
D2_VAL	0.233	0.069	0.084	0.879	0.018	0.188	0.032	0.040	0.044	4
D3_VAL	0.202	0.054	0.131	0.875	0.022	0.193	0.004	0.080	-0.029	4
D4_VAL	0.245	0.028	0.198	0.871	0.020	0.085	0.068	0.121	-0.025	4
D5_VAL	0.230	0.100	0.215	0.849	0.050	0.015	0.046	0.036	0.147	4
A1_VAL	0.149	0.112	0.141	0.066	0.886	0.101	0.104	0.026	0.025	3
A2_VAL	0.200	0.269	0.055	-0.004	0.877	0.049	0.053	-0.032	0.011	3
A3_VAL	0.279	0.379	0.077	0.025	0.730	0.092	-0.056	0.106	0.118	3
c3_val_rc	-0.256	-0.158	-0.088	-0.180	-0.137	-0.767	-0.048	0.024	-0.101	9
d8_val_rc	-0.223	-0.167	-0.366	-0.185	-0.097	-0.635	-0.088	-0.150	0.077	1
b6_val_rc	-0.385	-0.243	-0.040	-0.144	-0.018	-0.621	-0.127	-0.014	-0.124	9
B12_VAL	0.230	0.026	0.077	0.075	0.064	0.201	0.808	0.165	0.047	1
D10_VAL	0.129	0.146	0.237	0.297	0.041	-0.005	0.129	0.788	0.056	7
D9_VAL	0.281	0.311	0.293	-0.014	0.073	0.244	0.077	0.492	-0.232	7
C5_VAL	0.370	0.267	0.414	0.177	0.193	0.126	0.132	-0.047	0.470	1
Cronbach	0.9481	0.83 (.91)	0.8871	0.9462	0.8976	0.7947	-	0.5997	-	
% of Var	37.59	9.26	5.90	4.46	3.92	3.40	2.76	2.32	2.16	
Cumul %	37.59	46.85	52.75	57.21	61.13	64.52	67.28	69.61	71.77	

Appendix K: PCA Scree Plot
for Satisfaction — Main Data

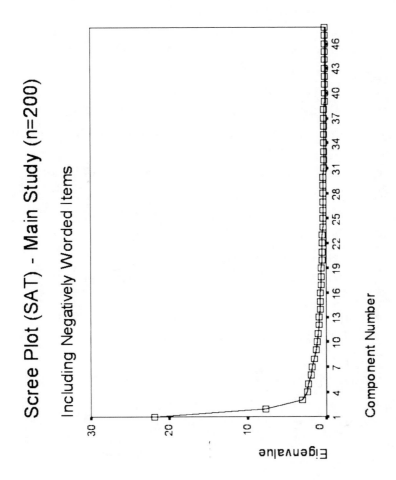

Scree Plot (SAT) - Main Study (n=200)

Including Negatively Worded Items

Appendix L: PCA Scree Plot
for Value — Main Data

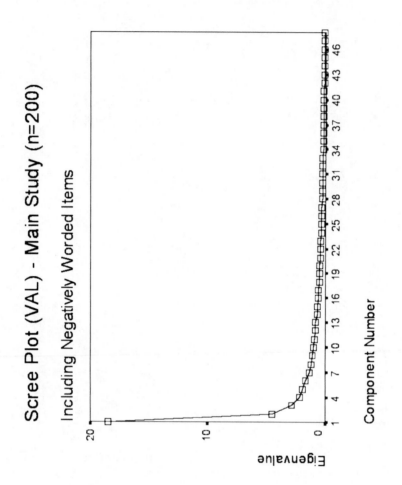

Appendix M: PCA for Satisfaction with Four Reflection Levels

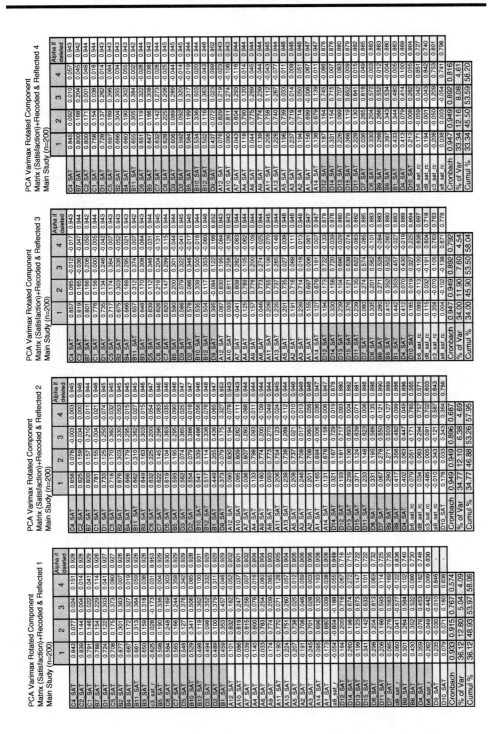

Appendix N: PCA for Value with Four Relection Levels

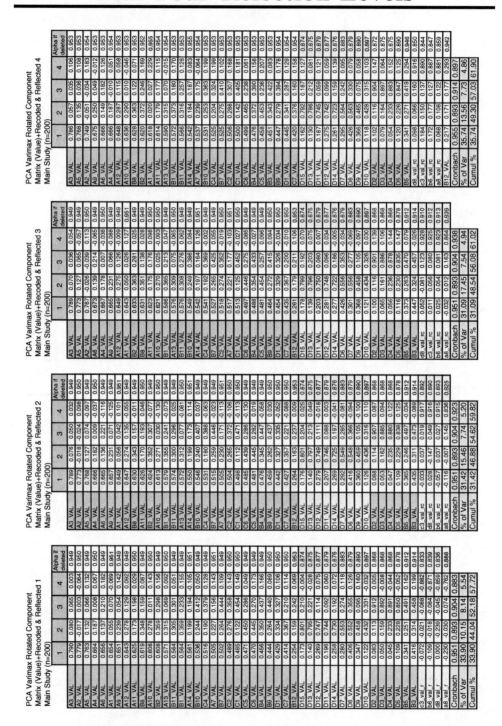

Appendix O: PCA Vector Analysis for Satisfaction

Factor Loading BiPlot
48 Questions (SAT) Recoded & Reflected

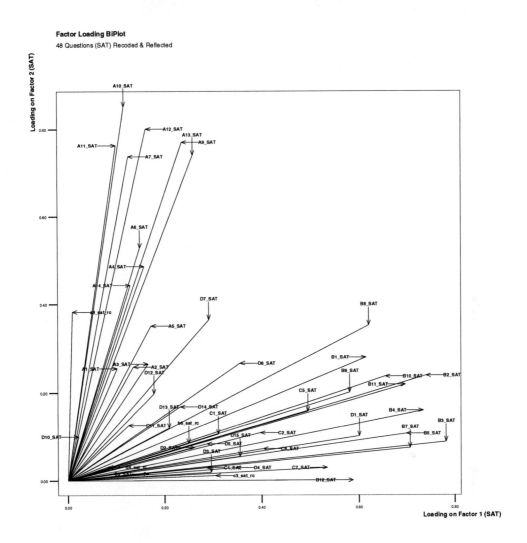

Appendix O: PCA Vector
Analysis for Satisfaction (cont.)

Factor Loading BiPlot
48 Questions (SAT) Recoded & Reflected

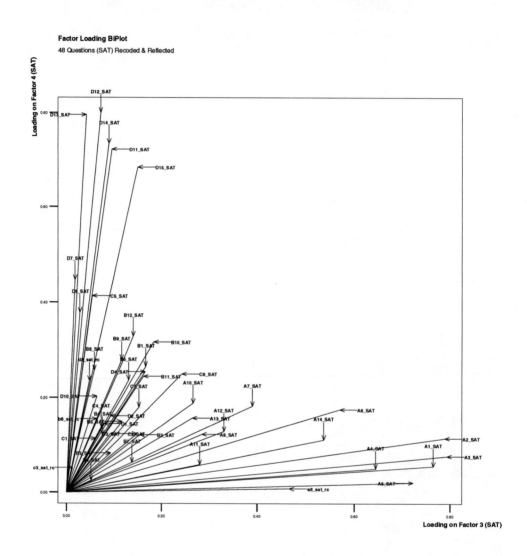

Appendix P: PCA Similar
Vector Analysis for Value

Factor Loading BiPlot
48 Questions (VAL) Recoded & Reflected

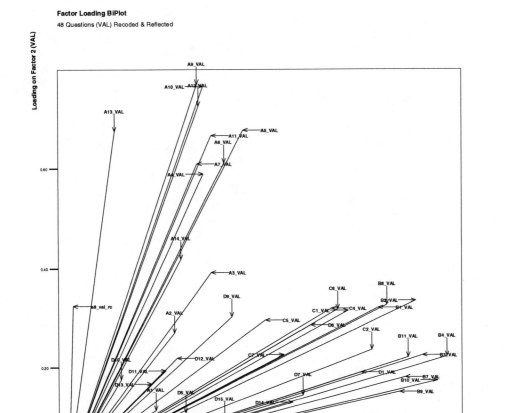

Appendix P: PCA Similar
Vector Analysis for Value (cont.)

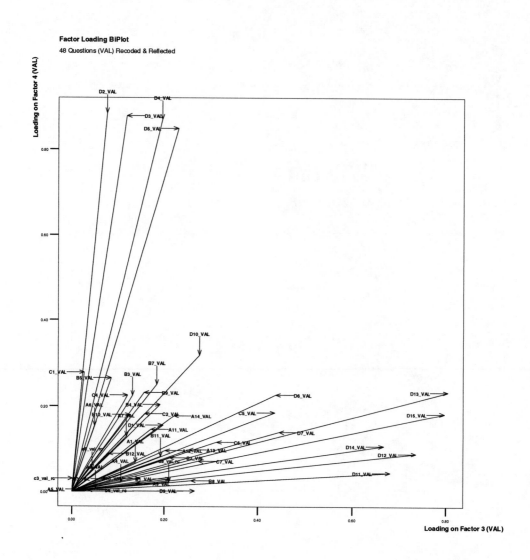

Factor Loading BiPlot

48 Questions (VAL) Recoded & Reflected

Appendix Q: Final Survey Instrument

Online Learning Experience

The following is a list of items related to the **Courses and Professors** (across all online courses) of online learning.
Please read each item and rate your level of **satisfaction** you attribute to each item when learning online.
Please rate the level of **satisfaction** for each item from: 'Extremely Unsatisfied' to 'Extremely Satisfied'.

A. The following items related to courses and professors:

Items *(Old Item)*	Level of Satisfaction					
A1. Quality content of courses *(B2)*	☐ Extremely unsatisfied	☐ Very unsatisfied	☐ Unsatisfied	☐ Satisfied	☐ Very satisfied	☐ Extremely 'satisfied
A2. Amount of material in courses *(B3)*	☐ Extremely unsatisfied	☐ Very unsatisfied	☐ Unsatisfied	☐ Satisfied	☐ Very satisfied	☐ Extremely satisfied
A3. Interesting subject matter *(B4)*	☐ Extremely unsatisfied	☐ Very unsatisfied	☐ Unsatisfied	☐ Satisfied	☐ Very satisfied	☐ Extremely satisfied
A4. Difficulty of subject matter *(B5)*	☐ Extremely unsatisfied	☐ Very unsatisfied	☐ Unsatisfied	☐ Satisfied	☐ Very satisfied	☐ Extremely satisfied
A5. Enjoyment from the courses/lessons *(B7)*	☐ Extremely unsatisfied	☐ Very unsatisfied	☐ Unsatisfied	☐ Satisfied	☐ Very satisfied	☐ Extremely satisfied
A6. Gathering information quickly *(B10)*	☐ Extremely unsatisfied	☐ Very unsatisfied	☐ Unsatisfied	☐ Satisfied	☐ Very satisfied	☐ Extremely satisfied
A7. Organization of courses (content of courses, organization of assignments, etc. across all courses) *(B11)*	☐ Extremely unsatisfied	☐ Very unsatisfied	☐ Unsatisfied	☐ Satisfied	☐ Very satisfied	☐ Extremely satisfied
A8. Amount of professor-to-student online interaction *(C1)*	☐ Extremely unsatisfied	☐ Very unsatisfied	☐ Unsatisfied	☐ Satisfied	☐ Very satisfied	☐ Extremely satisfied
A9. Professors' attitude (across all professors) *(C2)*	☐ Extremely unsatisfied	☐ Very unsatisfied	☐ Unsatisfied	☐ Satisfied	☐ Very satisfied	☐ Extremely satisfied
A10. Quality of professor-to-student online interaction *(C4)*	☐ Extremely unsatisfied	☐ Very unsatisfied	☐ Unsatisfied	☐ Satisfied	☐ Very satisfied	☐ Extremely satisfied
A11. Freedom of learning (selective seeking and processing of information) *(C5)*	☐ Extremely unsatisfied	☐ Very unsatisfied	☐ Unsatisfied	☐ Satisfied	☐ Very satisfied	☐ Extremely satisfied
A12. Submission time window for assignments and quizzes *(C6)*	☐ Extremely unsatisfied	☐ Very unsatisfied	☐ Unsatisfied	☐ Satisfied	☐ Very satisfied	☐ Extremely satisfied
A13. Online workload of courses *(C7)*	☐ Extremely unsatisfied	☐ Very unsatisfied	☐ Unsatisfied	☐ Satisfied	☐ Very satisfied	☐ Extremely satisfied
A14. Learning a lot in these classes *(D1)*	☐ Extremely unsatisfied	☐ Very unsatisfied	☐ Unsatisfied	☐ Satisfied	☐ Very satisfied	☐ Extremely satisfied
A15. Amount of interaction with classmates *(D2)*	☐ Extremely unsatisfied	☐ Very unsatisfied	☐ Unsatisfied	☐ Satisfied	☐ Very satisfied	☐ Extremely satisfied
A16. Quality of interaction with classmates *(D3)*	☐ Extremely unsatisfied	☐ Very unsatisfied	☐ Unsatisfied	☐ Satisfied	☐ Very satisfied	☐ Extremely satisfied
A17. Classmates' attitude (across all courses) *(D4)*	☐ Extremely unsatisfied	☐ Very unsatisfied	☐ Unsatisfied	☐ Satisfied	☐ Very satisfied	☐ Extremely satisfied
A18. Being part of a 'class' although it was online *(D5)*	☐ Extremely unsatisfied	☐ Very unsatisfied	☐ Unsatisfied	☐ Satisfied	☐ Very satisfied	☐ Extremely satisfied
A19. Overall, how would you rate your level of **satisfaction** with the **above items**?	☐ Extremely unsatisfied	☐ Very unsatisfied	☐ Unsatisfied	☐ Satisfied	☐ Very satisfied	☐ Extremely satisfied

Appendix Q:
Final Survey Instrument (cont.)

Online Learning Experience

The following is a list of items related to **Technology and Support** of online learning (across all online courses).
Please read each item and rate your level of **satisfaction** you attribute to each item when learning online.
Please rate the level of **satisfaction** for each item from: 'Extremely Unsatisfied' to 'Extremely Satisfied'.

B. The following items related to technology and support:

Items *(Old Item)*	Level of Satisfaction					
	Extremely unsatisfied	Very unsatisfied	Unsatisfied	Satisfied	Very satisfied	Extremely satisfied
B1. Quick answer from technical support	☐	☐	☐	☐	☐	☐
(A1) via phone						
B2. Quick answer from technical support	☐	☐	☐	☐	☐	☐
(A2) after-hours via e-mail						
B3. Quality of technical support	☐	☐	☐	☐	☐	☐
(A3)						
B4. System operation time (up-time)	☐	☐	☐	☐	☐	☐
(A4)						
B5. Reduced system errors	☐	☐	☐	☐	☐	☐
(A5)						
B6. System security (discourage hacking,	☐	☐	☐	☐	☐	☐
(A6) secure access, etc.)						
B7. Access to courses from anywhere	☐	☐	☐	☐	☐	☐
(A7) in the world (via the Internet)						
B8. Learning at anytime of the day	☐	☐	☐	☐	☐	☐
(A9) (schedule flexibility)						
B9. Submit assignments from anywhere	☐	☐	☐	☐	☐	☐
(A10) (via the Internet)						
B10. Different system tools (chat, bulletin board	☐	☐	☐	☐	☐	☐
(A11) or discussion forums, etc.)						
B11. Access of all courses from one area	☐	☐	☐	☐	☐	☐
(A12) (My WebCT)						
B12. Taking quizzes remotely	☐	☐	☐	☐	☐	☐
(A13) (off-campus)						
B13. Review course audios	☐	☐	☐	☐	☐	☐
(A14)						
B14. Overall, how would you rate your level of **satisfaction** with the **above items**?	☐	☐	☐	☐	☐	☐

Appendix Q:
Final Survey Instrument (cont.)

Online Learning Experience

The following is a list of items related to **Learning and Interface Support** of online learning (across all online courses).
Please read each item and rate your level of **satisfaction** you attribute to each item when learning online.
Please rate the level of **satisfaction** for each item from: 'Extremely Unsatisfied' to 'Extremely Satisfied'.

C. The following items related to learning and interface support:

Items *(Old Item)*	Level of Satisfaction					
	Extremely unsatisfied	Very unsatisfied	Unsatisfied	Satisfied	Very satisfied	Extremely satisfied
C1. Availability of course content *(B1)*	☐	☐	☐	☐	☐	☐
C2. Ease-of-use (with content of courses, navigation, interface, etc.) *(B8)*	☐	☐	☐	☐	☐	☐
C3. Similar of interface across all online courses *(B9)*	☐	☐	☐	☐	☐	☐
C4. Your comfort with online learning and technology *(D6)*	☐	☐	☐	☐	☐	☐
C5. Your Internet and computer skills *(D7)*	☐	☐	☐	☐	☐	☐
C6. Reduced travel cost/time (to and from campus) *(D11)*	☐	☐	☐	☐	☐	☐
C7. Ability to travel while taking online courses (for business or other) *(D12)*	☐	☐	☐	☐	☐	☐
C8. Employer support and your ability to work while learning *(D13)*	☐	☐	☐	☐	☐	☐
C9. Attendance to family responsibilities *(D14)*	☐	☐	☐	☐	☐	☐
C10. Family support *(D15)*	☐	☐	☐	☐	☐	☐
C11. Overall, how would you rate your level of **satisfaction** with the **above items**?	☐	☐	☐	☐	☐	☐

Appendix Q:
Final Survey Instrument (cont.)

Online Learning Experience

The following is a list of items related to **Cost** of online learning (across all online courses).
Please read each item and rate your level of **satisfaction** you attribute to each item when learning online.
Please rate the level of **satisfaction** for each item from: 'Extremely Unsatisfied' to 'Extremely Satisfied'.

D. The following items related to Cost:

Items *(Old Item)*	Level of Satisfaction					
D1. Cost of courses *(D9)*	☐ Extremely unsatisfied	☐ Very unsatisfied	☐ Unsatisfied	☐ Satisfied	☐ Very satisfied	☐ Extremely satisfied
D2. Cost of ISP and Internet *(D10)* access	☐ Extremely unsatisfied	☐ Very unsatisfied	☐ Unsatisfied	☐ Satisfied	☐ Very satisfied	☐ Extremely satisfied
D3. Overall, how would you rate your level of **satisfaction** with the **above items**?	☐ Extremely unsatisfied	☐ Very unsatisfied	☐ Unsatisfied	☐ Satisfied	☐ Very satisfied	☐ Extremely satisfied

Global Questions:

G1. Taking into account all your previous answers about **satisfaction** (including this section and the previous three sections), what is your overall **SATISFACTION** level from the online learning?	☐ Extremely unsatisfied	☐ Very unsatisfied	☐ Unsatisfied	☐ Satisfied	☐ Very satisfied	☐ Extremely satisfied
G2. Taking into account all your previous answers on **satisfaction** level (including all items in this section and *(G3)* the previous three sections), how would you rate your **overall educational LEARNING** outcomes?	☐ Extremely Poor	☐ Poor	☐ Slightly Poor	☐ Slightly Good	☐ Good	☐ Extremely Good

About the Author

Dr. Yair Levy is an assistant professor of Management Information Systems (MIS) at the Graduate School of Computer and Information Sciences at Nova Southeastern University, USA. Prior to joining the school, Dr. Levy was instructor and director of online learning at the College of Business Administration at Florida International University. During the mid to late 1990s, Dr. Levy assisted NASA to develop e-learning platforms as well as manage Internet and Web infrastructures. He earned his bachelor's degree in Aerospace Engineering from the Technion (Israel Institute of Technology). He received his MBA with MIS concentration and PhD in Management Information Systems from Florida International University. His current research interests include value of information systems, value of online learning systems, IS and online learning effectiveness. His research publications appear in the *Journal of Computers & Education, International Journal of Information and Communications Technology Education (IJICTE)*, as well as in several conference proceedings. Additionally he published an invited chapter for *Distance Learning and University Effectiveness* book, as well as in the *Encyclopedia of Information Science and Technology* and the *Encyclopedia of Online Learning and Technology*. Dr. Levy is the recipient of the IJICTE 1(3) Editor's Award of Excellence for his paper titled "A case study of management skills comparison in online and on-campus MBA programs." He served as the executive chair of the technical program & proceedings committee for the IEEE SoutheastCon 2005 conference as well as a co-chair of the information systems track in the same conference. Dr. Levy was the editor of the *Proceedings for the IEEE SoutheastCon 2005*. Additionally, he chaired and co-chaired multiple sessions/tracks of his research area in recognized conferences. He served as a member of the technical/proceedings committee for several conferences. Moreover, Dr. Levy has been serving as a referee research reviewer for numerous national and international scientific journals, conference proceedings, as well as MIS and information security textbooks. He is also a frequent speaker at national and international meetings on MIS and online learning topics. Dr. Levy's teaching interests and courses taught include e-commerce, management information systems, information systems security, telecommunications and networking, system analysis and design, as well as enterprise architecture and infrastructure in the graduate programs. To find out more about Dr. Levy, please visit his site: *http://www.proflevy.com/*.

Index

V

value
    2, 18, 90, 118, 124, 143, 213,
    242
value factors 146, 157, 161
value item 156
value of e-learning systems 22
value ranking instruments 139
value theory 2, 5, 6, 10, 14, 19,
    93 213
Value-Satisfaction and effective-
    ness grids 184
Value-Satisfaction Dimension Grid
    187, 190
Value-Satisfaction grids 4, 8, 116,
    123, 150, 155, 212, 217
Value-Satisfaction overall grid 212
vendor support 57
VLS (virtual learning systems) 1

W

weak-difference independence 37
Web-based survey 147
WebCT™ 216, 228

2004 RELEASE

Distance Learning and University Effectiveness:
Changing Educational Paradigms for Online Learning

Caroline Howard, PhD, Emory University, USA
Karen Schenk, PhD, K.D.Schenk and Associates Consulting, USA
Richard Discenza, PhD, University of Colorado, USA

Distance Learning and University Effectiveness: Changing Educational Paradigms for Online Learning addresses the challenges and opportunities associated with information and communication technologies (ICTs) as related to education. From discussing new and innovative educational paradigms and learning models resulting from ICTs to addressing future student needs and international issues, this book provides comprehensive coverage of the paradigm, teaching, technology and other changes that may be required of universities to remain in the new competitive marketplace of online learning.

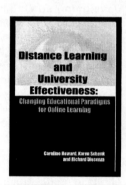

ISBN 1-59140-178-X (h/c) • US$74.95 • *ISBN 1-59140-221-2(s/c)* • US$59.95
• *368 pages* • *Copyright © 2004*

"To succeed in distance education, faculty members must be willing to change their teaching methods and reward expectations. Universities will need to transform their structures, rewards, and policies to accommodate the needs of distance education programs. In summary, the influx of distance education into the system is forcing universities to rethink their foundations and shift their paradigms."

- Caroline Howard, Emory University, USA,
Karen Schenk, K. D. Schenk and Associates Consulting &
Richard Discenza, University of Colorado in Colorado Springs, USA

It's Easy to Order! Order online at www.idea-group.com or
call 717/533-8845 x10
Mon-Fri 8:30 am-5:00 pm (est) or fax 24 hours a day 717/533-8661

 Information Science Publishing
Hershey • London • Melbourne • Singapore

An excellent addition to your library